The Ladykiller

Other books by
DENNIS BARDENS

MYSTERIOUS WORLDS

CHURCHILL IN PARLIAMENT

GHOSTS AND HAUNTINGS

PRINCESS MARGARET

FAMOUS CASES OF NORMAN BIRKETT, K.C.

LORD JUSTICE BIRKETT

ELIZABETH FRY

PORTRAIT OF A STATESMAN [LORD AVON]

A PRESS IN CHAINS

CRIME DOES PAY: A GALAXY OF NOTABLE RASCALS

The Ladykiller

The Life of Landru, the French Bluebeard

DENNIS BARDENS

PETER DAVIES : LONDON

Peter Davies Ltd

15 Queen Street, Mayfair, London W1X 8BE

LONDON   MELBOURNE   TORONTO

JOHANNESBURG   AUCKLAND

© 1972 by Dennis Bardens

First published 1972

432 01140 4

Printed in Great Britain by

Willmer Brothers Limited, Birkenhead

For Marie and Peter

Contents

Illustrations

Acknowledgements

This is a biography of a man who has been called a mere petty crook but who has become a legend. My reasons for reporting retrospectively on the life of a social nuisance are given in the Preface. It may seem an odd metamorphosis, from biographies of Elizabeth Fry, Princess Margaret, Lord Avon and Sir Winston Churchill to the life of a French crook who took to mass murder for trivial rewards, but, like his more distinguished fellow-mortals, he was a human being, a product of genetics, his times and his environment.

The research has been heavy, and I am greatly indebted to Madame Jeanne Harburger, Conservateur of Archives at the Préfecture of Police in Paris, for her wonderful help, understanding and patience in making available to me long-forgotten material and valuable records; and to Monsieur Coutarel for his assistance in assembling official documents. My thanks are also due to Mr Brian Stoneman, of *Agence France Presse,* for translating the immense *Interrogatoire Définitif* from police records, which is itself the length of a large novel. I am grateful to many others—Mr Paul Spitzer, for assistance with research; Miss Dawn Tindall, for preparing a bibliography and list of sources; and Mrs Gladys Phillips and Dr George Morey, LL.D., for their checking of the finished work. My thanks are also due to Mr S. W. Derrick, Chairman of the Paris Branch of the National Union of Journalists, to Mrs Betty Bethenod, and to M. Claude Roland, Secretary-General of the Committee of the Union Interalliee for the hospitality of their very beautiful club. There are others, too who have helped me to find my way around and do my job, and though they are not named here, they may be sure their help is warmly appreciated.

Savage Club,   DENNIS BARDENS
86 St James's Street,
London SW1A 1PL.

Preface

IT IS JULY 1971. The summer season is in full swing. Intent on 'doing' Paris, perspiring but determined women tourists in the Boulevard Michel gesticulate in what they hope is Latin fashion, and demand frantically in schoolgirl French, laced with strange native accents, where the devil Napoleon's tomb can be. Loose-limbed students with beards and enormous buckled belts (handy to undo and use as weapons if a quarrel with the police blows up) stroll peacefully with their girls, pausing occasionally for impatient dalliance. The temperature is in the mid-eighties, and those who can, and are so disposed, sit lazily at the outside tables of the boulevard cafés, sipping their aperitifs or coffee, and watching the world go by.

This, indeed, is what I would like to do myself. Laze in the cafés, browse amongst the Left Bank bookstalls, seek refuge in the hushed monastic quiet of Notre-Dame near by, window-shop in the rue de Rivoli, or get some air by sailing down the Seine on a *bateau mouche*. The present is difficult enough to chronicle or comprehend, but to recall the past....

Yet this is what I am here for. The ghosts of the past must be summoned, without benefit of sigil or pentalpha, but by the prosaic means of research and often unwelcome physical exertion. I am looking for a man called Henri Désiré Landru. I mean that I am trying to form an accurate mental picture of him—he was guillotined fifty years ago for having murdered ten women, most of them middle-aged, and a youth of seventeen. He was short in stature, bald, bearded, melancholy, some-what sinister in aspect and he had inordinately deep-set, almost hypnotic, eyes.

Inspector Belin, who arrested him in 1919, and who died recently, maintained that Landru was nothing but a petty crook and unworthy of all the fuss made about him. Nevertheless, the Landru legend persists. How did this insignificant and unattractive man succeed, in his late forties and fifties, in getting amorously involved with 283 women? How did ten known women fall in love with him to the extent of entrusting everything they possessed to his keeping? Why did Landru put such fiendish ingenuity into his murders and crooked dealings for such paltry financial rewards, when the same effort and thought could have made him so much more money honestly? Is it credible that a man who came from a respectable and happy family, who loved music and poetry, who devoutly assisted at Mass in one of Paris's most famous churches, could have dismembered and burned the bodies of eleven people?

A lot of questions to ask on a hot day, but they seem worth asking. Landru was a human being, and a remarkable one. He was questioned for nearly two years by the examining magistrate, yet never once lost his aplomb or confidence, parrying questions and accusations, failing to answer, making witty rejoinders, or throwing the ball contemptuously back into the court. Not once did he admit his guilt and, indeed, maintained his innocence to the last, even in those few seconds before he met his death. He never confessed to murder, still less to what he had done to the bodies.

Was he a woman-hater, then? Not at all. He was married, and had children. He seems to have provided for them. Women found it possible to love him—or impossible not to. Mlle Segret, his attractive mistress, kept his photograph by her bedside until the very last day of her life. Surely a man has to be something more than a petty crook to engender devotion such as this.

The Landru case was a *cause célèbre*, which made daily reading for a world sickened by the endless slaughter of the First World War. It is almost ironic that the world should have become so absorbed with the fate of eleven victims all, except one, unspectacular people when chess-board massacres of thousands of men a day had been an accepted routine for years. But perhaps such attention to individual human life came as a relief, a sign that society had belatedly regained its sanity.

In Versailles, I visit the court which for several weeks was the focus of the world's attention as the international press reported the most sensational murder trial of the century (thus far). There is nothing very remarkable about the court now. The only touch of colour is the barristers, impeccable as usual and exuding the requisite air of knowledgeable importance as they stand talking to their clients, the trend of whose fortunes can be read in their faces.

A court official explains that during the German occupation of World War Two some of Landru's papers, including his famous little black book, in which he noted the names of his victims and the meagre amount of cash he expended on each of them, disappeared. The documents in the case are now dispersed, and nothing of interest in the Landru case remains in Versailles.

Clearly, I must get at some original source. Surely the Préfecture of Police in Paris must have something?

I leave the bustle of the Latin Quarter, the Sudanese patisserie with its students eating monstrous, plate-sized rolls stuffed with spiced vegetables, the groups of gendarmes patrolling in fours or sixes, and stroll over the Pont St Michel into that part of Paris which was a famous city even two thousand years ago. The Romans knew what they were doing when they constructed a stockaded settlement on that island in the Seine. The Île-de-la-Cité is still virtually impregnable, its bridges well guarded. Successive governments have chosen the island as the logical site for police headquarters and for the Palais de Justice.

I turn left into the Quai des Orfèvres, the Scotland Yard of Paris. Here is the huge stone edifice that figures so much in the brilliant detective novels of Georges Simenon. An impeccable gendarme waves me into the courtyard. I go out of the stifling summer heat into the cool, thick stone building, up, up, up the seemingly endless flight of 218 stairs, along a corridor through whose half-open doors shirt-sleeved detectives seem to be either phoning frantically or sitting deep in thought. Ah, here are the archives. The door is of steel; there is no bell to ring, no knocker to knock, no handle to push or pull.

I rap on the door and it opens. There is an examination of credentials, then follows a silent peregrination through the 'Black Museum'. I pass an infernal machine, for all the world like a series of parallel, horizontal gas pipes on a simple frame, but capable of firing a dozen explosive charges at once. Here are some fearful shackles, almost an inch thick, which chafed and held captive prisoners long forgotten and long dead. There is a strong tree stump set in a pedestal, an execution post used by the Germans in one of their torture chambers in the last war. It is much pitted with bullets, yet, strangely, not blood-stained. And who is this? As I pass life-sized models in full authentic uniforms of the gendarmes of previous centuries, I see in a dark glass case a familiar face—since I started my researches I have got to know every feature of his face. *Landru!*

His deep-set eyes glower from the fading albumen; the mixture of insolence, affected charm and secrecy still show through. Juxtaposed is a heavy, old-fashioned pair of curling tongs, the sort that used to be heated over an open flame, an everlasting instrument to be used by everlasting women. But this had belonged to one of Landru's victims. Who, nobody can say. Landru could have done, but chose to keep his silence. I am reminded of the fact that he cannot do so now. Then, a gruesomely realistic guillotine, complete with its horizontal victim and a decapitated head lying in the adjacent basket, makes its point.

But in the office of the Chief Archivist, all is calm and quiet. The antique desk is clear of clutter. The shelves are lined with books bound in hand-tooled calf and morocco. There is a sense of unhurried order, intelligent planning, of timelessness.

'Landru, ah yes. I'm afraid the Court records disappeared during the war, but we have here many relevant documents, the *Interrogatoire Définitif* for example, photographs, documents of various kinds....'

Now I am in a room on my own. The parquet flooring is polished, with never a speck of dust. The shelves are lined with records exquisitely kept. France has always had a deep sense of history, a feeling for the value of archives, and the care of their maintenance is a revelation to me. Boxes and boxes of documents are brought in. There are bulky files for all his victims, hundreds of pages of the incessant interrogation to which he was subjected before the trial began, bundles of letters to the presiding Judge, folios of photographs. Millions of words!

It is to Gambais I must go next. A place that doesn't mean much to people nowadays, except, perhaps, to the handful of

Parisians who use it as a weekend hideaway. But it was in Gambais that Landru rented a certain villa.

My companion and I speed out of Paris in the scorching sun, the black vinyl upholstery almost red-hot with the heat. The roads are crowded with motorists racing away from the city as though the devil himself was after them. But at last we are on the tree-lined road to Dreux, and passing through rich agricultural country. There is a fast-moving panorama of lush, green meadows, fields of waving yellow corn, of sleepy-looking farmsteads, tool sheds and Dutch barns. At last we turn off the M 12 highway, towards Gambais.

With what high hopes had many women made this journey! Women, often plain-looking and middle-aged but still yearning for love, deceived by Landru's promises of marriage, on their way to his villa, to find on their arrival an almost totally isolated house, scarcely furnished, cold and gloomy. It was only when the front door opened and they sensed the dank and dusty chaos of the house, that disillusionment and suspicion may have come upon them. . . .

The countryside becomes more deserted. Here are more tree-lined avenues, some handsome stone entrances leading to elegant and secluded country houses. We pass trim, new-looking villas, obviously weekend houses.

We move into thickly-wooded country, the forest of Rambouillet, which stretches for fifty miles, and in whose dense undergrowth and muddy lakes some of the victims may lie buried. For most people Rambouillet conjures up re-collections of the romantic paintings of Watteau, the play of sunlight on shimmering leaves; and of the Château, now the country residence of the Presidents of France, a sort of equivalent of the English Chequers—at least in purpose. The Château is more elegant and more ancient.

Now we are coming into Gambais itself. It is barely distinguishable from countless other French villages, yet it is impossible for me to suppress a gathering excitement. Yes, at first glance, the victims of Landru could well have felt that this was their haven of love—a country retreat where, away from prying eyes and gossiping tongues, the ardent wooer could assert himself. Here are ivy-covered barns, fences with wild roses trailing carelessly over them, the old Lodge, with its classic shutters, the eighteenth century town hall in the rue des Gabelles, with its stone basins of brilliantly coloured flowers. The town hall, I notice, displays an announcement: COLLECT DE SANG. The mention of blood donors reminds me of my mission. Where is Landru's villa?

We stop at the Auberge de la Poule Faisane. It is a pleasant, low-built inn, and was flourishing half a century ago. Here Landru often ate, and perhaps even brought his women, though he was not one to advertise their presence.

Well fortified with the inn's excellent food and wine, we emerge once again into the sunlight to find Landru's villa. I have an old photograph of it as it looked fifty years ago. We come across it after a while, not as far from the village inn as I had expected, and I am surprised to discover it abutting the road, at least the garden fence and the original wrought-iron entrance gates. But half a century earlier it must have been very remote indeed.

Landru's villa, now called La Lézardière (The Lizard's Haunt), has changed little in half a century. But of course it looks better kept. The garage gates are of wrought iron. To the left of the house, and behind it, stretches a magnificent lawn, enlivened by a romantic rose arbour. The house has merely two floors, with the usual, traditional shutters at the windows, the *mansardes,* or dormer windows being very close to the chimneys from which, police reports of the time alleged, acrid, evil-smelling smoke belched forth. The front windows look out upon rolling countryside, woodland and forest.

There is a high fence around the villa, now used as a week-end home by a Paris couple. The wide walls to the right of the house, I see, have had windows let into them.

The house's sinister history does not worry the present tenants. On the contrary, they are astonished at the curiosity it excites. Fifty years after the *cause célèbre* the tourists still call, but never get further than the threshold.

Clearly, M. and Mme C. do not believe in the association of ideas. A refrigerator has replaced the evil-looking stove in which, it is believed, at least six of Landru's victims were incinerated. The C.s enjoy cultivating the large garden, tending the fruit trees. They have even raised sheep: a final pastoral touch. Renaming the house was a forlorn hope, for it was doubtful that the nine hundred inhabitants of Gambais could ever think of this house as anything but the home of the 'sad squire' of Gambais—'Bluebeard', whose beard is described by various writers as black, blue, bluish-black, ginger, red and brown. Not everyone would want a house with such a reputation as a weekend retreat.

The previous occupant of Landru's house was a restaurateur who realised that the house's notoriety could be turned to good commercial use. What had been a granary during the killer's lifetime was converted into a loggia, where from the time of Landru's execution until the outbreak of the Second World War, Parisians would eat, wearing hired bowler hats and buttoned boots as a period touch, and visit the 'museum' in which apocryphal relics of the murdered women were on show.

And now it is a home again. It has had many names (even La Villa Tric, after the name of the owner who rented it to Landru) but for Gambais it remains La Maison Landru.

The local tobacconist does a roaring trade with a coloured picture postcard of Landru's villa. It carries a witty rhyme:

> *Pour prouver que l'amour est un feu qui dévore*
> *A son foyer, un jour, Landru les invita*
> *Ardentes et joyeuses, avides d'aimer encore . . .*
> *Puis l'étincelle jaillit . . . et la poêle ronfla Moralité:*
> *Il en cuit de fréquenter les hommes à poêle.*

which, very freely translated (since it will not translate literally), could be rendered:

> Love, we are told, is a consuming fire
> In seeking which, strange courses we pursue;
> None stranger than those women who aspired
> To fan the flame of Désiré Landru.
> Hoping to kindle passions long since dead,
> They crossed the threshold—and the fire was fed.

But of course this misses the play on *poêle,* which can mean 'stove', and on *à poil,* meaning 'naked'.

I take a brief look at the cemetery, which may well contain rather more bodies than were legally buried there, and a last glance at Landru's villa. At the edge of the adjacent field blood-red poppies wave in a gentle breeze and catch the sun—poppies which later invested the nightmarish battlefields of France with an air of sylvan beauty. They seem symbolic.

We return via Rambouillet. The drive through the forest

merely confirms my original impressions. Nobody will ever know if any of Landru's victims lie here. Were not the lakes dredged at the time of his trial? Too late did informants come forward with weird tales of hunks of putrescent flesh being drawn up by indignant fishermen, of strange sacks floating, or of what sounded like a body being dumped into a pond late at night. It is difficult enough to identify a drowned corpse after a period of months, let alone after years; Landru knew this, for he made notes of the impossibility of identifying human remains after a lapse of time in the water. Advances in forensic medicine would modify many of Landru's optimistic assumptions, but they were probably valid then.

It seems almost a crime to be thinking of such things in such idyllic surroundings. I visit the Église St Lubin, and in the park of the Château de Rambouillet inspect the fantastic dairy farm created by Louis XVI for the amusement of Marie-Antoinette, with its dream-like statue of a nymph and the goat Amalthæa, wet-nurse to the Greek god Zeus. Its fairy-like grotto seems an oddity in a dairy-farm—but before the Revolution burst upon France there were no eccentricities too wild or too extravagent.

Nevertheless, along these roads, half a century ago, at dead of night, Landru came alone. Did he ever come with any of his victims, and destroy them there? Did he ever tempt into these forests victims whose names did not even feature in the little notebook which proved his undoing? Only an examination of the evidence accumulated at the time can provide the answers, or such answers as can be given.

Back in Paris, I arrive at the Church of St Louis-en-L'Île just in time for a wedding. Excited little bridesmaids chase each other in and out of a local sweet shop, while the Mayor and keyed-up relatives await the arrival of the bride and bridegroom. The church stands on the corner of the main street of the old medieval city and the rue Poulletier—still a fine church in the Jesuit style, finished in 1726. Its exterior features are a handsome clock and a 'wedding-cake' steeple reminiscent of Wren's Church of St Bride in Fleet Street, London.

I hadn't expected so grand and ornate an interior. Pope Pius VII celebrated mass here on March 10, 1805 and about eighty years later a handsome, quiet, lad called Henri Désiré

Landru assisted at Mass. There is a sober majesty about the interior, with its large arcades, high windows, the pilasters topped by Corinthian capitals, the superb stained-glass windows. There are a wide variety of chapels, one to St Vincent de Paul, another to Holy Geneviève, patron saint of Paris, another to St Francis of Assisi and one, appropriately enough, called The Purgatory Souls Chapel.

Well, if Landru's soul was ever in purgatory (and if the soul is a reality, presumably Landru had one) then he could well do with the Mass that was said for him every year. It was not said for him in this church, however; all concerned hope that his soul now rests in peace, but Landru's association with the church of St Louis-en-L'Île is an historic detail tactfully omitted from the notes for visitors.

Finally, and nearby, I take a look at Landru's childhood home in the rue du Cloître, flanking Notre-Dame cathedral. It is an old stone house, but there are building alterations going on; it is being given a new façade. It is a respectable house in a respectable street, and reflects both the simplicity and orderly good citizenship of his devoted parents, who chose for their son the name of Désiré—the desired one. Well, it is always a hazardous thing to reflect your hopes for your child in your choice of name; it is almost like challenging providence. Name your son Hercules and he may turn out to be the hunchback of Notre-Dame. Name him Désiré and ... yes, I suppose that is the beginning of the story, the day that Landru was born. . . .

I

The Desired One

THE WORLD into which Henri Désiré Landru was born, on
April 12, 1869, was a world of shifting values, unstable
governments, revolutions, and wars or threats of war.

It was, one might say, the sort of world we live in today.

When the Franco-Prussian War burst upon France in 1870
he was a baby. As he had conscientious and loving parents,
the famine that gripped a besieged Paris, whose letters had to
be sent out by balloon post, left him untouched. He was still
a toddler when the brief and bloody Commune Revolution
filled the streets with wounded and dying, and was only two
when the enraged mobs pulled and pulled at the great ropes
that brought Napoleon's Column in the Place Vendôme
crashing down on to its specially prepared bed of dung.

He was three when the National Assembly, by a huge
majority, enacted that a national shrine, the Eglise du Sacré-
Coeur, should be erected on the heights of Montmartre in
thankfulness for the city's deliverance. And as he played in its
ancient streets in later years, wandered in the Tuileries
Gardens and watched the *bateaux mouches* weaving their way
down the Seine like monster fish with luminous eyes, he,
like so many Parisians, might have felt, with his contemporary
Alphonse Daudet, that

> Paris beamed upon me through her open shop windows; the
> Odéon itself seemed to nod affably towards me, and the white
> marble queens in the gardens of the Luxembourg ... appeared
> to bow graciously and welcome my arrival.

Landru's father, Julien-Alexandre Sylvain Landru, a stoker at
the 'Forges de Vulcain' (a famous Paris foundry still in
operation), had been born in 1835 and had, in 1853, married

Flore Henriquel, a 'small' dressmaker—sometimes described, inadequately, as a seamstress.

M. and Mme Landru had long wanted a son. Their daughter, Florentine-Margaret, had been born in 1854, a year after they married, and it was to be a long, long wait before they were to be blessed with their second and last child, a boy. Hence his second name, Désiré. His parents were God-fearing people and fervent Catholics, and so, from the earliest years, Henri Désiré, clutching the hands of his mother and his older sister, went regularly to church. Father worked hard and long, Mother cut and stitched incessantly, and Florentine, a good and devoted daughter, helped about the house and assisted her mother with the dressmaking long beyond the age when she would, in a more opulent home, probably have married. She was thirty-three when she did eventually marry Léon Ache, a mechanic, no doubt feeling that Henri Désiré, in accordance with the pattern of family life at that time, would keep a friendly and protective eye on his parents, and help with their support as they grew older.

Neither father, mother nor sister ever had the slightest brush with the authorities. Like many poor and struggling families, they were close-knit, sharing duties and sorrows and pleasures as a matter of course, making the most of what little they had, holding fast to that respectability which used to be, in a class-ridden society, the aim and ambition of the aspiring *petite bourgeoisie*.

Police records describe the daughter as 'irreproachable', while Landru senior was said by his friends to be 'sober, punctual, hard-working, of an equable temperament, held in high esteem by his colleagues and employers'.

Henri Désiré seems to have been healthy, cheerful and intelligent. There is no hint of any strained relations at home, although probably because of the chaos following the Franco-Prussian War and the Commune, the family did change addresses more frequently than was normal. Thus they left their homestead in the rue de Puebla (now called the rue Bolivar) for the Île St Denis, and then went to 18, rue de Cloître, where they lived from 1877 to 1888. The daughter married from there.

Until he was sixteen, Henri Désiré went to a school kept by monks in the rue Bretonvilliers, a short street near to

Notre-Dame and his home (which was literally opposite the cathedral), and from them he derived, along with the usual three R's, a liking for music and literature. The priests remembered him—according to police records—as 'one of their most brilliant pupils', while a schoolmate recalls him as 'a good little chap, with a nice character—playful, but intelligent'. He obtained his primary school certificate at the age of eleven and on leaving school went to work on September 15, 1885 in the office of M. Bisson, an architect. When his employer died in April the following year, he worked for a year for a M. Alleume, another architect, and then for a third architect, a M. le Coeur, until December 1888. All three gave Landru the most excellent character and competence certificates when he left their employment.

He was punctual, neat in appearance, very conscious of his rise from the working to the professional class—too conscious, in fact. And now we have our first hint that the former happy, smiling lad, who sang so beautifully in the choir of l'Eglise de St-Louis-en-Île, near Notre-Dame, and whose piety and love of ritual so impressed the priests that he was allowed to serve at Mass as a sub-deacon, was changing subtly in character.

Whereas he had been 'hail-fellow-well-met' with his school chums, he now began to 'high-hat' them. One of his school-mates said: 'Once he went to work he was no longer the nice little chap we had known at school. When he came back to the Ile St Louis, he was stuck up and cold towards his former chums; he avoided speaking to them, and when he did deign to address them, it was only to make it very clear that he was now working in an architect's office.'

Next to the church where he served at Mass was a laundry, and the young man conceived a vigorous passion for Marie Catherine-Remy as she dashed about with the smoothing iron. She was pretty and she was trusting, and when the young man with the courtly ways and mellifluous speech lied about his age, saying that he had already completed the statutory three years' military service and that he intended to marry her, she allowed him to seduce her. On June 4, 1891, a daughter was born who Landru officially acknowledged as his, and who was legitimised when the couple married, on October 7, 1893, after Landru had genuinely completed his military service.

The Desired One

He entered the Army on November 15, 1890 as a 2nd class soldier with the 87th Regiment of Infantry at St Quentin, passing fairly rapidly to the rank of corporal, then sergeant, and finally becoming assistant to the quartermaster-sergeant (*sergent-fourrier*). Such rapid progression, in the French Army of those days, suggests an acceptance of discipline and soldierly efficiency. Here he acquired—or at any rate, developed—his flair for meticulously kept financial accounts. We will see that this passion was to prove a very significant factor in shaping his destiny.

So here is Landru, with a wife and child to support, back in 'civvy street' and wondering where to turn next. Like so many whose rhythm of work is disorganised by military service, he found it difficult to settle.

There followed a succession of short-lived jobs, although his first appointment, as accountant to M. Designes, lasted only a month because the firm failed. He became accountant in charge of works to M. Raimbault, a firm of plumbing and roofing specialists from November 1893 to March 15, 1894, and it is in connection with this particular job that we find an actual instance of dishonesty in money matters (Landru had already lied to his wife before marriage). M. Raimbault gave Landru a deposit of 1,800 francs, a considerable sum in those days, which was never repaid. This fact somehow got twisted, as some authors allege that it was Landru who lent his employer the money, and that it was because his employer decamped without paying him back that he took to crime. I find no confirmation of this, which is hardly surprising, as a young, newly married man just out of the Army would simply not have had that amount of money to lend.

Landru then worked, from March 20, 1894 to May 31, 1895 at 'La Garantie Immobilière' of 52, rue des Victoires. It was a furniture shop, and here Landru acquired a useful knowledge of the buying, selling and storage of furniture—a knowledge which, again, he put to good use later on.

This was followed by two years' employment with a M. L. Henri, of 28, rue de Vaugirard, or so Landru maintained in later years. In fact he was his own employer. His wife always maintained that he, Landru, set up there, using a nom de plume derived from his real name—L(andru) Henri.

Here we perceive the first evidence of his fondness for

13

forgery. From the spoken lie, he effected a transition to the written lie. He carried with him a certificate dated January 3, 1897, signed by 'L. Henri' confirming that Henri Désiré Landru had proved quite brilliant as a toy-maker. In the most eulogistic language it praised his prowess as an 'engineer', his 'technical aptitude' and the 'improvements' of his own 'invention', which he had made in the workshop.

It is interesting to note that the signature on this certificate was not legally authenticated, as required by French law, and that the handwriting resembled Landru's.

The Landru family led a butterfly existence, with Henri Désiré changing jobs and addresses with bewildering frequency and suddenness. Poor, patient Marie was forever packing pots and pans and furniture and moving into different districts. After leaving his own employment in his toy factory, Landru lived in the rue Git le Coeur, a small street near the Seine off the Boulevard St Michel—within, prophetically enough, a stone's throw of the Préfecture of Police just over the bridge.

It was substantially no different then from now. Long after midnight the cafés and bars and restaurants would be buzzing with life, and deals of all kinds would be transacted over coffee and aperitifs. Marie got used to her husband keeping erratic hours. She abandoned all hope of maintaining any sort of regular domestic routine and was content to keep the household going and look after the children, of whom, in the course of time, there were four, two sons, Maurice and Charles, and two daughters, Marie and Suzanne.

The family moved successively to 283, rue de Vaugirard, to Soicy sur Montmorency, to Tournay and to Grand Montrouge, where Landru carried out various professions, of building contractor, furniture remover and bicycle manufacturer. It is clear that he must have been of an inventive turn of mind. His bicycle factory turned out good machines but showed little profit, while a motor-cycle which he designed was a complete failure.

During these years Landru is a shadowy figure. He moved around too much and changed jobs too often to make any real impact in any particular calling. His father, who had entertained high hopes for Henri and made great sacrifices to educate him, followed his 'progress' with bewilderment tinctured increasingly with suspicion and disillusionment. Landru senior had, in a financial and social way, managed to better himself. He had long since left the hard, back-breaking job at the Forges de Vulcain for that of a salesman at Masson's bookshop in the rue de Vaugirard. When he retired from the Bookshop at the age of seventy-five, he and his wife went to live with their daughter and son-in-law at Agen.

It was while Landru junior was occupying himself with the manufacture of bicycles at Montmorency that police suspicion first fell on him. From this time onwards he was in continual trouble with the police for fraud, embezzlement and a whole variety of offences. Many of these were extraordinarily petty, and of such a nature that his detection was inevitable—a sort of not-so-juvenile delinquency. For instance in 1900 he advertised for a traveller to work in Paris, a condition of the 'appointment' being that the applicant provided his own bicycle. When the work-hungry applicant appeared, Landru asked him to deliver a letter on foot, and in the meantime made off with his bicycle!

For fourteen years, until the outbreak of the First World War, Landru was a very amateur crook. His habitual 'uniform' was a neat mackintosh and bowler hat, a sober 'city' type suit as might be worn by a lawyer, engineer or other professional of the white collar class, and sober tie. Being now committed, by inclination or circumstance, to a life of deception, he saw in his appearance and speech and demeanour the absolute necessity for respectability. Probably he got away with a lot of offences which were never detected, and his now habitual technique of using whatever name came into his head may have saved him some sentences, yet he was in and out of prison all the time. In the Préfecture files, the Landru dossier grew and grew.

In 1900, 1901 and 1903 Landru was found guilty of false pretences and fraudulent misuse of funds, for which he was prosecuted, before being arrested *in flagrante delicto* while attempting a fraudulent operation with a savings bank and taken into custody after refusing to give any details about himself. During his detention he feigned suicide, and the prison doctor, Dr Vallon, after examining him, reported that Landru was a man of 'diminished responsibility' or, as we might say, a borderline case.

In 1902 he was condemned *in absentia* to three years'

imprisonment and a fine of 500 francs, and on May 30, 1904 this offence was linked with another and he was sentenced to two years' imprisonment and a fine of 50 francs.

It is worth noting the reduction in both sentence and fine. Dr Vallon's report obviously carried weight with the authorities. Here, according to the general view, was a social nuisance whose petty thefts and clumsy methods, when weighed against his seeming intelligence and respectable family background, suggested some emotional or psychological imbalance. It was a view which the authorities found reason to modify as Landru's convictions mounted. On May 19, 1906 he received two years' imprisonment for petty frauds committed in 1905. On May 28, he was given thirteen months' imprisonment and a 50-franc fine for a series of frauds against eleven victims, using the name of Dupont. These proceedings were linked with the earlier ones, and Landru was given a second mental examination. Another prison doctor declared that Landru was wanting in moral responsibility and should be treated with 'indulgence'. (We would say 'scarcely responsible for his actions, and not deserving of the punishment his offences would merit, were he a man of normal balance'.)

Indulgence or not, Landru persisted in his ways. Many of his victims were elderly or widowed women, taken in by his smart talk and smart clothes. He would offer to sell goods and then decamp with them, take money for non-existent property, and offer employment as a mere excuse to secure a deposit as 'a sign of good faith'.

As the list mounted, the patience of the police wore thin. On January 4, 1909, Landru was condemned *in absentia* to five years' imprisonment and a 300-franc fine for a fraud involving thirteen plaintiffs. On March 12, 1910, he was sentenced to three years' imprisonment and a fine of 100 francs, for fraud. He appealed, with the result that the two previous judgments were combined, to form a sentence of three years' imprisonment and a 100 francs fine.

Landru first realised that elderly, lonely women made easy victims in April 1909. Using the name of Paul Morel and claiming to be a manufacturer from Amiens, he inserted an advertisement in the newspaper *Echo du Nord* and induced a widow, Mme Izoret, to part with her securities.

All these offences were a great sorrow and anxiety to

Landru's family, and not least to his father, who felt utterly lost when his wife died in 1912. In response to almost desperate appeals from the unhappy Marie Landru, he returned to the Landru home in the rue Blomet and lived with his daughter-in-law and grandchildren for as long as he could bear it. But the disgrace of his son's perpetual criminal activities and sojourns in prison, coupled with the suffering he saw in Landru's home, proved too much for him. On August 27, 1912, he was found hanging from a tree in the Bois de Boulogne.

The last conviction recorded in Landru's dossier, prior to the outbreak of war, was for July 26, 1914, when he was sentenced, once more *in absentia*, to four years' imprisonment and transportation for life to the penal colony of New Caledonia; this was a case of fraud against fifteen people, perpetrated while Landru was running a garage at Malakoff, a suburb of Paris.

Let us picture Landru as he was on the outbreak of World War I. He is already forty-five years old. He has the air of a man-of-the-world. He is soft-spoken; everything he says carries quiet conviction. In all the reports of him (and before the Germans removed the voluminous records of his trial from Versailles to Berlin, they ran into millions of words) there is not one mention of him ever losing his temper or self-control. Considering the extreme complexity of his social, emotional and financial life, this is almost a unique achievement. Of course, it does not follow that everything he did is on record. But, if he were habitually bad-tempered, some story, amongst the hundreds that have survived, would indicate it.

Landru is dapper. As his metier is the confidence trick, and as part of him appears to be an actor hungering to be taken for a member of the professional classes, this is not surprising. His ample beard is well-trimmed. His white collar really is white.

He is a familiar figure in the teeming streets and labyrinthine alleys of Montmartre and the Latin Quarter, and has built up a considerable network of underworld contacts—thieves, swindlers, fences, pimps, prostitutes, bordel-keepers and undesirables of every type. He is never, so far as we know, threatened, blackmailed or robbed by any of them, which indicates that our M. Landru must be rather tougher than his 'refined' ways and nondescript physique at first suggest.

We can assume that not all his victims felt it worthwhile to complain to the police, and as he has already used so many pseudonyms, that even had they done so, their number could not be accurately assessed. But even the official total of plaintiffs numbers forty-four, from all of whom he seems to have obtained bonds, transferred them into an account opened under a fictitious name, and then drawn on the account afterwards. We see one conviction for a 'false marriage' (the French term is '*escroquerie de mariage*').

He is still living, sporadically, with his long-suffering wife. Marie, their first daughter, is now twenty-three, and the other children occupy too much of their mother's time for her to wonder, let alone discover, what strange missions keep her husband constantly on the move. But she must know that he has been in and out of prison. However, she has not given up hope that he will turn his hand to an honest living.

Landru is not a neglectful father. If he could elude scores of outraged and indignant victims, he could easily elude his family, but he never chooses to do so. Somehow, there is always money for rent or food.

Landru, we see, is a Jekyll and Hyde. On one hand, a family man; on the other, a ruthless opportunist, ever seeking new ways to make easy money.

There is one thought that makes him particularly ruthless. If he is caught again for whatever offence, grave or trivial, he can be certain of life imprisonment in a 'Devil's Island' type of fortress in New Caledonia. His future will consist of endless labour under harsh conditions, with poor diet, no hope of escape, and savage punishment for real or imagined misdemeanours.

But though he harbours this knowledge, there is about him not the least trace of apprehension or diffidence. His manner is quick, cool and confident. Is he too cocksure? After all, despite all his devious devices, he is constantly being caught. Or has he thought of some new formula for his trickery, some ways of ensuring that the evidence of his victims will never reach the police?

2

Two Kinds of War

WAR CLOUDS were already settling over Europe when Landru was released from prison in 1913, and busied himself with fresh swindles in connection with his garage at Malakoff. He had emerged from his prison cell penniless, and lost no time in remedying his situation. Soon the air was thick with complaints about his embezzlements and false pretences, and it would have been thicker but for his increasing use of pseudonyms.

As we have seen, he had begun to place small advertisements in Paris newspapers, and he soon became past master at economically worded announcements that brought elderly women buzzing round him like flies about a honeypot. He usually offered marriage, or financial advice, or else to buy and sell furniture. He was forever bundling furniture and scraps of property into one of his ancient cars and disappearing for weeks.

Landru left Malakoff on April 23, 1914, to avoid prosecution. He continued to visit his wife occasionally and to give her money, so his family do not appear to have been watched by the police. The fact is, that public nuisance though he was, he was not in the 'top class' of criminals. Not only did the police have bigger fish to fry, but police organisation was feeling the strain of impending war. More and more men were called to the colours, public administration functioned with a depleted number of civil servants, and society was to suffer a tremendous upheaval. These circumstances provided just the background Landru needed for his devious schemes.

Paris became a labyrinth of lonely widows and love-starved women. Although Landru had ignored his call-up papers and was subsequently listed as a deserter, he allowed it to be inferred that he was doing something important in the national

19

interest. In some cases he even stated outright that he worked for the secret service. As such services *are* secret, it was a safe claim to make, since nobody could or would prove or disprove it.

Among the innumerable women with whom he made contact at this time was a Mme Jeanne Cuchet (née Famast), a widow living with her seventeen-year-old son in the rue du Faubourg St Denis in Paris. She was thirty-nine and still an attractive woman, with full, sensual lips, bright eyes well-spaced, and finely arched eyebrows. Like many a lonely woman, she was beginning to think that if ever she was to marry again it would be better if she did it the right side of forty. She had for many years worked in a lingerie store in the rue Monsigny.

There are varying reports of how their association began.

One is that Mme Cuchet's son, André, called at Landru's garage looking for employment. It is not impossible, but surely not very probable. Mme Cuchet's home was a considerable distance from Landru's garage at Malakoff, from which he had fled in April in any case.

Another account suggests that Landru struck up conversation with Mme Cuchet one afternoon in the Luxembourg Gardens. Landru did make a habit of chatting, quietly, sagely, confidentially, to women he met in public places.

All the evidence suggests, however, that, like scores of others, Mme Cuchet was drawn by one of his advertisements in the matrimonial columns of the popular newspapers. The particular advertisement which she had seen was worded:

> Widower, with two children, aged forty-three, possessing comfortable income, affectionate, serious, and moving in good society, desires to meet widow of similar status, with a view to matrimony.

She answered, and received by return a letter from 'Raymond Diard', who described himself as an engineer. He wrote from an accommodation address in the rue Barbette, and is said to have 'borrowed' two charming little girls to accompany him on his first visit to her flat. Some reports say that these children were never seen by either Mme or André Cuchet after this first meeting. But this detail, I suspect, may be a mere legend, for subsequently Mme Cuchet fell in love with the quiet, professional gentleman with the charming manners, and shortly afterwards went to live with him—not for long, as it happens.

M. Diard proved most agreeable company. He took an instant liking to her son André, showing himself solicitous for his education and future, and he not only entertained Mme Cuchet in restaurants and bought her flowers, but sent her romantically-worded missives that might have been more appropriate from a love-sick youth swearing that he would climb the wistaria-entwined balcony at midnight. 'Without you I cannot live, my sweet one!' he used to write—probably in irritation and half wishing he had a rubber stamp for the phrase since he used it so much.

Mme Cuchet does not seem to have thought it anything but an unhappy coincidence that her son was taken ill twice after enjoying Monsieur Diard's kindly hospitality. Indeed, as we shall see, she was not only not a suspicious person, but could easily be dissuaded even when her suspicions were justifiably aroused.

Initially she was in conflict with herself. Some say she worried about the welfare of the two little girls whom Landru had brought with him on their first encounter, wondering how so affectionate a father could so easily reconcile himself to 'parking' them, as he claimed, with an aunt in Brest. She had visited his rather seedy villa, which he had recently rented, La Chaussée, near the Paris suburb of Chantilly, and it did not have the lived-in look one associated with a widower of means and a family man.

Despite this, she set up house with him at Chantilly, mindful of his promise to get married soon. It was towards the end of April 1914, and within a matter of days Landru, who had been living from hand-to-mouth and financing the initial stages of their association from the proceeds of other petty frauds, had opened an account for 5,000 francs with the Société Générale of Chantilly under the name of Diard.

Mme Cuchet's sister, Mme Friedmann, and her husband had met 'Monsieur Diard' at her flat in St Denis, and had taken an instant dislike to him. In vain they tried to warn Mme Cuchet that his background was too vague, his manner too slick, that it didn't make sense for an association between a woman nearing forty and a man in his fifties to exist on so passionate a level after so short and fortuitous an acquaintance.

'For goodness' sake make more detailed enquiries about him,' Mme Friedmann urged. 'Can't you see he's after your money? Does he *look* as though he cares a fig about love? So he's a widower? Have you checked where and when he got married before? He's an engineer, is he? Where's his office?' And so on, until relations between the two sisters, which had always been affectionate and close, became more and more strained. 'You're merely jealous because I've found love again,' snapped Mme Cuchet.

Even so, although there was this growing rift—which Landru did everything to make worse—between the two sisters, Mme Cuchet began to tire of her lover's continual prevarications over the subject of their proposed wedding. There was always some excuse—an urgent business proposition, some vague indisposition, or, when all other excuses had been exhausted, his claim that he had lost his military certificate.

Mme Cuchet spoke to her employer about this snag. 'No problem at all,' she said, 'it's quite easy to obtain a duplicate.' But Landru, when told this good news, simply glowered with annoyance. 'This is not something you should do. Why should a woman I don't even know be asking the military for a copy of *my* military certificate? I'll find it in due course—it's just that with pressure of business my private papers have got into disorder.'

At this, Mme Cuchet, feeling frustrated and humiliated, stormed out of the house and returned to her own flat.

We know that Landru was in touch with innumerable other women at this time, but found time to send after Mme Cuchet love letters protesting his utter devotion. 'I am very weary here', he wrote from Lyons, 'but I shall soon be back with you, darling. No hour passes but I think of you. I look forward eagerly to our day of supreme happiness. . . .'

'*Our day of supreme happiness*. . . .' It was more than Jeanne Cuchet could bear, and she broke down. She hurried round to her sister and brother-in-law, desperate with grief. 'I must see him, but I am ashamed of the way I've treated him. He will have gone to our villa in Chantilly by now. Please, please come with me, and I will try to make it up with him!'

But when the trio arrived at the villa, they found it empty. M. Friedmann suggested that they look around. The house seemed very ill-furnished for the home of a man claiming to be an engineer. It boasted the bare minimum of *petit-bourgeois* furniture, although there was some new linen, which had been bought at Mme Cuchet's suggestion when she had noted that there was none. The latter had been paid for by Landru out of 5,000 francs which she had loaned to him. There were piles of bricks, too, for what purpose it was not clear.

In one room was a box. 'I can't help it, I *am* suspicious of this man,' her brother-in-law insisted. 'Why don't we open this box? It's probably our only chance to get at the truth about him. Come. . . .'

Mme Cuchet was torn between seeking a reconciliation with Landru and easing her suspicions. 'All right, if you like. It'll prove you wrong and perhaps stop you grumbling about him.'

M. Friedmann found a sturdy chisel, eased it into the ledge of the box and forced it open. It was full of letters and documents, and a mere glance at these was sufficient to make his face cloud.

'Jeanne,' he said, gently, 'you won't like this, but it is as I suspected. This man is a charlatan and a rogue. Look! There are scores of letters to him, posted to different addresses—accommodation addresses, I should think. Some of them are addressed to him at newspaper box numbers. His name's *Landru*, not Diard. And he's married already. Many of these letters are from women.' He handed a few of them to Mme Cuchet. She inspected the box's contents herself. There was no denying the evidence. There were scores of letters from different women.

'So *that's* why he didn't want my boss to apply for a duplicate of his military certificate! Because his name isn't Diard and they couldn't have produced one! Just wait until I see him!'

'I wouldn't see him,' urged her sister. 'I'd break it off altogether before you get involved further with him.'

Mme Cuchet stood there, pale and shaking. 'I can hardly believe it. If only he were here to explain it all. . . .'

'He'd explain it all, no doubt,' Friedmann assured her. 'He spends all his time explaining things away. How would he account for trying to marry you, when he's married already? And look at the *dates* on some of these letters from other women. He's been in touch with them all the while he's been meeting you.'

The party left for Paris. Mme Cuchet felt utterly broken, but later seemed calmer, and her brother-in-law and sister felt that, cruel though the shock had been, she had been saved from a disastrous association. Jeanne did not tell her sister of her financial gifts to Landru. She must have known that had she done this, she and her husband would have gone to the police. There must still have been in her mind a lingering hope that the whole thing had an innocent explanation. She was in love again after years of loneliness, and found the thought of reverting to her old state intolerable.

Landru bombarded her with letters, which she ignored. Scenting trouble, he came to see her. There was a stormy scene. Since her visit to the empty villa, Mme Cuchet had received other disturbing information about her paramour. André, her son, had seen him walking jauntily, and arm-in-arm, with an Italianate woman.

But, as the Friedmanns had feared, Landru did, in fact, talk her out of it. He told Madame Cuchet what she wanted to hear: that he loved her, that he was unhappily married and seeking a divorce, and that he would marry her as soon as the necessary papers were through; that the letters from all those women were responses to advertisements placed long ago, when he was in a lonely state, and before he met Madame Cuchet. People often delayed for weeks before answering advertisements, and it had seemed to him only polite to acknowledge such letters, even if they arrived when his problems had passed and his needs met. Seen in the rue de Rivoli with another woman? Impossible! On that day he had been working in his garage at Clichy.

Relieved and happy, Mme Cuchet set up house again at La Chaussée. Landru inveighed against her sister's perfidy in attempting to break up their romance. How mean of them to begrudge her happiness! The Friedmanns, for their part, hearing that she had ignored all the warning signs and gone back to live with him, gave her up as a bad job. The rift was complete.

The end of August, 1914. Probably Landru had vanished in July in order to avoid call-up to the army, although he was, at the same time, making assignations with various women who had answered his matrimonial advertisements. He had disappeared just when Austria-Hungary declared war on Serbia —the tiny squib that was to explode a big bomb—followed by Germany declaring war on Russia on August 1, by Germany on France on August 3, and by Britain on Germany the following day. There followed a whole succession of declarations of war as the great powers lined up for the endless holocaust intended, vainly, to preserve what was known politically as the 'balance of power'. Montenegro declared war on Austria-Hungary; France, likewise, on August 7, followed three days later by Britain. Italy threw down the glove to Austria and Turkey, and so on.

The streets of Paris resounded to the tramp of soldiers on their way to points of assembly. As priorities switched from peace to war, all the wheels on which civilian life depends began to creak. But for Landru, all this was grist to the mill. By the time he was reconciled with Mme Cuchet, and privately planning his own little war, the greatest slaughter in history had begun. Belgium was overrun, Brussels entered, Namur had fallen, Louvain had been sacked, Antwerp taken. The 'small' British Expeditionary Force of 150,000 under Sir John French had reached France, the first two corps taking their place on the left of the Fifth French Army near Mons on August 22 and being brought into bloody conflict with the Germans the following day. Did Landru read about these tremendous battles, or feel any concern that his country— indeed, all Europe—was in the throes of a life-and-death struggle? Did he care that the Fifth French Army had been thrown back in confusion at Charleroi, that a breach had been made in the French lines, that the Third and Fourth French Armies were in retreat?

We know the answer. He was too busy rushing backwards and forwards in his van, from garage to garage, calling at newspaper offices for his bundles of letters or meeting his elderly women in cafés or parks. He did buy newspapers, but purely to study the advertisements. Astonishingly, considering his rather distinctive appearance, he was never detained for questioning or asked how he was getting his living. And he continued to support his family, mainly from money he had obtained from Mme Cuchet.

Perhaps because he no longer felt so confident at La Chaussée, Landru, having regained Mme Cuchet's trust, talked her into giving up her flat. On December 8 Landru rented a villa in Vernouillet, a little town in the Valley of the Seine. Far from being an attractive house, it was a squat, two-storied affair set back several feet behind a high wall, with a flight of stone steps leading to the front door. There were four windows in front, but one could not see into the rooms beyond from the narrow street. Landru had complained that the villa La Chaussée had too little privacy. Lovers, like murderers, like to be unobserved, and although André Cuchet had objected to the move to the dreary villa, his mother agreed.

The villa had a garden with fruit trees and beautiful lilacs and, a most important point where Landru was concerned, it had a small garage. Landru had promised Mme Cuchet marriage as soon as his divorce was through, and gradually, she made over all her property to him.

On December 8, 1914, Mme Cuchet, André Cuchet and 'M. Diard' were in residence at 47, rue de Mantes, Vernouillet. 'They kept themselves to themselves', as they like to say in England, but the average man with crime in his head would hardly have chosen such a place. The house was overlooked on both sides, and, because it was comparatively modern, the walls were not thick enough to be sound-proof.

On December 10, the director of La Paternelle, a firm of furniture removers and storers, was told by Landru to transport furniture from Mme Cuchet's home to Vernouillet. Landru busied himself putting flowers about the home and—a thoughtful, sentimental touch—placed upon their near-nuptial bed a sky-blue dressing-gown which he had had specially made for her. Sky-blue was Mme Cuchet's favourite colour. Landru knew that if a woman is pleased in small things her attention may be diverted from those that matter more.

Mme Cuchet and her son were scarcely seen in the town. Once or twice, early in December, she had called at the local shops to buy staples such as bread and coffee, but she exchanged few words. Her son was far from happy. He felt keenly the indignity of his mother playing the role of mistress when she had been promised marriage, and especially that Landru had deceived her in claiming to be unmarried.

Meanwhile, Mme Friedmann had gone to Landru's old address at Malakoff to make enquiries about him. These confirmed her worst misgivings. She wrote to her sister at Vernouillet, warning her that 'the man is a bandit, an unscrupulous rogue.... My dearest, please protect yourself.' The letters never reached Mme Cuchet. It is obvious that Landru must have intercepted them.

Mme Cuchet had rented the villa by an agreement signed on December 4, 1914. Later Landru had this agreement put in the name of M. Cuchet, whom he pretended to be, having abandoned the name of Diard. This agreement was not registered, as by law it should have been, and to make it valid a second agreement, dated March 31, 1915, was drawn up by Landru and formally registered. He had meanwhile obtained the personal papers of Mme Cuchet's dead spouse.

In the interim, Mme Cuchet and André her son had disappeared from the face of the earth. They were not well known enough locally to be missed much, and because of the family rift the Friedmann family felt there was nothing further they could do. In January, Landru had sold a tobacco-pipe that had belonged to André. M. Louis Germain, a brother-in-law of Mme Cuchet's, received a letter early in January from André Cuchet, in which he said he was lonely and not very happy, while on January 4, 1915 Mme Louise Morin received a letter from her friend Mme Cuchet which said little except that she had moved to Vernouillet and was waiting to marry her lover. Those were the last communications from either of them.

At about this time neighbours noted the most appalling, nauseating smoke coming from the 'Diard' residence. M. Meunier, a butcher in the rue de Mantes, was taking a late-night stroll with his wife when they saw and smelled the dense black fumes billowing from the villa's chimney. Whatever could it be? Most people in the area burned wood for fuel, as it was plentiful and could be had for the collecting. Rubbish, perhaps? Meunier's keen butcher's nose sniffed something unmistakeable—the smell of burning fat. He and his wife stood in the shadows of the little street, faintly illuminated by a single gas lantern. 'It's very late. Perhaps we won't bother now, but I'll mention it to the police in the morning. It shouldn't be allowed.'

Nor were M. and Mme Meunier the only outraged citizens. A doctor from Triel, on a professional visit to a patient in the Rue de Hameau had, like his patient, been caught in the awful stench, which he roundly condemned, in a protest to the police, as a menace to health.

The following day a policeman called at La Chaussée to investigate. Landru received him with polite surprise. 'I was burning a little rubbish, that's all. If every citizen disposed of his own rubbish in this way, imagine the trouble and expense we should all be saved!'

'If everyone made the offensive smell which you are reported to have made, sir, Vernouillet would be uninhabitable. Who else lives here?'

'My wife and her son André—but they're on a visit to her sister at the moment. They were here with me, and can confirm my statement when they return. . . .'

'Which will be . . . when?'

'Tomorrow.'

'Very well, I will call tomorrow. May I say, sir, that I don't think that *three* different people would be under the same illusion. They all maintain that the smell from your chimneys was very offensive, a real nuisance. I trust that before we speak again about this matter, there will be no further cause for complaint. . . .'

'I have not acknowledged, Officer, that there is any cause for complaint. I merely acknowledge your right to make enquiries if a complaint is made, and I am sorry you have been bothered over so trivial a matter. But do please call again, if you wish.'

With suave assurance, Landru saw the gendarme to the door.

Once his visitor was out of sight, he left immediately for Lyons where, from the Terminus Hotel, he wrote to the Brigadier of Police at Mantes. He had, he explained, to come away on business which would keep him away from Vernouillet for a few weeks. 'I made an appointment with the policeman who called upon me to come again and see my wife. But she has been called to London on a family matter.' He would let them know when she had returned, he said, adding that as the complaint was a slight one, he trusted they would not find the delay in following it up any inconvenience.

The depleted police force was hard-pressed at this time,

and in the middle of a war had more to think about than smoking chimneys. Landru had played for time, and won.

He now called on his wife, and gave her some money and some pieces of jewellery that had belonged to Mme Cuchet. In his cravat he wore a cheap tiepin which had belonged to André. On April 20, 1915, he fraudulently sold André Cuchet's insurance policy for 145 francs. Later in the year he sold a bond belonging to Mme Cuchet for 925 francs at the Remandon Bank. Not only had he styled himself M. Cuchet, but he now possessed all the dead M. Cuchet's identification documents.

And so Mme Cuchet and her son passed into oblivion. Mme Friedmann's letters were no longer ignored, but returned marked 'gone away'. Certainly the addressee *had* gone away—but where, and when, and how?

Landru seems to have realised that his letter to the Mantes police, explaining his absence and promising to call upon them on his return to answer questions, could not be his last word in the matter. If he should fail to contact them, as he had promised, their suspicions might be aroused and enquiries pursued, instead of being dropped. He therefore called upon them, apologised for any nuisance he might have caused by the burning of rubbish, promised to exercise more care and consideration for his neighbours in future, and explained that his wife, Mme Cuchet, and her son, had gone to England on pressing family matters.

The police were satisfied with this explanation. It was as well for Landru that they were. They did not know that Mme Cuchet had disposed of all her assets, and was therefore penniless; that to go to England in the middle of a war, when her own country was being invaded, was both a hazardous and pointless undertaking; that she had no family there; that André Cuchet had written to his friend, M. Morin, that he was expecting to spend the summer at Vernouillet, and do some canoeing, and assured him, as well as his uncle, M. Germain, that he was awaiting his call-up for the French Army and was quite ready to do his duty bravely at the Front. To the letting agency, in seeking to get the house in his name, Landru had said that his wife had gone to America in connection with her fashion house, while to a neighbour who enquired he had said that his wife and stepson had gone to England. But in the chaos and anxiety of war these inconsistencies did not arouse the concern they might have done in less troubled times.

At this point Landru became involved with a forty-six-year-old widow, Madame Laborde-Line, whose husband had been a hotel-keeper at Oloson, Santa-Maria. She had been living in Paris (at 95, rue de Petey) with her son, a postal clerk, and her daughter-in-law. Her relations with the latter had never been good; they quarrelled frequently. Although the son and his wife may have been relieved when he was appointed to a position in Nancy, it left Mme Laborde-Line lonely and unoccupied, and she advertised in a Paris newspaper for work as a *dame de compagnie*.

Among the few replies she received was a letter from Landru, calling himself M. Fremyet and writing from a room he had taken on March 16 at 152, rue du Faubourg St Martin. He addressed himself to her with that mixture of ardency and aristocratic concern for the proprieties which he had made his own special art. 'Brésil', as he described her cryptically in the little black notebook he carried perpetually in his inside pocket, called on him in his apartment in the rue des Petits-Champs, was captivated by his manner and quiet confidence, and within a day had agreed to hand over to him all her furniture, for which he assured her he could obtain better prices than anyone else. Within two days he had sold everything she had to a dealer in Batignolles.

For reasons on which we can only speculate, Landru now made an audacious move. Well knowing the suspicion with which the Friedmanns regarded him, he called upon them. He countered their angry and anxious accusations with the skill of a ping-pong champion. The correspondence with other women? Why, yes, he had been lonely, he had pined for a woman's solace—what normal Frenchman wouldn't? Certainly he had replied to some in terms of encouragement. In what other terms could one reply to a lady who had answered an advertisement from a man seeking matrimony? Why yes, he *was* married, but unhappily. Was a man who made an unwise choice of mate to be denied the right, forever, of finding the right person to share his life? The odds and ends of women's clothing scattered about the villa? He was in the second-hand business; there was no limit to the odd items that passed through his hands. There could be jewellery, furniture, the simplest domestic utensils, clothing of all sorts.

Mme Cuchet? André? Ah, yes, he understood their concern. It was unlike either of them to leave for England without first informing them, but they had no choice, for their work was secret. They had been assigned to secret work for the armed forces and were specifically forbidden to give even a hint of it beforehand. But they would hear in due course.

It seems odd, in retrospect, that the wary Friedmanns should have been taken in by the latter explanation. They were not to know, of course, that all the documents of identification that the average person would not dream of parting with, were still in Landru's possession. At that time the most ordinary people, in the chaos of war, were assigned to extraordinary jobs. If they did not believe it, they could not disprove it.

Landru at this time had several other addresses, but clearly he did not want to leave the Vernouillet villa yet, as he would certainly have to do if the Friedmanns pursued their original threat to inform the police of Mme Cuchet's disappearance. Such a complaint, coinciding with the complaints already made to the police of offensive burning smells coming from his house, might have set them thinking. It was a dangerous situation in which he had no choice but to take a dangerous risk. It is an interesting example of his cool nerve and audacity. But, the incident leaves one question unanswered. Would Landru have attempted to kill the Friedmanns, had he found them intractable?

These two complications being resolved (the complaints about his smoking chimneys, and the Friedmann's concern over Jeanne and André Cuchet's disappearance), Landru, in his apartment, set about filing, with the utmost method, his enormous correspondence from love-hungry women. Just as he itemised the most trivial item of expenditure, so every letter was placed in a neat pile according to its category. 'Reply later'; 'File'; 'Reply immediately'; 'Ignore'; '*Soupçons de fortune*'. He kept an exact index of the women's names, with little biographical details as to their physical and moral qualities, their family situations, their work, interests and style of living. It certainly was an awful lot of work for a man to be doing when he was committed to marrying a Mme Cuchet, whose disappearance he had accepted so philosophically.

Poor Laborde-Line! She is a dim and shadowy figure. She was seen at Vernouillet in June 1915, picking flowers in the garden. She told the concierge that she was going to stay with her future husband at Vernouillet—told him with a mixture of casualness and excitement, with the air of a woman anxious to have it known that she was sought after, but permitting no inference that she was over-anxious. Landru and Laborde-Line were seen walking together in the village.

Her son was by now fighting at the Front. He felt unhappy about the rift between his wife and his mother. Every fighting man likes to feel that his emotional life, at least, is secure. From his miserly soldier's pay, he sent his mother, by registered post, 200 francs which he had borrowed from her, to help with the cost of the removal. She never received it, and the unhappy youth wondered why she did not even acknowledge it, for it was accompanied by a letter written in his usual affectionate terms, and written under the daily risk of death.

To her friends in the provinces, too, Mme Laborde-Line had written in high excitement to say that she was about to marry, and was off to stay in the country villa of her fiancé, at Vernouillet.

For them, too, followed silence. Their letters were unanswered, and, later, returned. After June 25, she was never seen again.

Landru's next fiancée might best be described as *une dame formidable*. Her misfortune was to meet somebody as hard and calculating as herself—which is not to say that she deserved whatever fate overtook her.

Mme Guillin was fifty years old and living alone in a flat in the rue Crozatier. She was a woman of strong character, as her astute eyes and firm jaw confirm. She had for many years worked as companion-housekeeper to an old man in Melun, who had left her a legacy of about 22,000 francs.

She was lonely. She missed having somebody to care for, and the companionship of a man. And then, one of Landru's numerous advertisements caught her eye:

M. 45 ans. Seul, sans famille, situation 4000. Ay. inter. Désire épouse même age, situation rapport. G.I. 45 Journal.

Could this be true? A mature man alone, without a family,

and with a modest financial nest-egg, wanting to meet a woman of the same age?

She replied. The mere mention in her letter that she, too, had a little money to measure up to his was sufficient to bring the beady-eyed Romeo in his putty-coloured mackintosh and bowler hat to the door of her flat. It earned her a special pseudonym in the little black notebook.

To Mme Guillin he introduced himself as M. Petit. He was 'something in the Government' and was to be rewarded for services to his country which he was too modest to specify, but which she could only assume to have been connected with the war. His neatness, his assurance, gave colour to his story. And his reward? He was to be appointed Consul in Australia. It would be a wrench to leave his beloved France, but duty called. Australia was a long way away—a huge sprawling country, but with a fine climate and such luxuries as were long forgotten in war-torn Paris. But it would be unthinkable to take up his important duties without the right woman to support him, to share his duties and pleasures and, in particular, entertain local notables and important visitors from France.

He had a villa in Vernouillet as well as a town flat. A quiet weekend was all that was needed to arrange details. But she should get rid of her furniture while a price could still be had for it, for, what with the risk of bombing, dealers were increasingly reluctant to buy. It would not be worth taking to Australia. As for jewellery or anything like that, it would be better entrusted to his custody.

Although his story about being appointed as a Consul could so easily be checked, it is possible to see how she was taken in. Here was a well-dressed man with good manners, a man-about-town, imperturbable in the face of wartime upheaval, well known in many restaurants, a man who possessed a car— a considerable luxury at this time—and a villa. She was completely captivated by him and at once gave him charge of her property.

On August 2, 1915, Mme Guillin moved into the villa at Vernouillet, bringing with her a large brown trunk which Landru had advised her to buy for the journey to Australia, thoughtfully leaving her to pay for it herself. On August 4 Landru was at her flat in the rue Crozatier supervising the removal of her effects, by the firm of Laffitte, to a store at Neuilly. It was one of the numerous storage places which he used over the years, this one being at 43, rue Parmontan.

A box of jewellery he took custody of himself. It also contained Mme Guillin's false hair. Subsequently he sold the jewellery but kept the hair, one assumes less from sentiment than the thought that it might be sold for a few francs one day. The concierge enquired kindly after her.

'She's very well, thank you,' said Landru, looking anxiously around to ensure that the removal men did not miss the smallest item. 'She is going to Australia.' This is what Mme Guillin had herself told the concierge on giving notice to leave. She had written, excitedly, to various friends in similar terms.

Mme Guillin was never seen again by anyone after August 2. It has been alleged, but not by the French authorities, that Landru murdered her immediately on her arrival, put her in her own trunk and despatched it to 'Mme Jacques, Gare Arachon, to be called for'. Nobody did call for it, but unpleasant evidence that it did not contain normal luggage induced the railway staff to prise it open six months later and discover the decomposing corpse of a middle-aged woman. The find was never positively connected with Landru. Certainly Mme Guillin had brought a large trunk with her to Vernouillet, in obedience to Landru's suggestion, but it was second-hand, and only Landru could have said if the trunk found at the Gare Arachon was the one purchased by his 'fiancée'.

A few days after Mme Guillin's disappearance, Landru sold some bonds belonging to her, for the sum of 971 francs. He then proceeded, by forgery and deception, to collect her money from the bank, showing considerable audacity in the process.

His first step was to hire a room in the Avenue MacMahon in Mme Guillin's name. He forged a type of Deed of Attorney (the term used is 'general procuration') alleged to have been signed by 'Widow Guillin' and, using the name of Georges Petit, called on M. Lesbazeilles, attorney of the Meyer Brothers bank in the rue St Lazare. He explained that he was acting for his sister-in-law because she had become paralysed and unable to attend to her business affairs. She had authorised the withdrawal of her stocks and bonds and other credits from the Banque de France and wished them to be placed to the credit of himself, Georges Petit, in an account he had opened on December 15.

It seems to have been surprisingly easy for Landru to have appropriated to himself all the assets of Mme Guillin entrusted to the safe keeping of the bank. From November 4 to December 15, 1915, he collected from the Banque de France, under false signatures, a total sum of 8,382 francs, and 5,450 francs from the Meyer Bank by selling other bonds which Madame Guillin possessed.

Mme Guillin had written a letter to her daughter and son-in-law from Vernouillet, dated August 3 or 4, saying that she found the villa and its surroundings charming, and was looking forward to embarking for Australia and a new life. When she disappeared, it was no surprise to them that they did not hear from her. Australia was a long way away, posts were uncertain and, anyway, the ship could have been torpedoed.

And so Mme Guillin followed Mme Laborde-Line, Mme Jeanne Cuchet and seventeen-year-old André Cuchet into oblivion. Four people had disappeared without trace within a year, from a house hemmed in by others. All had some kith or kin, and in every case there were family factors that prevented enquiries being energetically pursued. Poor Mme Cuchet became estranged from her sister and brother-in-law because she obstinately ignored their warnings; Mme Laborde-Line's son attributed his mother's silence to her quarrel with his wife; Mme Guillin's daughter, not too affectionately disposed because she had been brought up in an orphanage and felt her mother had neglected her, accepted her mother's disappearance as a normal thing.

As for Landru, he was still busy careering around in his car, transferring furniture, selling odds and ends, inserting new advertisements, and indifferent to the fact that at Loos, where he was once in prison, a mighty battle had been fought, and that the British had held and taken it. What if a million British and two million Frenchmen were trying to hold back the German hordes? Landru had his own war to fight, his own very private war.

3

The Lonely Love-Nest

IT IS CLEAR that in the middle of May 1915, just after the disappearance of the Cuchets, Landru was busily engaged lining up other victims. Indeed, in the course of 1915 he was working from no less than four different addresses, apart from his villa in Vernouillet, his garage at Clichy and the family flat in the rue Blomet. For the purposes of his deceptions he had taken apartments at 152, rue du Faubourg St Martin (March 26, 1915–July 27, 1915); 8, Place Budapest (August 9, 1915–August 15, 1915); 15, rue Lamartine (August 27, 1915–September 18, 1915); and 57, rue Tallier at Lavallois (October 1915–January 1916). During this same period, apart from his garage at Clichy, which was the cloak for all sorts of activity, legal and illegal, he stored furniture at various *gardes meubles*—2, rue de Château at Neuilly; 43, rue Parmontan at Neuilly; 137, rue Sicouffetard, and 21, rue Etex. From January 1916, he rented a further storage place, at 6, rue Maurice, Clichy, and this address, as well as those in the rue de Château and the rue Sicouffetard, he retained until the very end of the war.

I give these details, which inevitably are of no more than passing interest, to indicate the complexity of the programme he had set himself. He must have been a man of quite extraordinary energy to have been rushing around on the railways, riding his bicycles (as he often did) or driving his cars from one place to another. He was a skilled and expert driver and a good mechanic, and could undertake the longest journeys, confident that he could deal with any breakdown or setback. He was also physically strong, humping chairs, wardrobes and other heavy furniture about with the nonchalance of a bummaree at Smithfield Market.

Apart from attending auction sales for a bit of legitimate

36

trading, he had his voluminous correspondence to collect, answer, sift into categories and follow up. Sometimes a whole day would be taken up in meeting and 'interviewing' likely subjects. In handling the letters, he applied fairly stringent eliminative processes. He never bothered to investigate a reply further unless there was some evidence of money. But even so, there were many, many more assignations and appointments than there were victims, since women looking for a mate have been known to exaggerate.

It is easy to imagine Landru driving from Vernouillet to Paris, collecting his mail from the *Echo de Paris*, retiring to his Paris room to inspect the letters, busying himself with his pen as he composed those dignified, educated missives so perfectly blending formality with an undercurrent of gallantry. Through his pebbly glasses he would look for tell-tale signs such as he sought—a good quality envelope, perhaps tissue-lined; a good handwriting; die-stamped letterhead. But what he favoured most was the particular sort of victim he knew to be the easiest and most vulnerable—the middle-aged and lonely.

It must have been hard work sometimes, following up all the enquiries. In this he applied the most methodical techniques, listing names and addresses and special information. Within days of ensuring the disappearance of the Cuchets, he listed his appointments for a single day:

9h 30.	Tabac, Gare de Lyon. Mlle Lydée.
10h 30.	Café, Place St Georges. Mme B.
11h 30.	Metro Lancry. Mme L.
2.30.	Metro Concorde. Mme L. [as above, but not necessarily the same person]
3.30.	Tour de St Jacques. Mme D.

There were others that day, but we can see that, allowing himself ample time for lunch, as every good Frenchman does, he was a very busy man.

Funds were running low towards the end of 1915, however, despite his frenetic petty swindling and his capacity to make people disappear. He seems to have become less confident about Vernouillet as a base for activity, and we find him exploring the countryside in search of a more suitable spot.

Somehow, although nobody knows in what exact circumstances, Landru found himself exploring the area that lies between the vast dense forests of Dreux and Rambouillet, some parts of which are so dense they are seldom visited. In this area of pleasant villages linked by lonely roads, he came at last to Gambais. Near a church and its cemetery, and almost concealed by trees, was a villa advertised to let.

True, it was very close to the road. But the road itself was quite isolated. No houses overlooked the villa or its extensive garden; its windows opened on to sweeping countryside and distant woodland. Landru noted with satisfaction that the garden ended in a ploughed field, and was well fenced off from another adjacent field. Indeed, the whole house was surrounded by substantial fences, and the windows had those solid, old-fashioned steel shutters. Also, for Landru a primary consideration, there was a good garage.

Landru was seen wandering in the church cemetery, deep in thought. A solitary mourner thought he was a relative paying a duty visit. Whatever his thoughts were, he was not, like Gray at Stokes Poges, composing an elegy.

Landru made enquiries locally, called upon the villa's owner, M. Tric, signed a lease for the house and paid three months' rent in advance. M. Tric observed with satisfaction that the 'engineer', M. Petit, was punctilious in matters of money, paying the exact amount due, on time.

One woman who had responded to Landru's advertisements at this time was Mme Heon, a widow, born in Havre in 1860 and therefore fifty-five years old. She was plain to the point of ugliness, 'ill-favoured' as the English used to say. Married in 1882, she had been a widow since 1907 living in a flat in the suburb of Ermont.

Mme Heon was lonely and grief-stricken and desperate for company. Her daughter had lived with a M. Kowalski, a tailor, in the rue de Rennes, but he had been killed at the Front in August 1915. Then her own son had died at the Front. Her daughter died. The friend with whom she was living at Ermont died. She was left with scarcely anybody near to her, and when Landru called upon her, soft-voiced and protective, she gladly accepted his proposal of marriage and, having no further need of it, entrusted the sale of her furniture to him.

Landru described himself as 'M. Petit' and claimed to be the representative of a big concern in Brazil. He was already 'courting' Mme Heon when planning to marry Mme Laborde-Line and Mme Guillin.

While his relationship with Madame Heon was developing the way he wished, and finding himself, for whatever reasons, free of the possessive intentions of (the late?) Mme Laborde-Line and Mme Guillin, Landru, alias 'M. Petit', set about making The Hermitage, as M. Tric's villa was called in Gambais, fit for the reception of his latest love.

He had his own set of priorities. First, he bought a quantity of fire-proof bricks and cement, and purchased in Paris a solid iron oven which seemed rather large for the requirements of a middle-aged couple. The stove he installed himself, supplementing it with a brick oven which linked up with the same flue, and thence to the chimney.

In September 1915, Landru arranged for Mme Heon's furniture to be bought for 820 francs by a merchant in Montmartre, giving him a receipt signed 'Petit'. Mme Heon, meanwhile, had been telling friends, in a state of high excitement, that she was going to remarry, a very charming gentleman who was something important in Brazil, to which country they would no doubt go when the ceremony had been enacted in Tunisia.

Landru supervised, also, the removal of his furniture from his villa in Vernouillet to Gambais. He did not trouble overmuch about making the home attractive. It was almost as though he did not contemplate a very lengthy stay. There was not a room which could be said to be adequately furnished as a bedroom. For example, in the whole of the house there was only one camp bed, not at all the sort of standard of comfort you would think acceptable to a self-professed Lothario.

On December 8, Landru and Mme Heon boarded the train in Paris for Gambais. Perhaps she did not hear him ask for the tickets at the booking office. If she did, she does not seem to have thought it unusual that he ordered one return ticket and one single. The provisions they were taking with them were rather frugal for a weekend in the country, but she supposed there was plenty of food to be had locally. At any rate, she must have observed on arrival that the house would be warm, for there was such a splendid new stove and no less than half a ton of coal, which Landru had ordered from a local merchant. Most local inhabitants used wood, which was both economical and plentiful. Mme Heon may have thought his choice of fuel extravagant or eccentric.

Extravagance, however, was never one of Landru's failings. He had been engaged in angry correspondence with a tradesman for weeks, over a matter of a refund of six francs, and never rested until he received it. His saving on the single ticket to Gambais, which he bought for Mme Heon when the pair left Garanceières, was a mere 1 franc 45 centimes. But why waste money? With his usual care, he had recorded in his *carnet*: 'Gare de Garanci, return 3 francs 85; single, 2 francs 40.'

Mme Heon had been hurt, though apparently not puzzled, by Landru's indignation at her telling friends of her impending marriage. He had been even more displeased when, while walking together in Paris, they had met some of them, and she had proudly introduced him as her fiancé.

From the moment of her arrival at Gambais, the poor, plain, lonely widow Heon was never seen again. On the same night Landru appeared at his home and spent the rest of the night with his wife and children. In the morning he disappeared again on his mysterious missions.

In a day or so, three friends of Mme Heon received postcards written by Landru—on her behalf, he said, as she was so happily busy about the home and preparing for her new life abroad. When they heard no more, they assumed that she had gone her new, happy way.

Where *had* she gone? Only Landru knew.

I wonder if he also knew anything about Mme Chouillet, concierge of the block where Mme Heon's daughter had had her flat.

When Mme Heon (who adopted this name in memory of a sister, for her original name was Gondouin) started meeting up with Landru, he came several times to dinner and lunch with her and Mme Chouillet.

After Mme Heon disappeared, Mme Chouillet also disappeared. It seemed entirely out of character that this elderly widow, whose husband was killed in the war, should elect to leave the security of her job and home and live, as she said she intended to, in Switzerland. She sent a postcard saying 'Have arrived in Switzerland quite safely'. The card bore a Swiss postmark. 'It is very cold,' the card went on, 'but life is much gayer than in the rue de Rennes, and I have no regrets at having left Paris.'

It is highly improbable that an elderly concierge, whose life in the rue de Rennes had certainly never been gay, but whose life was wrapped up in the street and her few friends there, would have said that life was gayer in Switzerland, and that she did not miss Paris. Furthermore, the card was not in her handwriting, but in that of a man.

The first gas attack by the Germans had come and gone. The battles of Neuve-Chapelle, Ypres, Festubert, and Loos had taken their terrible toll of French and Allied troops. The world gasped in horror at the sinking of the *Lusitania*. The disastrous Dardanelles landing had been effected by the British Army, and by December 8, its evacuation had begun. Nurse Cavell had been arrested by the Germans, tried, and shot. Some of the prettiest parts of France were a shambles of mud; enormous poplar trees, slashed by shell fire, veered tipsily into streets and streams. Battlefields were a quagmire of mud, splintered duckboards, collapsed trenches and stinking shell-holes in which corpses floated.

And yet, as always in war, people clung ferociously to habit and tradition. So much of normal life continued cheek-by-jowl with wartime anarchy. The cafés still kept up a semblance of their usual routine. And the newspapers still came out, much to the relief of Landru, whose advertisements continued to appear in the matrimonial columns, attracting an enormous correspondence. Whatever else might happen in this war, France would never run short of widows. They were being created at a rate of thousands a day.

Another of the correspondents who answered his advertisements was Mme Anna Collomb, aged forty-four, a widow whose husband had worked in the silk trade. Had come to settle in Paris after his death, and was now working as a typist in the offices of La Société de l'Union Prévoyante. She had been working as a companion in Marseilles before coming to Paris, where she lived at 15, rue Rodier with a lover, M. Bernard.

She was still living with her lover when she replied to Landru's advertisement on May 1, 1915. Womanlike, she gave her age as twenty-nine. She had had a child by Bernard, and had placed it in a convent in San Remo. If somewhat wayward in temperament, Mme Collomb was certainly warm and gregarious. She was fond of her parents, M. and Mme Moreau, and especially affectionate and protective towards her younger sister, Mme Pelat, who adored her in turn.

Mme Collomb was a good-looking woman. She was also feminine enough to be flattered by the incessant gifts of flowers and the deluge of impassioned letters which her reply to Landru had sparked off. He visited her at her flat, and she in turn stayed occasionally all night with him at his apartment in the rue Chateaudun. There is no doubt that she found him attractive, and she lost no time in telling everyone she knew that they were in love and about to be married. Landru pretended that he was a rich refugee from Lille, living in Paris and Gambais under the name of Dupont. He pretended to have means, and as a result received the reciprocal confidence that Mme Collomb had about 8,000 francs in the bank.

Her family did not like Landru, and said so. But she insisted that this was 'the real thing' and spoke animatedly of setting up house in the south with her fiancé, in the Var or the Midi.

Mme Moreau pleaded with her daughter: 'Please, Anna, make careful enquiries about this man of yours. I can't say why, but I simply don't like the look of him. He seems to be using *two* names—Fremyet and Cuchet. He says it's to draw benefits as a refugee in two names. Even if that's true, it wouldn't be honest....'

'Mother,' Mme Collomb would say, and say quietly, for she never quarrelled with her parents, 'please trust my judgment. He's a real gentleman. I love him, and I know he loves me. He says such beautiful things to me, and even when he can't be with me, because he works so hard, he sends me lovely letters....'

'Anything that makes you happy, makes me happy. But I implore you, please, please be careful. I can't help it. I have my doubts. But, believe me, I don't want to stand in the way of your happiness.'

On Christmas Day, 1916, Mme Collomb had lunch with her mother. She left, saying that she would come and see her again two days after Boxing Day.

The next day she and Landru caught the train to Gambais. Once again he asked for a return ticket for himself and a single ticket for her. She had given up her flat in the rue Rodier on November 19, and Landru had removed and stored her furniture in one of his garages. She had since been living with him in the rue Chateaudun, and now, at his pressing invitation, was off to spend a happy holiday with him in the romantic seclusion of his country villa. Tradesmen who called at the villa during her brief stay noticed her in a blue dressing-gown— the same one that he had originally had made for Mme Cuchet.

Mme Collomb disappeared. Landru noted in his little private notebook the cost of the train fares for both of them, referring to her by a code name. There was also a cryptic entry in his book: '4 o'clock.'

The money she possessed had been gradually withdrawn from her account from the day she first met him, so that by the time she went to Gambais with him she possessed only 300 francs of her original balance of 8,000.

None of Mme Collomb's family had any further direct communication from her. She owed a wine merchant for two bottles of wine, and Landru's son Maurice called on his father's instructions and paid for them on her behalf, returning the empty bottles at the same time, and saying that Mme Collomb was in good health and had gone to Valencia.

Landru sent Maurice on another errand—to Mme Collomb's sister, Mme Pelat, with a basket of mimosa, inside which was a visiting card. The flowers were supposed to have been sent to her from Nice. But both Mme Pelat and her mother were puzzled and worried. Why hadn't Anna, an effectionate, dependable daughter, kept her promise to see her parents on December 28? Why had she sent no personal word of her inability to do so? Where was she now, and why hadn't she written to tell them of her new address? Why did the card with the flowers give no indication of her address in Nice? Why, if the flowers really came from her, hadn't she sent them *directly* to her sister from Nice, instead of through Landru's son? And if she couldn't have brought the flowers herself, for whatever reason, why hadn't her fiancé brought them, instead of sending them by his son?

The concierge at the building where Mme Collomb had been living received a visit from Landru personally, to convey

Mme Collomb's good wishes, and her delight in her new-found happiness with the man of her dreams. She missed Paris very much but was happy in her new home in the South of France.

'Of course, our forthcoming marriage is very secret. I know we're not that young, but we've as much right as anyone else to be romantic,' Landru told her, and she nodded with understanding, 'so keep all this to yourself until you hear we've been married. I know you know how to keep a secret—it's part of the job you do so well. I have always appreciated your discretion, and your concern for Mme Collomb's best interests.'

Landru handed the concierge a ten-franc note as a tip, which she accepted with discreet good grace.

4

More Vanishing Ladies

LANDRU'S CONTACTS with women in need of companionship or
solace were achieved not only by advertisements in Paris
newspapers; he was also a frequent visitor to matrimonial
agencies, and even to employment agencies.

Any woman possessing property or cash was of interest to
him; age and looks scarcely mattered. The means of initial
contact did not matter, either. He would accost women in
cafés, in the streets, in the parks, on the Metro trains and,
come to that, in the stations too.

There is one woman in France today who can remember
being accosted by the ingratiating stranger. She is Mme
Madeleine Serin, now aged seventy-one. As a young girl, in
World War I, she was travelling on the Pereire-Montmartre
tramway when a distinguished-looking man, bald, bearded and
neatly dressed, who was sitting next to her, inclined his head
slightly in her direction and whispered, softly, through his
beard:

'Are you married?'

'Yes.'

'Happy?'

'Yes.'

'But you might still need a sincere friend, in whom you
could confide—someone like myself, for example.'

They continued their journey in silence. When Madeleine
Serin got off the tramcar, Landru followed her, caught up with
her, and suggested that they take a cab.

'I don't take cabs with men I don't know,' she said, now
finding his attentions a nuisance. Eventually she reached her
grandmother's house, and raced up the steps. Safely inside, she
watched the bearded stranger through the window. He paced
up and down for at least two hours before leaving.

The Ladykiller

It might be supposed that a man in his fifties, with a wife and four children to support, with the worry of maintaining a garage at Neuilly, a villa at Gambais and of transferring and selling furniture and odds-and-ends of property, might be too tired by the pattern of his constant travelling and the hazards of his frauds, to be amorously inclined. But as he was subsequently found to be in ardent correspondence with 283 women, whose letters to him were often couched in uninhibited language, we must not take his virtue for granted. Mme Serin was fully entitled, when she related her story about the bearded ogre to her children, to finish with the catchline: 'So you see, my dears, if you hadn't had a virtuous mother, you wouldn't be here today.'

The case of poor Andrée Babelay is the only *known* instance of Landru courting a woman without property of any kind. Unless he wanted to enjoy her ample charms, there seems no reason why 'Bluebeard' should have deliberately sought to get involved with her, nor that he should have had any motive for causing her to disappear.

It was in February 1917, that Landru, waiting for a train on the platform of Opéra station on the Paris underground, caught sight of an attractive, neatly dressed girl of nineteen. She looked very unhappy, was crying to herself, and occasionally dabbing her eyes with her handkerchief.

When the train came in, he followed her into the carriage and sat down beside her. When she alighted he followed her, and said to her sympathetically, 'Sometimes strangers can be friends when one's own friends have become strangers.'

Andrée Babelay stopped and stared at him in the gaslight.

'I saw you were crying. I can't bear to see young people suffer. You are too young, and too pretty, to suffer. If I can help you. . . .'

They walked on through the crowded, darkening streets, reached a café and went inside. Thankfully, Andrée Babelay accepted a coffee and a liqueur and poured out her story.

She was working for a fortune teller, Mme Vidal, in the rue de Belleville in Paris. She had just quarrelled with her mother, Mme Collin, and had nowhere to sleep for the night, nor money to pay for a room.

'My name is Lucien Guillet,' he told her, 'and I have a

small flat in the rue de Mauberge. You are welcome to my hospitality, and you will be in safer hands than you would be wandering the streets here, where every type of villain is roaming about.'

Andrée smiled thankfully, and Landru produced his little black notebook and dutifully recorded her name in it.

Andrée stayed on in the rue Mauberge, doing his cooking and sharing his bed, reconciled to his frequent absences when, in fact, he was collecting his mail from the newspapers, or visiting his wife and children, or meeting other women who had responded to his offer of matrimony. She gave up her work with Mme Vidal, telling her that she was in love with a charming man of thirty-five, who wanted to marry her. She visited her mother, hugged her little sister Adrienne with joy, and announced to them both that she was going to be married, and that although her fiancé wanted the wedding to be a private affair, she would see to it that they came to stay with them at the beautiful villa where she was going to live.

Landru had introduced Andrée Babelay as his niece, up from the country. Bearded old men do have nieces, and it seems the concierge took little note of the pair, except to observe that Landru, known there as Lucien Guillet, was a particularly affectionate uncle. Andrée was, in effect, a second wife to him. She cleaned, cooked, ran errands and, as she imagined, shared his secrets. There were many secrets she did not share, such as the fact that he was married and the father of four children, to whom he referred in his notebook by numbers—3, 4, 5, and 6. References to himself were always to 'I'. Marie Landru, his wife, was No. 2.

Since Landru enjoyed her company, and clearly tired of it far slower than was the case with his previous brief courtships, one wonders why, within a short time, she was to join the ranks of the vanished women. The explanation may be different from that behind the disappearance of the other women.

Mme Cuchet's brother-in-law was still not convinced by Landru's pretences, that all was well, and that both Mme Cuchet and André were alive and well in England. He believed that they had, in fact, vanished in mysterious and sinister circumstances, and as a result had gone to the police. The police at Mantes did not think this sinister; in wartime so many people change their addresses suddenly or vanish from their usual districts. Thousands of women had done so. Nevertheless, the concern which Mme and M. Friedmann expressed over Mme and André Cuchet's disappearance caused them to make enquiries. If the couple could be traced, that would dispose of the matter, so they allowed the press to know that they wished to trace a M. Diard, who had rented a villa in Vernouillet, and a Mme Cuchet and her son, who had lived at the villa with him. All had vanished, but M. Diard had been seen.

A report to this effect had been published in a newspaper, *Bon Soir*. Andrée Babelay had bought a copy of this to read, and happened to notice the report. There is no reason to suppose that she actually suspected Landru, at least at this stage, but she may well have thought that the description of 'M. Diard' was rather similar to M. Guillet.

On March 12, Andrée was taken ill while staying at Landru's flat. He took her by taxi to a doctor, carefully noting the date and the cost in his notebook. Not the smallest item of expenditure ever went unrecorded.

On March 29, 'M. Guillet' and his bride-to-be set off for Houdan, the nearest station to Gambais, the final lap of the journey being completed by coach. With that fine sense of economy which was second nature to him, he once again booked a return ticket for himself and a single ticket for his lady companion, recording the details as usual.

When they arrived at Gambais, Landru noted with concern that his stocks of coal were exhausted, and set about laying in plenty of wood for fuel, as coal could not be bought in Gambais. It is believed that, during Landru's frequent absences, Andrée went exploring through the house and, opening a box, found documents pertaining to Mme Cuchet in it. If this were so, and the authorities seemed to think it probable, she might certainly have put two and two together. If the authorities were looking for a M. Diard, whose description tallied with that of the man she was with, and were also trying to trace Mme Cuchet, with whom he had been in contact, then M. Diard and M. Guillet could be the same person.

If this did happen, then Landru must have been extra-ordinarily careless, because it had been a similar discovery which had made the Friedmanns so suspicious when they prised open the box in his villa at Vernouillet. But the pattern of his life had become so complicated that mistakes were easy to make.

Thereafter Landru's notebook shows that he bought small presents of sweets and cakes for Andrée Babelay. He spent five francs on her on April 2, and a similar sum on April 10. On April 12 he noted that he had bought two *stères* of wood (two cubic metres); the price of a Metro ticket; the money he had spent on meat and bread; and the figures '4h.3'.

From four o'clock on April 12, 1917, Andrée Babelay was never seen or heard of again. Mme Collin, who had not been a bad mother to her and had certainly never forbidden her daughter the house—Andrée used to visit her every week, and was devoted to her younger sister—worried and fretted about her daughter's fate and happiness. She assumed that Andrée must have got married, as she had said she would. But why the utter silence? It was unlike her. And why did her letters never get answered?

However, Andrée had always been mercurial and impulsive, and had presumably married her bearded lover who, surely, must have been older than the thirty-five he claimed to be.

What happened to Andrée Babelay? As she had only been earning a little over a pound a month, she had no savings and could not have gone off anywhere. Usually, after one of Landru's visitors vanished, his chimney belched nauseating acrid black smoke, so the experience of Dr Jean Monteilhet, who in 1916 was serving with the 1st Regiment of Engineers at Versailles, has a certain interest:

About the end of May or the beginning of June of the year in question [1917] I cycled from Versailles to Gambais to spend the day with my aunt, who was the Lady Superior of a convent there. About nine o'clock in the evening I cycled to Houdan [near Gambais] to catch the train back to Versailles.

After passing by Gambais Church and the Cemetery, I was surprised to note that M. Tric's villa had been let. It was a superb moonlit night, and I noticed before the door a little motor wagonette with its nose pointed towards Versailles, and its lights out. There was a light in the villa on the ground floor, and a thick column of smoke was issuing from the chimney. The stench chocked me, and I thought: 'Whatever can M. Tric be burning?'

I continued on my way. While running down to the Etang des Bruyères, a pond about a mile away, my tyre burst. The pond at this point borders on the road. I got down, filled my *képi* with water, and set to work to mend the tyre.

I had just finished when I heard the sound of a motorcar coming from Gambais. My first thought was to ask the driver to give me a lift to Versailles, so I waited. To my disappointment and astonishment the car stopped some yards from the pond, and then I saw that it was the little wagonette that I had seen in front of Tric's door. The chauffeur, instead of being in uniform, proved to be a little man in a light coloured overcoat and cap.

He jumped down lightly, and I saw that he had a black beard. He began to walk along the side of the pond away from the road, and carried something; but I could not distinguish its size or shape. On reaching the path leading to the gamekeeper's lodge, he turned on to the earth causeway running to the centre of the pond. At this point he was hidden by rushes, but a moment later I heard something flop into the water. I thought it was a poacher throwing a net into the water, and as there was no hope of a lift to Versailles, I continued on my bicycle. . . .

The pond is a wild, lonely spot known only to poachers and wild duck hunters. It is shallow along the borders, but twenty feet deep in the middle.

The engineer's story is interesting, as his experience happened just about the time of the disappearance of the poor servant girl. Her precise ending was never proven, nor her body found. All that remains to be said about her is that, like all the women visitors to the Gambais villa during Landru's tenancy, she disappeared irrevocably, and without trace.

Sometime in 1915, a Mme Celestine Buisson, a pleasant, home-loving widow of forty-four, answered one of Landru's numerous matrimonial advertisements.

At that time he was busy—that seems a reasonable word— arranging to secure the property and assets of Mme Cuchet and a succession of equally unfortunate women. In between, however, he had met and maintained frequent contact with the widow whose letter he placed neatly on the pile headed *soupçons de fortune*. Quite an expert, by now, at assessing and confirming the assets of complete strangers (he would have done well with a modern credit status agency), he had ascertained that she was worth about 10,000 francs and that the furniture in her Paris flat in the rue de Banquier was her own.

Landru had written from the Hôtel de France et d'Angleterre at Beauvais, explaining that he was a prosperous manufacturer who had fled from Lille as the Germans advanced. It had been agony for him to abandon his estate there, to lose touch with friends and relatives (not family, he was careful in his choice of words) and to become a refugee. Fortunately he had not kept his financial reserves in Lille. All this, however, was poor consolation to a French gentleman of cultivated tastes and ardent disposition. He was lonely. What was life without a woman to share it?

What, indeed? Mme Buisson had been a widow for three years, and did not greatly like it. She too was not without human warmth. 'I will love you well,' she wrote to him. 'I will soon make you forget your unhappiness in face of the German invaders.' Landru followed this up with a succession of wildly passionate letters which set her middle-aged head swimming.

They had met in and around Paris, and even stayed together for a few days in Beauvais and Biarritz, sometimes in a middle-class hotel or a comfortable *pension*. The First World War was one in which the air raid was a comparatively rare thing, mostly limited to military objectives and limited in its destructive potential. While millions were locked in battle elsewhere, there were still pockets of peaceful, and even comfortable, living. Mme Buisson grew very fond of the busy, romantic M. Fremyet, as he now called himself.

Why did Landru wait so long before bringing their relationship to a conclusion?

It may be that his earlier victims were easier to deal with, although he had taken a considerable risk in the case of Mme Cuchet and her son. Only the fact of a war being on, the police being over-worked, so much of the population on the move, and his own frequent changes of name and address had saved him from arrest and questioning.

Mme Buisson, whose late husband had been a hotel-keeper, introduced Landru to her mother and to her two sisters, Mme Paulet and Mlle Lacoste. Reluctantly, Landru had dined with them all in her flat, possibly wishing that there were some easy way to make them all disappear and acquire all their furniture. He had also been pressed to see Mme Buisson's illegitimate son, but this he had refused to do, fearing arrest in Bayonne. Celestine was devoted to her blind son, whose sad state seemed at times to move Landru almost to tears.

In 1917, just after the disappearance of young Andrée Babelay, Landru pursued Mme Buisson in earnest. In his little private notebook he put against her name the significant number '7'. Six of his former 'fiancées' had vanished without trace. Mme Buisson was his seventh.

Landru's first job was to isolate Mme Buisson. Her blind son was placed in a home, away from their love-nest in Gambais. Mme Paulet had died as their friendship developed, and Landru won himself even further into Celestine's confidence by undertaking all the funeral arrangements (no doubt, like Seddon the poisoner, charging a commission on the coffin). In June, Mme Buisson ordered a wedding dress from her dressmaker. She brought Mme Paulet's children to Gambais to spend a weekend there, and they romped and played with 'Uncle Fremyet' in the rose-arboured garden. They spent a fortnight in Paris together, then returned to Gambais on August 19, this time without anybody else.

In Landru's little book another entry was made:

1 single ticket, Tacoi	...	...	...	...	Frs. 2.75
1 return	...	...	...	...	...	Frs. 4.40

There was no point in buying a return ticket for Mme Celestine Buisson, whereas in purchasing a return ticket for himself he saved over one franc. Tacoi is the station before Houdan, and is also used for Gambais.

While Mme Buisson was agog with thoughts of her forthcoming marriage and planning to return to Paris to collect her wedding gown, Landru thoughtfully made his own contribution towards her trousseau—some bed linen and underclothes that had belonged to the missing Mme Cuchet. He had collected them from one of his numerous store rooms.

Mme Buisson was seen, fleetingly, by a few inhabitants of Gambais. Landru by now was known to have such a succession of women that a new face occasioned no great surprise. She was never seen again after September 1, 1917. On that day Landru noted in his diary '10hr. 15.' On the same day his cash assets increased from 88.30 francs to 1031 francs.

Mme Buisson, with that clockwork regularity one now

expects of Landru's guests, had disappeared on the very eve of her wedding. No woman, least of all one of a certain age, or at least not in the period we are at present considering, would have dreamed of getting married without telling those nearest to her, and a lot of people whom she knew only casually. Mme Buisson had told her mother, her two sisters (although Mme Paulet had since died), her blind son, the concierge of the block of flats in the Boulevard Ney, the lady who was busy making her wedding gown, and Mme Simon, a friend she had asked to serve as a witness at her wedding.

This comprised a formidable catalogue of curious people. Landru had won, with difficulty, his initial battle to thin the ranks of those who stood between him and a lonely assignation. His greatest difficulty had been to avoid getting involved with Mme Buisson's blind son. Naturally enough, his mother was loath to part with him and had at first suggested that the three live together. Landru, anticipating having to do twice the work for the same amount of profit, and remembering, possibly, the disappearance of his first guests, Mme Cuchet and her son, was wholly against it. 'A boy needs a father's guiding hand,' he told her, 'and I am always running around on business. My interests take me everywhere. If he once got used to me, he would fret when I am away. It would be cruel to let him live with us under those conditions.'

Mme Buisson by no means followed this reasoning. Would her son not have *her* company? But Landru's attitude persuaded her that her marriage might be in jeopardy if she insisted on her son joining them. On a previous visit to Gambais she had found it necessary to reassure him in a somewhat pathetic letter: 'I am afraid that you will be annoyed at the presence of my son. Do not be uneasy. He will not trouble us much. And he will soon be leaving us. All I ask is for the chance to love and cherish you.'

Well, a blind son, grieved at the thought that his mother had deserted him because she was starting a new life with a new husband, was not likely to be much of a nuisance. But the dressmaker! Landru, to whom every *sou* was an important matter, justifying the most laborious entries in his little notebook, must have found this a quandary. To leave the dress unclaimed would start too many enquiries, for what dressmaker —least of all one who knew her customer personally—would be content to have wasted time and material on a wedding dress that would only fit a lady of the same ample proportions?

On September 4, 1917, the dapper, hollow-eyed little man called courteously at the shop. 'I really think it's a woman's job to collect her wedding-gown, don't you?' he laughed, 'but Madame is so busy with the wedding preparations and getting the home ready that she asked me to fetch it.'

He received and paid for the gown, with its intricate appliqué work and orange blossom and clouds of tulle. With such civilities as one would expect from a man courteous and gentlemanly by nature, and by circumstances happy, he carried the box away—inwardly cursing the waste of money, we may be sure, and consoled only by the thought that he had paid for it with her money anyway, and that, like Mme Cuchet's blue dressing gown, it could make a useful addition to his growing museum of hand-me-downs. There would be a use for it sometime.

To Mme Lacoste, Mme Buisson's only surviving sister, a postcard was sent, signed allegedly by Mme Buisson but in another handwriting. Mme Simon received one too. It seemed oddly perfunctory and vague, mentioning no specific date for the wedding and ignoring the fact that she, Mme Simon, had been asked to be a witness. The handwriting seemed different, too; more like a man's handwriting. Oh, well ... perhaps she was so busy that she had asked the charming M. Fremyet to write it for her. No doubt she would write again. But she didn't.

M. Paulet, her brother-in-law, was hurt and puzzled by her disappearance. Why had she vanished in this strange way? Why did she neglect to write to her blind son, of whom she was so fond? It didn't make sense, somehow.

Mme Lacoste was also uneasy, and by no means mollified when Landru assured her that her sister was well.

The concierge at Boulevard Ney was suspicious, too, when Landru called towards the end of September to give, on behalf of Mme Buisson, notice to quit and arrange for the removal of her belongings. The signature seemed unsatisfactory.

'I am sorry, M. Fremyet,' he said gravely, 'but I am not authorised to accept this. I cannot allow the removal of Madame's property without her assurance that this is in order. She must see me personally.'

M. Fremyet drew himself up, his deep-set eyes smouldering with a mixture of anger and amazement. 'Are you implying that a concierge is entitled to summon his tenants to his presence?' he said.

'Of course not, monsieur,' said the concierge, shocked at the inference that he would ever show such disrespect, 'you appear to misunderstand me. . . .'

'I understand you perfectly. Monsieur, I am a busy man, not only with my factories, but in connection with my war work. Have you forgotten there is a war on? At any rate, I have neither the time nor the disposition to argue with you.'

'I am only trying to do my duty to my tenants, to protect their interests. . . .'

'Madame is away in the south, managing a canteen for American troops. Are you saying that you deny her the use of her property unless she deserts these brave soldiers in order to return and satisfy your mean suspicions?'

'Oh no, Monsieur . . . it was just the signature. . . .'

'Her signature? Are you suggesting that she is too illiterate to write properly, or to know her own mind? Or are you suggesting that I, M. Fremyet, am troubling to present you with a false document? If this is so, I will refer it to my attorney. Even in the middle of a war, slander of an honest citizen is not permissible!'

The notice to quit was accepted, and Landru set about selling her furniture, storing the remainder in a garage in the rue Maurice.

On August 17, Mme Buisson (née Celestine Lavie) had taken out her securities from the Crédit Lyonnais and entrusted them to her fiancé's custody.

Whether Landru's family knew what Landru was doing at Gambais, we do not know. Certainly they knew that he had rented the villa there, since they had several times persuaded him to give it up, as a useless expense. He had said that it was useful as a storage place for furniture, an excuse that could hardly have made sense to them, as he was known to have several other storage places, and we know that Maurice had frequently helped his father in removing and storing furniture and other belongings.

Following the disappearance of Mme Buisson, Landru enlisted the assistance of his wife in forging Mme Buisson's signature and impersonating her, so that the securities could be cashed. She signed her name 'Lavie'.

Throughout all his frauds and crimes, Landru remained a good husband and a good father, in the sense that he lived with them harmoniously—whenever he was at home—and kept them as well supplied with money as his own fluctuating fortunes permitted. Over the years, the family had been so accustomed to his pattern of living, his frequent absences on unspecified errands, his running around in a succession of motorcars, his humping furniture here and there, that nothing really surprised them. It seems doubtful that they can ever have suspected anything actually sinister behind some of the rather odd gifts and presents he brought with him. Mme Landru was a simple, homely woman who strived bravely to bring up her four children in these rather chaotic and insecure circumstances. Would she have enjoyed owning the gold watch her husband had given her, if she had realised it had belonged to the vanished Mme Cuchet? We cannot know for certain, but I doubt it.

5

Numbers 8, 9 and 10

WE WILL CALL Mme Jaume, née Barthélemey Louise, Number 8. Towards the end of her life, such a description would have surprised her, but in M. Landru's notebook, that was what she was.

She appeared in his notebook under other pseudonyms, too, such as 'Lyanes'—because she lived in a stuffy, bourgeois flat at 23, rue des Lyanes, off the historic rue de Bagnolet in the 20th *arrondissement*. The flat was close to a great number of churches—only a few steps from the old village church of Saint Germain de Charonne, whose seven-hundred-year-old belfry so often called her to Mass. This section of Paris retained, and today still retains, something of its original countrified appearance. This was as well, because one day Mme Jaume would go to live in the country, in a very remote spot known as Gambais, somewhere near Dreux, Seine-et-Oise.

There were cemeteries within easy distance, too. There was the little local cemetery, and the great, sprawling Cimetière du Père Lachaise. Come to that, Mme Jaume's *milieu* also included a 'Hermitage' and a rather famous one, the Château de Bagnolet, the marvellous home bought and rebuilt by the Duchesse d'Orléans, legitimated daughter of Louis XIV, 'The Sun King'. And just as Landru's garden had its display of roses, so was Mme Jaume's local churchyard famous for the tomb of Magloire Lebegue, the market gardener, who gave his unusual Christian name to the Magloire rose.

We do not know if any of these coincidental similarities registered with Mme Jaume, for her acquaintanceship with Gambais was to prove a brief one.

Her relationship with Landru himself lasted a little longer. It started in March 1917. In the *Echo de Paris*, she noticed the following advertisement:

Gentleman, aged fifty, for many years a widower, with no children, skilled and educated with frs.20,000 capital and a good job, seeks marriage with like-minded lady. DEROY, Bureau 26.

A gentleman! And with capital, too! And his age—old enough to have waged marital battles, yet still young enough to begin another campaign. She herself was thirty-eight, but she looked younger. To such a man she would seem a young girl! But what of her own slender means, her humble position? Would she be good enough for him? But then ... a gentleman would not be marrying a woman for her money. He would be content with love and a well-run household.

From the stacks of letters which Landru collected from the *Echo de Paris* offices, he selected Mme Jaume's and placed it neatly in a pile of 'possibles'. On March 11, two days after she had written to him, he replied, suggesting that they meet. He signed himself 'Lucien Guillet' and explained that he was an engineer, a refugee from the Ardennes, and engaged on national defence.

In between helping Mme Collomb to disappear and arranging to entertain the pretty—but inquisitive—Andrée Babelay, 'Lucien Guillet' called upon Mme Jaume at her flat and appraised her furniture and her figure in the usual order of priorities. Her furniture was unremarkable, but solid and saleable.

Apart from this visual inventory, there were the usual enquiries to be made. She had what she described as a modest capital. A pity it wasn't more, but Landru had learned to appreciate small things. It was really rather a pity that he hadn't met her before her abortive marriage to the absentee M. Jaume, to whom she brought a marriage portion of 20,000 francs. Her husband had been a ne'er-do-well, and, having spent the dowry, deserted her and went to Italy as a commercial representative for a Paris firm. Since then she had tried living with her father, maintained sporadic contact with some relatives by the name of Maurice in the Midi, and subsisted on her minuscule allowance, plus meagre earnings as a dressmaker, working for Mme Lherault at 26, rue de la Chine in Paris.

On March 17, 1917 Landru noted in his little book: '6 1/4 Gambetta Metro a Chine 0fr.30.' And even later, in a wicker-work basket in which he kept his detailed records of his innumerable amours, he noted:

Barthélemy, 26, rue de la Chine, 36 ans, parait plus jeune, air provincial, séparée de son mari parti en Italie; mariée à 28 ans, 6 à 7 ans avec son mari, age de 33 ans, avec qui elle vivait fraternellement. . . .

Ten days after Andrée Babelay had disappeared from Gambais, Landru was sufficiently intimate with the lonely, deserted wife, to record in his notebook: 'Metro à Lyanes 0.20, fleurs 1.20.' 'Lyanes' was his code word for Mme Jaume. The flowers, we may take it, were the best he could procure. They were, so to speak, part of his stock-in-trade. Many of the women he met (from amongst those who survived, of course) testified to his exquisite taste in flowers, and his generosity with them.

But Mme Jaume was fervently religious. Oh, well. One must be all things to all women. Had he not served Mass in the Église de St Louis-en-l'Île? Did his expression, as a youth, not impress his priestly elders with its piety and decorum? Well, then, why not a little nostalgia? It was all in a good cause.

Days later Mme Jaume met Landru at a new flat he had taken at 76, rue de Rochechouart. He was soberly dressed in dark clothes, his white collar pristine, his shoes polished. The street is near the Boulevard Rochechouart which, like Clichy and La Chapelle are in the heart of Montmartre. Landru was a frequent visitor to the famous Chat Noir at No. 84. And so, one evening, with Madame Jaume linking her arm in his, they made their way from the rue de Rochechouart to the Boulevard Rochechouart, down the narrow, gaslit, cobbled rue Saint-Rustique, and from there to the Sacré Coeur on the heights of Montmartre overlooking the great city. Within its hushed interior, by the lights of countless votive candles and to the strains of its great organ and the intonations of the choir, they knelt in prayer. Perhaps, as they took Mass together, Landru managed a sidelong glance at the modest jewellery she was wearing. It is a safe assumption, because not the slightest pecuniary detail was unworthy of his notice. Later, in his note-book, he recorded—with what feelings we can only imagine: 'Offertory plate, Ofrs.20.'

Although Landru had contacted Mme Jaume in March, and

saw her at intervals until May, he was too preoccupied with his other plans and assignations to pursue her further at that time. But now, in September, Mme Buisson had been despatched, and there was no reason to delay. He proposed to her—if she could get a divorce, of course. He pretended to be very anxious that she should, and applauded her boldness, understanding her religious trepidations, in seeking a divorce, by asking the assistance of a M. Columeau.

A barrage of flowers and sweets followed, and a virtual flood of love letters, copied in good calligraphy from a standard book on how to address sweethearts, kept falling through her letterbox. In so heavy an atmosphere of romance, who could think of the war, of the battles of Arras, Vimy Ridge, Bullecourt, Messines? Of Amiens, Bapaume, The Somme? Early that year, during the Somme battle, a sergeant in the 15th Australian Battalion had had to break ice in the trench in order to melt it for water. It was only after days of chipping that they came across a pair of boots sticking out, and discovered that the boots were attached to a body. There was Arras, shattered and deserted, a few terrified inhabitants cringing in cellars, above them shattered rafters, wallpaper and plaster waving in the wind, and floors and furniture crazily tilting. The 'strafing', the indescribable shell-fire, the rocket-lights giving a deceptively decorative effect belying their deadly purpose, the tanks lumbering over men, corpses, the wounded and muddy debris—like monster metal black-beetles—Landru was far from it all, although he told the admiring Mme Jaume that his mysterious missions and absences were connected with the war effort.

On September 30, Landru took her to Gambais. She was enchanted with the place and on her return to Paris could not stop telling her employer, Mme Lherault, her daughter Mlle Lherault, and her friends, Mmes Masson, Geoffrey and Leburi, about it. It was a wonderful villa, she said, so peaceful and remote from busy Paris. As soon as she could be free she would marry the marvellous M. Guillet. Meanwhile, in order that he could collect his thoughts away from the turmoil of battle (where M. Guillet implied it was often necessary for him to be) she would stay occasionally with him there, and try to mitigate the burden of his war work.

In October, Mme Jaume quit her job with the dressmaker,

explaining that she was going to marry Guillet and needed time to prepare the home. He saw her frequently in that month, dining with her on the 3rd, 14th, 16th, 18th and 28 October. He did not see her on the 13th, as he had important domestic matters to attend to, including the purchase and arrangements for delivery of a considerable quantity of the best quality, quick-burning coal, which cost him, as he recorded irritably, '30 francs 90 centimes'.

On November 24 Mme Jaume moved out of her flat, Landru supervising the removal of her furniture and belongings, assisted by his son Charles.

The next day Landru and his 'fiancée' left by train for Houdan with tickets marked respectively '*aller*' and '*aller et retour*'. They cost, as of course he recorded, '2 francs 70 centimes and 4 francs 40 centimes'. By taking a return for himself he was saving a franc. By not taking a return for Mme Jaume 1 franc 70 centimes. It was on this day that they went to Mass at Sacré Coeur, and Landru also noted his contribution to the collection.

They arrived at Houdan in bleak weather, took the old, lumbering *diligence* to Gambais. But the following morning Landru returned to Paris and stayed with his wife and family. Mme Jaume was not seen again. Her friends waited for news of her forthcoming divorce and marriage, but in vain. On that day Landru's cash in hand jumped by 374.60 francs, which was the amount Mme Jaume had taken with her, while on November 30, he negotiated with the Banque Alleaume, using the name of Fremyet, for a sum of 1394 francs which Mme Jaume had deposited there. As usual, he used a forged authority.

Mme Lherault, her employer, became uneasy, but Landru sent her a letter by pneumatic tube—a speedy device which cuts out most of the transport time involved in postal delivery, and which is still used today in Paris—claiming that Madame Jaume had gone to America. Later, on New Year's Eve, Landru called on Mme Lherault and presented her with a box of chocolates 'from Mme Jaume.' In fact, he had bought them himself that afternoon in the rue de Rivoli.

He did not think it necessary to tell her that, a few days earlier, he had sold Mme Jaume's shoes for 15 francs. Leather was scarce at the time, and he found an easy buyer.

The Ladykiller

Mme Anne-Marie PASCAL, née le 5 Novembre 1880, ayant divorcé en 1913 à Toulon avec M. Gabriel, son mari, dont elle avait en un enfant mort en bas âge....

So begins a long police dossier on a tall, handsome brunette, with bright merry eyes and dark lustrous hair, who became Landru's mistress and believed that a new, exciting, feckless chapter of a wildly misspent life was about to begin.

She has been described as a lady of easy virtue—a puzzling description, since virtue was the one thing she found most difficult. She had experienced—possibly enjoyed—a long series of love affairs covering a whole spectrum of age and class.

She lived in a humble apartment in the rue Stendhal, was born in Toulouse, and since her divorce in 1913, had lived in Paris, her small dressmaker's business serving also as a cover for prostitution. In this she seems not to have prospered, for when Landru met her, she was earning a mere subsistence and her entire worldly property was worth scarcely more than twenty pounds.

Landru's motives towards her, and the manner in which he pursued them, are in some respects puzzling. Firstly, unless it was sex, what did he want from her? He was too experienced in assessing people's means not to know that she was nearly penniless. Well, some may have thought his appearance unprepossessing, or his background dubious, but women took to him very easily. 'What! Give up Lulu (Landru)? Never! He is sublime!' declared the pretty Andrée Babelay shortly before her disappearance.

Mme Pascal felt precisely the same about Henri Désiré Landru. 'I adore you!' she wrote to him. 'I am no more than a common mistress to you, but I am content.'

Feeling particularly lonely when she heard that her husband had been killed at the Front, Mme Pascal answered one of Landru's matrimonial advertisements, in which he described himself as forty-seven years old and possessing a modest modicum of 4,000 francs. Landru had written to her on September 22, 1917, fixing a rendezvous with her four days later, at six o'clock in the evening, at the 'Martin-Nadaud' Metro station. Three days later he noted the cost, in his famous notebook, of a letter sent by *pneumatique*, and a few days after that lavish bunches of flowers were delivered at 2, Villa Stendhal.

A most curious development, which must have had some purpose behind it, but about which we can only speculate, is that on the same day he wrote to her in impassioned terms, from a totally different address, and using a completely different name, M. Berzieux! Did he suspect her in some way, knowing that she had many lines into the underworld, and was he checking up on her by this curious means? For his advertisement, he wrote as M. Forest, living at an imaginary address of 43, Avenue de Chatou, Vesinet.

Despite protestations of affection and the usual gifts of flowers and sweets, Landru was far from pleased to discover that Anne-Marie Pascal had a pretty niece, Marie Jeanne Fauchet, who sometimes stayed with her and helped her aunt with the work. 'Damnation!' one can imagine Landru muttering to himself, 'is there nobody really alone in the world?' Something of this resentment may have registered with Mme Fauchet, Mme Pascal's sister. She did not like Landru. She did not like his background, the vagueness of his frequent absences and journeyings, and especially his eyes. Mme Pascal insisted that he had the most beautiful eyes she had ever seen in a man. It was not long before she was expressing an entirely opposite opinion.

'He's a mystery,' Mme Fauchet insisted. Thereafter, although she was always civil, if distant, to him in her sister's presence, she referred to him as 'Monsieur Mystère'.

Mme Pascal had also a close friend, Mme Carbonnel, and through her we have an interesting clue to Henri Landru's split personality. None of the fiancées except one had ever even hinted or implied that there was anything *sinister* about Landru. He was so courteous, so considerate, so gallant, so stable and mature and dependable. But Mme Pascal did have an odd experience that frightened her—unfortunately not enough or for long enough.

In March 1918 she went to stay with Landru at Gambais. He had promised her marriage but was continually postponing the making of any definite arrangements on one excuse or another. She had said she was content to be his mistress, but many a woman says this to retain, until she can soften him up, the company of a man disinclined to marriage. She was therefore having an affair with him.

One evening Mme Carbonnel heard a frantic banging on her apartment door. Her heart pounding, she raced to see what was the matter. Outside was her friend Mme Pascal. She was as pale as a ghost and shaking with a nameless fear.

'My God, whatever is the matter?' cried Mme Carbonnel, 'has that M. Mystère been up to something?'

She gave her friend a cognac and rushed to get some hot coffee. At last, as her panic subsided, Mme Pascal poured out her story.

It was evening in the lonely villa. Landru had closed the shutters. There was absolutely no sound except the howling of the wind and rustling of the trees. Landru had suddenly gone very quiet. He told her to sit in an armchair with her hair hanging down her back. He knelt before her and stared at her so fixedly that she suddenly felt faint. She found herself unable to move, as though paralysed. She became unconscious until the next day, when she fled from the house and caught the next train back.

'What did I tell you?' her friend said, and pleaded with her, earnestly, *'Please* give this man up. There's something that tells me he isn't the man for you. What normal man would behave like that. . . .'

'Normal men do do odd things,' murmured Jeanne-Marie, reminiscently, as though moved to protect her lover's good name.

'Not *that* sort of thing,' Mme Carbonnel insisted, 'what was he up to? Is he Mesmer, or something?'

It would seem that Landru, past master at extricating himself from awkward situations, regained her confidence somehow. Probably by conventional means, although her story suggests that he used hypnotism. Soon they were out together again. She told her concierge, and others, that she was soon to marry.

The drama now ran to pattern. On April 4, Landru, assisted this time by his son Charles, helped to move Mme Pascal's furniture from her flat in the rue Stendhal, noting carefully every single item, even the most trivial, in his notebook.

On April 5, 1918, Landru and Mme Pascal, accompanied as far as the station to his great disgust by her faithful friend Mme Carbonnel, took the train for the lonely house on the outskirts of

Rambouillet Forest. Mme Pascal carried, in a wickerwork basket, her little cat, for she could not bear to be parted from it. Nor, it seems, did the cat approve of all this upheaval. It meowed pitifully and continuously, while Landru tapped his fingers in irritation. Desperately, Mme Carbonnel tried to get her friend away from Landru to say a few words in private, but it was impossible. Landru held her arm. The train came in.

'You *will* write to me, won't you?' pleaded Mme Carbonnel. She felt suddenly distressed.

'Of course I will, darling.'

'Immediately you get there? Just to let me know you've arrived all right?'

'Of course.'

'You promise?'

'I promise.'

'We shall miss the train. It is leaving now,' said Landru, his voice less dulcet and soothing than usual. He tried to take from her, with a rough gesture, the basket containing the cat, but she instinctively drew it away from him, and followed him up the steps into the carriage.

Mme Carbonnel stood on the platform of The Invalides station and watched the train disappear into the distance. Mme Pascal waved all the time, until she, too, disappeared into the shadows.

There is no doubt that the couple arrived at Houdan. The driver of the *diligence* which took them from the station to the Villa Tric knew Landru well by sight, although quite accustomed by now to the sight of strange women with him. There is no doubt that they ate. His notebook records groceries costing 3.50, meat for 2.30, 0.35 for bread, coffee, 0.90, carbonate 0.35 and tobacco 1.25 and 1.40. The same notebook contains the cryptic entry: '17.h.15.' No woman who ever stayed at Gambais was seen after the hour thus cryptically entered against her name.

The following day Landru returned alone to Paris. He was in a hurry to get back because, irrespective of what had transpired at the Villa Tric overnight, he had waiting in his flat in the rue de Rochechouart an extremely attractive mistress—of whom we will hear more soon—Mlle Segret. She had been living with him for some time, unknown, of course, to Landru's other loves or to his wife.

Mme Pascal was never seen again. Nor was her cat. Her sister received a postcard from her in Toulon, with the original date written over. The original date was April 4—the night she had arrived. It had been altered to correspond with the postmark, which was April 19.

Mme Pascal did implement her promise to her friend Mme Carbonnel. In the silent house, she had enough time to write:

> We arrived quite safely, although there was a little rain. We slept soundly, without worrying about Gothas. I find it a little strange here, it is so quiet, but the weather is fine, and I enjoy the fresh air. One of these days I will come and see you and tell you all about my new home. My best love to you. Lucien sends his kind wishes.

'Gothas' were of course the German heavy bombers, used, like the twin-engined Handley-Page, from 1917 onwards for tactical bombing and assault on cities. 'Lucien' was for 'Lucien Guillet', alias Landru. But written inside the envelope of the letter—which was never delivered to Mme Carbonnel was this pencil message in a shaky hand: *'In case of accident, let my sister, Madame Fauchet, know.'*

In the days that followed, Landru sold her few pitiful belongings: some furniture, on April 12, for 500 francs; two days afterwards, he obtained 5 francs for her worn cloak. Within two weeks he had almost sold out.

But one article proved less saleable and did not go until June 4, 1918, when Mme Pascal's only set of false teeth went for fifteen francs.

Mlle Marchadier—Marie-Thérèse—was thirty-six, pre-possessing, high-spirited and full of resource. She was born in Bordeaux on October 27, 1881 and since 1913 had been living at 330, rue St Jacques. She had prospered reasonably well as a prostitute, managing to save 8,000 francs in the process, and, feeling that the time had come to rest on her reputation and impart her empirical skills to others, she had taken rooms in the rue St Jacques and established there a *pension* or *maison de tolérance*.

She was popular with her friends, a familiar figure in Montmartre and Montparnasse. The business cares of running the establishment proved tedious to her restless and fecund temperament. It was making far less money for far more effort than had previously been the case, so she decided to sell her furniture and return to her old and more profitable way of life.

Accordingly, towards the end of 1918, she inserted the following advertisement in the Paris press:

Would sell contents of 10 bedrooms, complete, in good condition. To view, apply 330, rue St Jacques.

A house agent, M. Moret, noticed the advertisement and, having ascertained that what was entailed was a mere sale of furniture rather than an exchange of property, he decided to earn himself a small commission by introducing Mlle Marchadier to a M. Guillet, whom he knew to be a buyer of miscellaneous furniture and belongings.

Landru, under the alias of M. Guillet, called upon her and showed the liveliest interest in her furniture. Even more agreeable, he showed an interest in her. He praised her clothes, her figure, her conversation. His worldly knowledge of the underworld (gained, as he implied, as mere relaxation from his arduous and widespread commercial activities) impressed her. So did the arrival of modest bouquets of flowers, and of sweets. She might have enjoyed them less had she known that such gifts formed part of what was, by now, an operation of almost military precision; letters; meetings; flowers; sweets; Gambais; oblivion. Once the barrage of flowers and sweets had started, the recipient was not likely to be seen around much longer.

There was one thing, above all else, that commended the bearded gentleman to Mlle Marchadier. M. Guillet was so kind to her two pet dogs. Sometimes it was a tid-bit of biscuit. There was always an affectionate pat. Yet the dogs didn't reciprocate, snarling or whining or snapping as though they did not like him. Mlle Marchadier was apologetic. 'No need to apologise, Mademoiselle,' said Landru, gallantly, 'for that is how dogs should behave. They are quite right to take their time before deciding to like somebody other than their owner. Their primary job is to protect you—and that makes me love them, whether they like me or not.'

'You are so understanding,' sighed Marie-Thérèse.

Landru's lease on the villa at Gambais was due to expire in December 1918. He had profited very little by the disappearance of Mme Pascal and, indeed, had made only the barest living by his frauds on all the other vanished fiancées. Life was proving expensive. He had his wife and children to keep. He had his flat in the rue Rochechouart to maintain, where Mlle Segret was now ensconced. In July 1918, in his desperate search for funds, Landru attempted to sub-let the villa to a M. Lambert. The latter quite liked it but drew Landru's attention to the deplorable state of the kitchen stove. 'It seems to have had very heavy use,' he complained, 'why, look—you can see that the stovepipes are completely worn out.'

'They must have been of poor quality,' said Landru, 'for I only bought the stove in Houdan in 1915. It was the finest stove they had. As you can see, it is sound and fit for use. Perhaps because of the war the stove pipes were not so good as they should have been.'

'Whatever the explanation,' replied M. Lambert, 'I must insist as a condition of a lease that the stovepipes and the other worn parts of the stove are replaced by brand new fittings.'

'Of course, of course,' murmured Landru, concerned only with the securing of a deposit.

But Landru, in any case, had further use for the villa. There could be no other tenant until he had 'entertained' one more guest. He had promised marriage to Mlle Marchadier. Delightedly she had confided in her concierge: 'I have found a charming man who is taking me into the country. I shall have my own house, my own car, my own servant, and we are to be married.'

The wooing of Mlle Marchadier took longer than Landru found comfortable. He was running so low in funds that in December he was perpetually borrowing small sums from his wife—10 francs on December 1, another 10 francs on the 3rd, yet another two days later, and so on.

His quarterly rent for the rue Rochechouart apartment was becoming due. The rent on his garage in the rue Maurice needed paying. It was a very frugal Christmas for the Landru family, for by this time his personal fortunes were reduced to 24 francs 60 centimes. By Boxing Day he had only 15 francs 50 to his name.

By every post Mlle Marchadier received impassioned letters. Would she marry him? Yes, said Marie-Thérèse at last, she would. And would she exchange the bustle and glamour of Paris for the quiet, Arcadian bliss of a country villa? Of course!

It would be bliss to be with him anywhere, but alone, and in a country villa! One thing, though—anxiously—she could take her dogs? Of course, said M. 'Guillet', the country was just the place for them.

Now things moved with the speed that Landru preferred. On January 10, 1919 he made arrangements for her furniture to be sold or stored. The following day, assisted by Charles, he supervised the removal of the furniture. On January 13, she left her apartment, telling the concierge that she would be back on the 15th to return the keys and attend to a few other formalities. A friend of hers, Mme Poillet, had asked her to take charge of her dog for the day. This she agreed to do, being fond of animals, and made a rendezvous with her for after mid-day, the 15th.

She left with Landru and the three dogs from St Lazare—at that time the Seine was in flood and departures from The Invalides were stopped. They journeyed to Houdan, where, because of the bitter weather, so he explained, and the fact that he had only just been able to renew the lease on the Villa Tric (actually, by promising to buy the house in January), Landru stopped to buy three sacks of coal. Obligingly, Mlle Marchadier helped him to carry them to the coach that was to take them to her new home.

Nobody ever saw her again.

On January 14, Landru was busy paying off urgent debts. On the 18th he was back in Gambais again, although not for long. Neighbours had good reason to know that the strange bearded man was in residence again, because, although some way from the village of Gambais, sickening smells could be detected coming from the villa. At nine o'clock Mme Lecoq, her daughter and Mme Najac were appalled by the smells borne on the evening wind.

'It's not an ordinary fire,' remarked Mlle Lecoq, with nausea, 'it's burning flesh. The smell's unmistakable. Remember now? When did we last smell anything like this?'

'You're right,' declared Mme Lecoq, 'it was when M. Thibault had that terrible accident in his home, and was burned to death.'

'And what domestic fire would make a glow like that,' said Mme Najac. 'Look! See how brilliant the glow is through the windows. Whatever can he be doing?'

69

The Ladykiller

By a coincidence, for the site of the villa was quite remote in those days, a M. Andrieu, taking his evening stroll, passed by the Villa Tric on the evening of January 18. The air was thick with black, nauseating fumes, while the gardens at the rear were illuminated by a brilliant light from the windows, like theatrical stage lighting.

He stood for a few minutes, puzzled. Whatever could make so bright a light? And what sort of fuel could a man be using to produce such evil-smelling smoke, a filthy, swirling mixture of black and yellow ochre? He sniffed uneasily. Oh well, a man's home was his castle, even in wartime, and strange things were happening everywhere. One might pass a remote spot and come upon a gunsight, or a temporary munitions store, or tents being pegged or struck. Many secret things went on during a war, and with children at the Front, he had troubles enough.

He shrugged his shoulders and passed on. Yet when he looked back when half a mile away, the smoke was still billowing to the sky, and the windows flickering with that strange, unearthly light.

There were others who had momentary suspicions about Landru's restless comings and goings—by car, or bicycle or on foot, wandering around lonely fields, deserted roads and tracks, lurking near used or disused quarries, loping along in the dense woods, on no obvious mission. But then, cannot we all speculate upon the demeanour and activities and motives of people we do not know? There was never anything in Landru's observable activities to justify a tangible suspicion, although the relatives and friends of the fiancées who disappeared one after the other were, naturally enough, apprehensive or downright suspicious.

Mme Poillet waited in vain for her friend to return on January 15, as she had promised to do, with Mme Poillet's pet dog. What had happened? It made no sense. She loved her own dogs so much, and surely knew what pain and anxiety it would give her to be deprived of her own pet. And where was she? She had given no address when she went away. 'It's a strict secret,' she had told her friend. Well, reflected Mme Poillet, a *demi-monde* perforce has secrets. It seemed unremarkable. And had not Mlle Marchadier said, 'I'll see you the day after tomorrow?'

Well, she never did. Nor the day after that. Or after that. Or after that. She and the three dogs all disappeared, and not all the enquiries that she made in the underworld could throw any light upon it.

But, in a Paris flat, by the light of an oil lamp, Mme Friedmann sister of Mme Cuchet, Landru's first 'fiancée', stopped her knitting, looked over at her husband, and declared:

'I believe Jeanne has been murdered. I'm certain of it.'

6

Nemesis

IN A SMALL FRENCH TOWN or village the Mayor is very much 'father of the town'. While keeping to the formalities of office, and discharging many dull but necessary duties, his office is the place where the town's heart can be heard to beat. Usually, he knows every member of a local family, and even several generations of it. Every street, every house, is often familiar to him.

But this familiarity is more difficult to maintain in lonely and scattered places, and especially in wartime.

In May 1918 the Mayor of Gambais received a letter from Mlle Lacoste, a domestic servant working in Paris, sister of the missing Mme Buisson:

Dear Mr Mayor:

Since September 1917 I have not been able to contact my sister, Mme Celestine Buisson. She came to live in your charming village with her fiancé, M. Fremyet. I have written both to her and to him several times, and again recently, without ever receiving a reply. I can't understand this, as we were always so close to each other. I am wondering if the address I have been using is incorrect or incomplete. Could you let me know the correct address? In 1917, I went with my sister to Gambais, and could if necessary point out the house to you without question. It is a little villa some way from the centre, along the side of the road...

The Mayor read the letter several times, as though its simple message took much understanding. His secretary waited for a response. At last he spoke.

'Didn't we have an enquiry about something similar some time back?'

'Yes, M. le Maire. I remember it well. Somebody wrote in to say they had lost all trace of a typist, a Mme Collomb....'

'Find me that letter.'

Within minutes he was reading a letter from Mme Pellat, sister of Anna Collomb: '... I simply do not believe that my sister would disappear, as she has done, without a word to those who loved her. It is something so opposite to everything she has done in the past, something it was not in her nature to do. . . .'

The Mayor thought to himself, 'But this woman went to live in a local villa with a Monsieur Dupont, who came from Rouen. She says it was a lonely house, which M. Dupont had taken on a lease. I wonder if she means the Villa Tric? It's isolated, near the cemetery, on the edge of Route Nationale 183. It belongs to a former public works contractor, M. Tric. Well, it's a fine day, and I've done all I need to do here—I'll go along myself.'

There was little about the villa to tell him much. The windows were closed and shuttered, the gardens neglected and overgrown, the woodwork starved of paint. He enquired in the local inn, and from a few neighbours. He spoke to the local shoemaker, who had given the keys to M. Dupont.

'What sort of a man was he, this Dupont?'

'Well, M. le Maire, I only saw him once. I think he was a Westerner, came from Rouen, I think—yes, he did, because I remember he said he lived in rue Darnetal.'

'What did he look like?'

'He was about fifty, I should say. Bearded. Bald. And a rare one with the ladies. I think that's what he took the villa for, for he was always with a different woman, so I'm told. Yet once they went in, nobody ever saw them come out again. He must have had a regular harem there—but he was a very discreet man, was Dupont.'

'Did he have any friends? Does the name Fremyet convey anything to you? Did he have a friend of that name living with him there?'

'Oh, no. The bearded one was the only man there.'

The Mayor walked back to the Town Hall. Was he making too much of this? No, not really. Surely it was a duty, for both of his correspondents had been very unhappy and apprehensive. There was nothing to show that the two cases were connected, but they were certainly similar. There were not many properties in his area corresponding to the Villa Tric and available for rental. Could Dupont and Fremyet be the same person? It seemed unlikely, yet some people, actors and writers for instance, sometimes used more than one name. Why not, then, put the two enquiries in touch with each other, so that they could compare notes and, perhaps, help each other in their quest?

Back in the town hall the Mayor dictated his reply:

Mademoiselle:

I am sorry to inform you that I have been unable to trace anyone of the name of Buisson within the area of my administration. Nor have I been able to trace a gentleman by the name of Fremyet.

However, from your description of the house, it would appear to be the Villa Tric, so named after its owner, a retired engineer who worked in Melun. It is certainly near the cemetery. Our records indicate that the present tenant is a Monsieur Dupont, and we have no record of a Monsieur Fremyet having ever been a tenant there.

I find that we have received a somewhat similar enquiry from the family Pelat, concerning a Madame Collomb, who is also missing. It might be of interest to you to contact the Pelat family...

It was a kind and considerate letter, with added expressions of concern and sympathy.

Mlle Lacoste lost no time in contacting the Pelat family. Mme Pelat, and her father-in-law, received the poor servant girl very civilly and listened attentively.

'Celestine would never have vanished like this of her own accord. Something terrible must have happened to her. You see, Celestine was lonely. When she was working as a maid in a hotel in Bayonne, she married the owner, M. Buisson. He died in 1912. He left a little money, and the furniture, but not enough for her to live on, so she came back to Paris to do domestic work again, hoping to pay her way and keep her small savings. She didn't like living alone, she wasn't the type. I knew she wanted to marry again.'

'And what did this M. Fremyet look like? Did you ever meet him?'

'Oh yes. I didn't really know what to make of him, he seemed so mysterious. But Celestine, she was infatuated with him.'

'Yes, but what did he look like?'

'His eyes were the main thing—so deep-set and penetrating.

74

They went right through you. Then his beard—he was very proud of his beard, and I'll admit he looked a perfect gentleman. He was rather pale, wore a bowler hat and a sort of stone-coloured mackintosh with outer pockets.'

At this point Mme Pelat was feeling faint, and gripped her father-in-law's arm. 'It's an absolute description of M. Dupont. I'm sure Dupont and Fremyet are the same man.'

'And what you tell me of the house makes it certain that it is,' said M. Pelat, 'but what a pity so much time's been lost. However, we, too, haven't pressed the matter as often as we might have done. We told the police of our misgivings, but they have got nowhere. We had better see the police together, and compare notes. . . .'

The Great War was over. Paris, drab and tired but still retaining the air of a great city, was gradually reverting to normal. The talk now was of squeezing Germany 'till the pips squeaked'—or reparations, and revenge. The winter of 1918–19 had been severe, and when on April 6, 1919, Commissioner Dautel of the Paris Préfecture of Police, reached his office at half past seven in the morning, he stamped noisily into the room, beat his arms against his chest to keep warm, blew on his hands, and settled to his desk. The old-fashioned stove was unlit as they were economising on heating.

Dautel examined the schedule of enquiries on the large foolscap sheet before him. As he did so, he lifted from his basket the appropriate file, and examined it cursorily. It was for him not at the moment a matter of detail. He would have to spread the work amongst seventeen inspectors.

It looked routine stuff to him. A case of blackmail, and a few petty thefts.

At eight o'clock the inspectors filed into his office for the daily conference. One of them was Jean Belin, an athletic, alert, dark-haired young man with a deceptively amiable smile. He was a Burgundian, from Dijon in the Côte d'Or and his education, which was good, put him above the level of the average recruit when he joined the police in 1909. Because of his height, which was below the set standard, he was allowed to train as a detective, and was greatly helped by the fact that he didn't look remotely like one. His tough and wiry look, coupled with well-tailored clothes, fashionable ties and neat trilby hat, suggested, rather, a playboy-roué who had done a bit of boxing and could still manage it at a pinch.

Belin was not popular with Dautel. Dautel was more ponderous, bureaucratic, dogged, cautious. Belin was the opposite—ready to sprint, his mind rapier-like, imaginative, speculatively probing. Dautel felt towards him as the average bureaucrat, set in his ways, feels towards an impulsive, enthusiastic newcomer. He resented the inference that there can be quick ways of doing things that took him a long time.

'Have a look at this file, Belin.'

He handed him a grey file from the Mantes region, dated April 5, 1919.

'The Procureur [Attorney-General] has instructed us to enquire into the disappearance of two women. They're both widows and their names are Collomb and Buisson—you'll see all about it in the file. Mme Ann Collomb, a shorthand typist from Paris, disappeared in 1917, and Mme Buisson hasn't been seen since September 1917. The first went to live with M. Dupont, of Rouen, who had taken a lease on the Villa Tric in Gambais. The second was the mistress of a M. Fremyet, who also used to live in Gambais, but the Mayor knows nothing about him.'

'What about D.K.V. [Missing persons department of the Préfecture]?'

'Oh, they've tried. The families of these two women are convinced there has been foul play. They say frankly they're sure these women have been murdered, but there isn't a shred of evidence to support their suspicions. Inspector Adam, who has been following it up, says enquiries lead into a blind alley.'

'He couldn't find M. Fremyet?'

'No trace whatsoever. Nobody knows such a man.'

'And Dupont?'

'He's been seen, but not lately. We know broadly what he looks like, but don't know where he is now, or even who he really is. We don't know for certain that his name *is* Dupont.'

'Or that M. Fremyet is M. Fremyet?'

Dautel frowned. It was always the same with Belin. You tried to give him a simple instruction and then found yourself involved in a debate.

'I'm not asking you to speculate endlessly about this case,

or to cross-examine me, but to get some facts. Read the notes from M. Blaviet, the Public Prosecutor at Mantes, who has asked the help of the Sûreté.'

'Is there anything more, sir?' asked Belin, coldly.

'No. Study the papers and report back to me.'

Belin returned to his office and read the pile of papers, establishing the chronology of the enquiries so far. He noted that on February 3, 1919, the parents of Mme Collomb had brought a case against persons unknown in the court of Seine-et-Oise. Inspector Adam, of the missing persons department, had found no lead. In his report of March 11, 1919, he observed: 'If we are to find any traces of Fremyet, we shall probably find them in Gambais rather than in Paris, in which event it is better that the case should be sent to the court at Mantes.'

It seems that in Mantes, gendarme Brigadier Jules Hebbe had mounted his horse and ridden over to see M. Tric, owner of the villa. M. Tric was very ill, but managed to explain that he himself had never met his tenant, M. Dupont, because the local cobbler, M. Vallet, had, at his request, handled the physical practicalities of the deal, handing over the keys, and so on.

'But I have M. Dupont's address in Rouen,' murmured M. Tric, feebly, 'ah, here it is—it's in the rue Darnetal.'

On to Rouen. But there nobody in the rue Darnetal had ever heard of 'M. Dupont.'

Back to Gambais, and to the cobbler Vallet. The cobbler was talkative, but not especially informative. 'He was a little man who was always running around, coming for short stays, and always with a different woman. A regular Don Juan he was. The last I saw of him was last Christmas, when he came with a woman and three dogs. We exchanged a few words, but didn't talk long. I haven't seen him since.'

Inspector Belin read the file again. There *was* a mystery here and it had a sinister undertone to it. There was no proof, but a strong supposition, that Dupont and Fremyet were the same person, and that the mysterious tenant of the Villa Tric had murdered the two missing women. The false address in Rouen was a straw in the wind. There had been deception in the renting of the villa. Deception—for what purpose? As a cover for crime?

Soon he was back in Commissioner Dautel's office.

'Sir, I believe these two women have been killed in this one house, by a man using two different identities.'

Dautel gave him a look of glazed boredom. 'I did say that I wanted information, not theories. You can start theorising when you've put your hands on more facts than are in that file there. And as a start—an obvious start, I'd have thought— I suggest you go to Gambais.'

'I'd have thought, sir, that that would be pointless, as the file shows that the Mayor, the gendarmes and everybody else has pursued every possible enquiry locally. I would prefer with your permission to decide for myself the order and priorities of my visits for the purposes of enquiry.'

'You have my permission. All you have to remember is that I'm concerned with results.'

'Yes, sir.' In moments of anger Belin took refuge in excessive formality. A surfeit of politeness, when none is due, speaks for itself. He returned once more to his office, threw the file into his basket, and checked in his notebook of the address he proposed to visit: '*Mademoiselle Lacoste, 10 rue du Plâtre —sister of the missing widow, Mme Buisson.*'

From the rue Greffuhle, headquarters of the 1st Brigade Mobile, to the rue du Plâtre, which was near the Hotel de Ville, was only a short taxi ride. Within minutes he was on his way.

It was a well-to-do street where Inspector Belin called in search of Mlle Lacoste. She worked there as a housemaid.

The cook answered the door. She regarded the caller with undisguised disapproval.

'The staff are not allowed visitors,' she snapped. 'What do you want?'

Berlin produced his pass. If she was able to read it, she certainly did not understand it.

'Staff aren't allowed visitors,' she repeated. 'But since you're here, you can wait in the kitchen for a little while, if you want to.'

Belin sat in the kitchen amongst the pots and pans until Mlle Lacoste arrived. She was scarcely more co-operative than the cook, despite the fact that it was at her insistence that the case of her missing sister had been reopened.

'I want nothing to do with you,' she said, flatly, 'I've told Inspector Adam all I know and it's up to him.'

78

Patiently, Belin explained that the matter was now in his hands, and that he needed her co-operation if the mystery were ever to be cleared up.

'My sister was taken in by that man Fremyet, and I'm not going to be taken in by you. How do I know you're a policeman? You don't look like one!'

'Why not ring Inspector Adam and ask him? Here's his phone number, and if you care to compare it with the phone number you already have for him, you'll find it correct.'

Dubiously, Mlle Lacoste rang Inspector Adam. He reassured her that her visitor was genuine and persuaded her to answer Belin's questions and promise any help she could give.

Mlle Lacoste sat down and told her story, from beginning to end; how her sister had met M. Fremyet, how he had sold her furniture and promised her marriage, how she had left with him for Gambais and never returned. She had met him, so was able to describe him, and to confirm that relatives of Mme Collomb described him in exactly the same way.

'Now I don't know if we can get anywhere on this,' said Belin, 'but we're going to try, and try hard. And we need your help. I think, as you do, that Dupont and Fremyet are the same man. Probably neither name is genuine, so that we probably won't trace him from any records. But he might be seen about. You know what he looks like. You would recognise him instantly. So remember: if ever you see him, follow him until you see a policeman and then tell him that the man is wanted under a warrant for his arrest. Ask the policeman to telephone me immediately. Here's my card.'

'Probably I'll never see him again,' said Mlle Lacoste, doubtfully, 'but if I do, I'll know what to do.'

Belin also paid a call on the relatives of Mme Collomb. He was sure by now that he had a murder case on his hands. His colleagues ridiculed his theories, but he was so convinced that he was still hard at work at seven o'clock the same evening. Which was just as well, for his telephone rang then and, at the other end of the line, was Mlle Lacoste, almost hysterical with excitement.

'Thank God I've got you at last,' she almost screamed into the telephone. 'I've seen him! At the "Lions de Faience", a china shop in the rue de Rivoli. . . .'

'The rue de Rivoli?' Belin cursed himself for interrupting her narrative, but he had been momentarily surprised that a man with so many offences behind him would dare show himself in such a busy street.

'Well, I didn't meet him there at first. I saw him in the rue de Rivoli arm in arm with a young woman ... I followed them into the shop, where they chose a dinner service. I heard the assistant mention the price, 325 francs. He hadn't enough money with him, so he paid a deposit and left his card. ...'

'You didn't inform a policeman, while you were following him, that he was a wanted man?'

'No. I'm so sorry, really I am. And I was rude to you this morning, too. But I was so worried and excited. I just didn't want to lose track of him.'

'Where are you speaking from at the moment?'

'Where I work—the rue du Plâtre, where you came this morning.'

'Stay where you are and don't go out on any pretext. I'm coming over at once.'

'Yes, Inspector.'

Actually, Mlle Lacoste had shown considerable initiative in shadowing the couple as long as she did, for the rue de Rivoli was very crowded at the time. When the couple left the porcelain shop they had walked as far as Place de Châtelet and boarded a bus for Montmartre. She had tried to get on it too, almost bumping into 'Monsieur Fremyet' in her excitement.

Belin's heart sank. Had his quarry been warned?

'Do you think he saw you?' he asked.

'He must have done. He looked straight into my eyes.'

There was no time to lose. Belin dashed off to the shop, only to find it had closed barely ten minutes ago. He searched for the nightwatchman, got the address of the manager from him, hailed a taxi and arrived at the manager's house in the suburbs just in time to interrupt his dinner.

The manager had noticed and noted nothing. 'We have hundreds of customers during the day, as you can imagine, and I didn't see the man. But the assistant who served him might be able to help you. Just a minute. I'll get you his address.'

'Thanks. I'll get a taxi.'

'No. I'll drive you there. It's an awkward journey, and I can see you're anxious about it all.'

'We think he may be a man wanted on a number of very grave charges. We don't *know* of course—I'm saying nothing to reflect on the character of your customer. But on the basis of information in hand, we have to investigate—and at once.'

The assistant was at home. He remembered the bearded man and his attractive companion, and the imitation Limoges dinner service they had selected. But he couldn't remember the man's name, let alone his address.

'I know how you gentlemen will feel about this disruption,' said Belin, 'but the matter really is urgent. Would you consider opening up the shop and making a search for the customer's invoice and address? If your customer is the man we want, you may save a lot of women from fraud and danger. If he isn't—well, I can only apologise.'

The three returned to the china shop, rummaged through piles of papers, and at last the assistant produced the invoice with the customer's card attached. The buyer was not M. Fremyet. Nor was he M. Dupont. He was Lucien Guillet, an engineer, of 76, rue de Rochechouart, Paris.

Still it looked as though the taunts of Commissioner Dautel and his fellow-inspectors were justified. But why should he assume this? Was he not looking for a criminal and an imposter, who used whatever name happened to suit him at any particular time?

He asked the assistant: 'Would you describe this man to me again?'

'Rather dignified. Over fifty years old, I'd say. Balding, but with a neat, ample beard. His eyes were rather striking—deep-set and bright, as though they were boring through you.'

It sounded like the wanted man—and Mlle Lacoste had absolutely no doubt about his identity. But by now it was well past midnight. Everyone was very tired.

'Gentlemen,' said Belin, 'I must start work, but you finished yours long since and must be very tired. You have, I think, done a great service to the police and to the public. And now I must go and find your customer.'

It was a cold and dismal vigil for Belin, for he had no warrant for this particular man; he hadn't established yet that he was on the right trail. He merely felt he was. Unable to make enquiries until daylight broke, and unwilling to miss M. Guillet, he waited around outside until dawn and then awoke a protesting concierge.

It will be understood that Belin's enquiries were, at this stage, delicate. To have trod with the impulsiveness with which Dautel so often credited him would have ruined all his chances. The loyalties of a concierge are divided unevenly between tenant and owner. Any third party, any outsider, starts at a disadvantage. M. Guillet was absolutely no trouble at all, and the charming lady with him, Fernande Segret, was always polite.

The first, and disastrous, news was that the birds had flown. 'I don't know how long they'll be away, they come and go as they please,' the concierge muttered.

Belin organised a day and night watch on the premises. Would 'M. Fremyet' return? He hurried to get a warrant for M. Fremyet's arrest. Another inspector, Riboulet, helped to keep the place under discreet surveillance. Belin spent the next few days lounging around in local cafés and bars, and gained the confidence of M. Cerebus, the concierge. Belin had also alerted the police department to watch for any advertisements appearing under the name of Lucien Guillet (a watch had long been kept for the names of Dupont and Fremyet). They had come up with one. A Monsieur Guillet was advertising a car for sale from an address at Etampes.

A few days later, as Belin was having a drink in a bar, the concierge sidled up to him and whispered frantically: *'He's back!'*

Once more Belin cursed his luck, but he wasted no time doing it. He sprinted round to the building and stationed himself outside the door of the flat. Since, by French law, he could not conduct a search of private premises during the hours of darkness, he waited patiently until dawn.

Occasionally he put his ear to the door and listened. But there was not a sound. He had sent an urgent message to Inspector Riboulet to join him, praying that, on this night of all nights, he had not been called away on some other urgent case. Luck was on his side in this, for as dawn broke Riboulet, tall, beefy and smiling, tip-toed up the stairs to join him.

Although he suspected that Lucien Guillet was Fremyet, he had as yet no proof, and had no legal powers of forcing an entry into 'Guillet's' flat. He would have to get in by a subterfuge. Would it work?

At 9.30 a.m. Belin knocked on the door of the flat. There was no reply. He knocked again, more loudly and insistently.

At last a sleepy voice was heard.

'Who's there? What do you want?'

'I've come about the car—the car in the small ad.'

'I'm not even dressed! Come back later.'

'I can't come back. I've come all the way from Étampes and can't spare the time to come again.'

Riboulet and Belin waited, tense, to put their shoulders to the door and burst in the moment they got a chance.

Their chance came. A key turned slowly in the lock. A middle-aged man with hollow eyes and dark beard, clad in dressing gown, looked out through a chink in the door. In that instant, Riboulet and Belin put their weight against it, and thrust their way in, seizing him roughly in the process. 'M. Guillet' did not struggle. He stood there, looking at them both with an air of outraged dignity. Riboulet held fast to him as Belin snapped:

'Monsieur Guillet? Inspector Belin, Sûreté Générale. We wish to question you on various matters. Please get dressed and come with us.'

From an adjacent room came a woman's scream, followed by a heavy thud. Fernande Segret, a young lyric artist who was living with him, had fainted. She sprawled stark naked on the bedroom floor. 'Guillet' was allowed to comfort her. 'What do you want with my Lucien,' she moaned, as she came to, 'it is some terrible mistake. Lucien! Who are these men?'

Landru was very calm. 'I am Lucien Guillet, an engineer, born on September 18, 1874, at Verdun. What is the meaning of this intrusion?'

'I have a warrant for your arrest,' said Belin. This was untrue, for the warrant he held was in the name of Fremyet, and he had not yet established any certain connection between Fremyet and Guillin.

'Take him off,' said Belin, 'I'll come back later. Meanwhile, I want to see what I can find here.'

The two policemen were touched by 'Guillet's' concern for Fernande Segret. He spoke gently, soothingly to her, kissed her tenderly and long, and stroked her hair. Once dressed, he

D

took a look around the room and, to the accompaniment of her sobs, began singing des Grieux's adieu, from the chorus in *Manon*:

> *'Adieu notre petite table!*
> *Un meme verre était le nôtre,*
> *Chacun de nous, quand il bouvait*
> *Y cherchait les lèvres de l'autre.*
> *Ah! pauvre ami, comme il m'aimait*
> *Adieu, notre petite table, adieu!'*

It was a curious song for an innocent man to sing. For in Massenet's opera, it is sung when the young nobleman, des Grieux, is forced by his father to abandon his mistress, Manon, and sings this famous little aria, to the little dining table in their love nest at which they shared so many happy tête-à-têtes.

A third policeman had arrived. Riboulet and the newcomer took Landru down to the police car outside and whisked him away to the Sûreté. The car window was open, and Riboulet noticed his prisoner making a furtive attempt to extract something from his pocket and throw it outside. He checked him just in time. Riboulet prised it from his big, bony, tightly-clenched hands. It was a little black notebook.

'Interesting, Monsieur Guillet,' he said, putting it in his pocket. 'Now I wonder why you were so eager to get rid of this?'

Back in the rue de Rochechouart, Belin was searching the apartment—illegally, as he well knew, but in a good cause. In the pocket of one of 'Guillet's' overcoats he came across a scrap of old envelope with the name 'Landru' written on it. 'What a curious thing,' he thought to himself, 'why, that's the false name I once used when checking into a hotel with my girl friend for a naughty weekend.' The coincidence and nostalgia made way to a more serious line of thought. Was 'Landru' another of this man's aliases?

'Ever heard of Landru?' he asked Mlle Segret.

'Landru, Landru?' she asked, vaguely. 'No. Should I have done?'

'No, I just wondered,' said Belin, and went on with his search. This finished, he decided to get back as fast as he

84

could to 1st Brigade headquarters, as he did not want to miss anything of the initial interrogation of the prisoner. 'It would be helpful if you could come, too,' he told her, 'although you are not obliged to, and there is no question of any charge against you at this stage.'

'I don't mind at all,' said Mlle Segret. She seemed more collected now, although sad.

Belin took over the questioning. Landru had been stripped and searched. Apart from the notebook which Riboulet had prevented him from throwing away, Belin discovered a smaller notebook, or *carnet*. He did not reveal his interest for a moment as his eyes lit upon two familiar names, Collomb and Buisson.

'Identity papers?'

'I haven't any. I was born in Verdun and the town's archives were destroyed during the German bombardment in 1917. Now look here, what is all this about? Will you be good enough to explain all this intrusion and interference?'

'You're involved with murder.'

'Murder, or murders?' (Here Landru was indulging in a bit of untranslatable cheek. Belin had said, '*Vous êtes mêlés à une affaire assassinat*,' to which he replied, '*Avec s ou sans s?*'—'*assassinat*' sounding the same in the singular as in the plural.)

A splendid lunch, with a bottle of excellent wine, was brought in during the questioning. Landru picked daintily at a little of the food and almost ignored the wine, as though its quality was almost an affront to a man of his taste. Belin was losing his patience. The man's cool insolence, and the failure to loosen his tongue with drink, were a hindrance. But there were the notebooks. He took a detailed look at them while Landru waited in polite boredom.

'You seem to know an awful lot of women, M. Guillet. My colleague has counted 283 women's names. But I'm especially interested in two names, here, in this smaller notebook of yours, which I've just taken from your pocket. "Cuchet, A. *idem*, Brésil, Crozatier, Havre, Buisson, A. Collomb, Babelay, Jaume, Pascal, Marchadier"—Buisson, Collomb—do those names mean anything to you?'

'No. Nothing. I have nothing to say.'

Mlle Segret was questioned, but her innocence was so

obvious that she was allowed to take a tearful farewell of her lover and return to the flat. In the meantime, Belin was pondering what that reference to 'Landru' could be about. It was a long shot, but worth checking. He consulted the files of the prefecture, and came up in no time at all with the treasure trove he was seeking—the file on Henri Désiré Landru, persistent criminal with several jail sentences, and still wanted by the police for a crime committed in 1914.

The last piece of information was particularly welcome, for Belin now had ample legal justification for detaining him, irrespective of the course his enquiries might take in respect of his enquiries into the fate of the two missing women.

He confronted Landru over the desk.

'You are Landru.'

'Yes, I *am* Landru. Of course I had to hide and conceal my identity, for, as you know now, I was wanted by the police. But that doesn't make me a murderer. Prove what you say. Prove your accusations.'

'What I do know,' said Belin, 'is that you are Henri Désiré Landru, born in Paris in 1869, with eight convictions to your credit—or *dis*credit—in respect of forgery, fraud and false pretences. In fact, as you are well aware, there is a suspended sentence in respect of an offence in 1914. You are, therefore, under arrest, without bail, for your former offence, and we shall proceed rigorously with our enquiries into these other serious matters—which we believe are a matter of murder.'

Landru showed no obvious emotion. He did not avert his gaze as Belin spoke to him, but continued to look directly at him with deep, sombre eyes.

'Murder! That, M. Belin, is a very serious accusation to make, particularly as you are in no position to sustain it. . . .'

'At the moment.'

'Or at any other moment. I am innocent of any offence and have no idea why I am being detained.'

'We shall be taking your girl friend into custody. No doubt she will be less reticent than you.'

'There is not the slightest justification for worrying poor Mlle Segret. She is not responsible in the slightest degree for any of my business transactions or activities of any kind. It is not only ungallant, but I would have thought quite pointless, to make this lady the victim of your unfounded suspicions concerning me.'

Commissioner Dautel, and Inspectors Belin and Riboulet listened incredulously. Their prisoner was so cool, so confident. There was no *braggadocio* about him—merely a sort of bored detachment and the sort of quiet outrage a scholar might exhibit if interrupted whilst deep in thought on some vital problem. Could this insignificant little confidence trickster be a Don Juan with scores of women in thrall? Could he be a mass murderer?

'Your little notebook is interesting. So is your petty cash book. I see that under the date December 28, 1918, you have written "1 return, frcs. 4.95, 1 single, frcs. 3.95, taxi 2.75. Obviously you took a little trip with somebody on that day— but you came back alone, didn't you?'

'We're in April now, Inspector. December is a long way away.'

'What bores you, Landru, interests me. I happen to know that the nearest station to Gambais, where you rented this villa from which two women have disappeared, is Houdan. I know that the train fare from the Gare des Invalides to Houdan is 3.95 francs, and that you would need a taxi to Gambais itself, which would set you back about 2.75 francs. Now I wonder who you took to Gambais at the end of 1918, eh? It wasn't Mme Collomb, and it couldn't have been Mme Buisson. Does the Villa Tric mean anything to you?'

Landru did not reply.

Out of Landru's hearing, the Commissioner and his inspectors conferred. They agreed to keep questioning Landru in relays, so that they remained fresh while he became progressively exhausted. Belin, meanwhile, decided to visit Landru's garage at Clichy, whose address he had discovered written on a receipt for the rent.

The garage at Clichy revealed a strange multitudinous assortment of junk. There were some quite good pieces of furniture such as wardrobes, tables, chairs, and so on, and worthless bric-à-brac such as old washing basins, waterjugs, well-worn corsets, brassières and even false teeth. But a pile of documents lying in a dark, dusty corner were just the evidence Belin sought. They were personal documents relating to Mme Collomb and Mme Buisson, the sort of papers no person would part with, such as marriage certificates, birth certificates and so on. This discovery, and the revelation of his criminal record, allowed for sinister speculations. Yet Belin had to admit to himself that there was absolutely nothing in the man's records indicative of violence. Even his behaviour under arrest, obstructive and insolent though it was, had nothing of violence about it. At no point had Landru lost his head, become hysterical, abusive, threatening, self-pitying. He had just picked up the threads of detective work again after a long service in the army, and was anxious to prove his worth to a far-from-enthusiastic commissioner. The next move was obvious: to take Landru to Gambais and search the villa and grounds in his presence. But it was Saturday, and time was getting on.

Belin turned over some of the other papers. They concerned other women. Furthermore, some of these personal papers were even more unlikely to have been handed over voluntarily. Without personal identity papers most people are at a disadvantage in countless legal matters. What did this strange collection mean?

Five officials questioned Landru relentlessly. Alternately, they cajoled and threatened. He rejected proffered refreshments. The examiners seemed to tire more easily than he did. He was totally indifferent to the usual policy ploy that if he played along with them and told all he knew, he could expect more lenient treatment. He had been in police hands too many times to fall for that one.

Late in the evening, Danglure, a reporter on the *Petit Journal*, whose speciality was crime, made a routine call at the Préfecture. The day's cases were mostly run-of-the-mill stuff, but one of his informants among the detectives let drop a hint. Something important was brewing upstairs. A really important suspect. Murder, probably. Even several murders. A man with hypnotic eyes had been courting middle-aged women and taking them to a lonely villa near Paris from which they never emerged again.

Soon Danglure was hot-footing it back to his office with a scoop. Like Belin, he needed such highlights to keep his reputation bright and ensure promotion:

AN IMPORTANT ARREST. The police have arrested a smartly-dressed man, almost totally bald, with a black beard, who is wanted by more than ten local courts under a variety of pseudonyms, although his real name is Nandru [sic]. Previously convicted of stealing, swindling, and confidence tricks, this miserable individual who, they say, was helped by hypnotism, may well have to answer even more serious charges...

Danglure had been given a few hints, within the limits imposed by the fact that the man had only just been arrested. As in the USA, the sort of *sub-judice* restrictions which would inhibit a reporter in Britain in describing the arrest of a man awaiting trial, or, as in this case, merely held pending investigations, did not apply. Danglure had been given the tip that enquiries concerning ten women, whose names appeared in Landru's *carnet*, were involved. Hence the reference to ten local courts, although that number of courts was not involved. He had managed to take liberties with Landru's name, but was possibly given the wrong spelling in the excitement and haste.

The interrogation of Landru continued remorselessly until midnight, without any admission of any kind being extracted from him. Belin was almost desperate, because the French law as it stood then demanded that he should be handed over to the local court involved within twenty-four hours. Belin had only until mid-day the following day, Sunday, to do this. Since the administrative centre concerned was Mantes, about twenty-five miles from Paris, there was little time to lose. Would Landru confess? It would be a feather in Belin's cap if he could be induced to do so. Yet the physical arrangements for Landru's reception had to be made. The local officer concerned, although working at Mantes, lived in Paris, and explained, irritably, that if Landru was to be delivered into his hands on Sunday, and put in prison awaiting investigations, it would have to be done quite early in the morning, as he himself was giving a party in Paris and could not postpone it at such short notice.

This was a considerable nuisance. Landru would have to be taken to Gambais, where the police and mayor had been notified of the forthcoming visit, and it looked as though the search of the villa would have to be conducted in haste. Belin wanted to note Landru's reactions, for him to be confronted with any discoveries that might be made. It meant taking Landru down by car to Gambais, searching the villa, questioning Landru, and then taking him to Mantes, handing him over and completing all the formalities that the law demanded.

It goes without saying that by this time Belin, who had been on duty continuously for thirty-six hours without a break for sleep, was feeling very tired. So, too, was Landru. Fifteen hours of ceaseless questioning had left him exhausted. He slumped forward on the table, and snored loudly. All attempts to awaken him were hopeless. Whether he was asleep or feigning sleep they couldn't be sure.

On the following morning Landru, accompanied by detectives and of course by M. Belin, left for Gambais. Throughout the whole of the journey, and the visit to the villa itself, Landru showed nothing but indifference. He did not, however, persist in his pretence that he did not know the house. That, at least, he knew to be hopeless, as too many local people had seen him shopping, and the identity of the man who rented it from M. Tric could easily be established.

Belin was surprised at the dismal disorder and lack of comfort in the place. Could this have been the love-nest? In one room was a bed improvised on two chairs, in another a narrow, folding couch. In various corners there were heaps of soiled linen, and women's underclothing. A mattress seemed to bear bloodstains.

Landru seemed in a daze. 'Landru,' Belin said, 'you did kill these two women, didn't you? Confess it—you killed them, because you're mad. Mme Collomb, remember her? Mme Buisson. What did you do with the corpses?'

In one room Belin came across a good clue—a large trunk with the initials 'C.L.'

'Is this your trunk?'

'Of course—you can see the initials. Charles Landru.'

'You must think me simple, Landru. Your name is not Charles, but Henri Désiré. Those initials are those of Celestine Lacoste, otherwise Mme Buisson, whom you brought here. Besides, look at this label. It is from Bayonne, her home town.'

'I bought the trunk from her, and gave her a few hundred francs to get rid of her,' Landru replied.

'And where did she go?'

'Find out for yourself. I know nothing about it.'

In one of the rooms Belin came across a book about famous

poisoners. He thumbed the pages. It wasn't fiction. It was an accurate reconstruction of famous cases, with specific details of how they achieved their ends—with arsenic or strychnine, antimony or morphine.

'Interested in this sort of thing?'

Again no reply.

The garage was searched. It revealed nothing. It contrasted with the disorder of the house in that the tools and spare parts were in neat array, as one would expect in a garage kept by a dealer in cars.

In the kitchen, Belin inspected the heavy iron stove. Had this been used as a crematorium? He was convinced it had. To the left of the house was a small outhouse communicating with the kitchen, and a cellar below. Police found sand with what appeared to be bloodstains, and in the coach-house at the end of the garden were badly-charred scraps of bone, teeth, a fragment of fused glass and a hairpin. A 'Chocolat Meunier' box was open and empty on the kitchen table. The kitchen shutter, Belin noted with grim amusement, was in the shape of a heart—an ironically romantic touch.

These bits and pieces might sustain a limited amount of suspicion, but where were the corpses? Belin was getting desperate. Soon they must make their way to the jail at Mantes, where an irate official, obsessed with thoughts of the fine luncheon awaiting him in Paris, would make short of the whole proceedings.

The respectable bourgeoisie and country labourers were by now pouring from the little village church after the Palm Sunday service. Word had got around that things were happening at the Villa Tric, and they gathered around as Landru was questioned. The most dramatic find that morning were the skeletons of three little dogs found under a heap of straw in a garden shed. Some lengths of wire were found nearby, and Belin concluded that the dogs had been strangled.

'Well, Landru?' he asked.

'Their owner couldn't afford to feed them, and asked me to destroy them. They didn't suffer.'

'Who was this girl friend, and where is she now?'

Landru gave Belin a look of astonished reproach. 'Really, Inspector, a man of your experience should know better than to ask such a question. It is a most indiscreet thing to ask. It would be over-stepping the bounds of delicacy.'

In a high-pitched voice a spectator shouted over to the group, as they stood in the garden: 'Those dogs belonged to a fair young lady who came here!' Landru ignored it.

The scraps of calcined bone were put into bags. So, too, the pathetic remains of the three pet dogs. Landru waved airily towards the cemetery over the garden wall. 'Why don't you investigate there, too? They must have plenty of skeletons to spare.'

Belin was white with rage, yet dared not go beyond official bounds, at any rate in public. 'Now look here, we're going to have a good lunch at the local inn. You can have anything you like, because where you're going the fare isn't as good. Use your sense. You're on a capital charge, you know. You've got a wife and children to think of. If you give us a bit of help it may go easier for you at the Assizes. Confess that you murdered these women. Tell us what you did with their bodies.'

'Inspector, we are not, it seems, to spend much more time together. Let us not waste it in useless speculation.'

At lunch, Landru ate heartily of the excellent cheeses, omelette and delicious stewed rabbit cooked in regional style. Once more he refused the wine—a fine Burgundy. He accepted a bottle of Vichy water instead. It was not a drink calculated to loosen his tongue, and Belin fumed all over lunch.

After lunch, the car sped on to Mantes, and Landru was handed over to an infuriated official. 'Keep it short!' he snapped, 'I've missed my wife's luncheon party now. Where on earth have you been?'

'We have been searching his villa,' said Belin, coldly, 'a procedure which can't be timed to a second.'

As Landru was led off to his cell, a few paper formalities having been completed, Belin pleaded with Landru once more to confess. Belin said afterwards that, had he not been so rushed because the official was impatient to get to Paris for his lunch, he might have been able to soften Landru up and secure a confession. I can only say that, in the light of Landru's behaviour in the ensuing years, such a theory seems optimistic. In any case, we shall never know.

Incidentally, while Landru was being taken around the so-familiar villa at Gambais, a lady called Nina waited for him at the Gare St-Lazare, where she was to meet him and travel with him for a weekend at Gambais. Her letter had been intercepted by the authorities, but it carried no address and they never discovered who she was. If she read the popular newspapers, she would in due course have been thankful that her paramour was unable to keep his appointment. Meanwhile, his faithful and sorrowing mistress, Fernande Segret, who had lived with him while less lucky mistresses disappeared from the face of the earth, awaited developments in the rue de Rochechouart. She had been released by the police, after brief questioning, as it was obvious that she was not involved personally and, indeed, it was evident that she believed utterly in Landru's innocence. As she certainly was not naive, she obviously had to be uninformed.

In the Landru home there was utter consternation. The police had descended upon poor Mme Landru and her family, plying them with questions. They had grown so used, over the years, to Landru's butterfly activities that there was nothing remarkable in him renting another house, or acquiring, suddenly, another lot of furniture, or distributing such odd and unsolicited largesse as corsets, hair combs and well-worn underclothing. Mme Landru had forgiven him much in the course of his life, but stared at the police in shocked incredulity when informed that her husband had engaged in amorous correspondence (and often dalliance) with nearly three hundred women. And the revelation that Landru had a 'regular'—a comely mistress in the rue de Rochechouart—was a crowning humiliation.

How had Landru crammed all these activities into his frequent absences from home? Had the watch given to her really belonged to the Mme Cuchet who, like so many others, had disappeared from Landru's villa at Gambais? Had the sporadic housekeeping money come from the pockets of women who were murdered after their property and cash had been stolen?

The police wondered about this too, and arrested her in due course. Yet never, in the annals of French crime, had so many questions been asked to which there were so few satisfactory answers.

7

The True Heart

A MAN may be a villain, yet still find someone to love him. Eva Braun loved Adolf Hitler to the end, and died with him. Mme Petacci, mistress of the Italian dictator Mussolini, could have deserted him when his fortunes turned and he was a fugitive. But she stayed with him to the end, and died with him.

Landru had been loved by many women. There is no doubting that, of the scores of women with whom he had intimate relations, many were genuinely in love with him. Unfortunately, for most of them, such affection was a mere prelude to oblivion. Fernande Segret was the notable exception. To her he was civil, courteous, attentive, ardent and protective. Protection, as one has gathered from the narrative so far, was not Landru's outstanding characteristic.

Not only did Fernande Segret love him and live, she seems to have evoked real love in Landru himself. Also, whereas everyone else deserted Landru once the law caught up with him, she uttered no word of criticism and never failed to uphold his good name. Her love was rooted in trust, for, initially, she had little reason to trust him.

Their idyll began in 1917, in that most homely and democratic of places, the Paris tramcar. Fernande was sitting with a friend when she became aware of the man opposite, a man old enough to be her father. He was neat, bearded, bald and there was 'something' about him that demanded attention. His eyes, perhaps? He fixed her with a continual, direct stare that both repelled and attracted her. She and her friend laughed about it. What a peculiar old man!

They got off the car, and were soon accosted by the stranger, whose quiet and melodious voice surprised and charmed

94

Fernande. So, too, did his impudence—the sort of cheek a girl might expect from a much younger man.

'You're both too young and too attractive to be walking about Paris alone,' he chided.

'And who appointed you our protector?' laughed Fernande.

'I would scarcely deserve the description of protector if I waited to be invited. You know, too many young girls go about alone in Paris nowadays. There are some bad characters about.'

It was impossible not to burst out laughing at this approach. It was as Landru wished. Instead of a rebuff, the ice had been broken, and now he was walking along with them.

'What is your name?' asked Fernande.

'Lucien Guillet — G-U-I-L-L-E-T.'

'And what do you do for a living?'

'I'm an engineer from Rocroi, but I have interests in Paris, too. I have a garage here, and a country retreat in Gambais.' Landru talked volubly and amusingly on a variety of subjects, and was allowed to walk as far as her home at 7, rue Custine. He seems to have made a deep and instant impression, for Fernande made a date with him for the following day, and whenever he was not with his wife and children, or at Gambais on his unspecified errands, or at his non-existent factory at Rocroi, or at assignations with any of the other women with whom he was in correspondence, he would see her home from the furrier's shop where she worked. In describing herself as a 'lyric artist' Fernande was expressing aspiration rather than fact. She could sing and mime passably well, and her personality was vital and vibrant (she was certainly not 'a tall ugly girl' as one writer once put it—her photographs belie this absurdity). And she awakened (or sustained) in Landru passions which seem to have been absolutely genuine.

Fernande was certainly tall, but she was, as we say now, shapely. The ample-hanging garments of the time tend to conceal this. She had even, almost oval features, a delicate aquiline nose, full 'cupid's-bow' lips, graceful neck, good hair and extremely expressive, well-spaced eyes. She had passion and humour, spirit and docility, kindness and strength, and was pre-eminently feminine. She was the catalyst who could prove that Henri Désiré Landru had a human side, which many were entitled to doubt.

Would she have 'disappeared' had not their idyll been so

cruelly interrupted? This we will never know for certain, but as she survived while others 'disappeared' we must accept that their relationship, in the context of Landru's life, was unique. His relationship with his wife seems to have been a matter of habit—an odd bourgeois side to a man utterly unconservative in his secret life. Some of the biggest villains of this century have had this grotesque 'conservative' side to them. Hitler, in the middle of planning genocide and murders, would hold formal receptions, taking care that his collar was snow-white and his boots polished like mirrors.

The day after their first meeting they met by the Étoile, the huge triumphal arch that had cost over half a million pounds to build. It has seen history enough. Victor Hugo's bier was set up under the vault on the night before his burial in 1885. In two successive world wars, Allied Armies marched in triumph beneath it.

Their meeting was one of the Étoile's minor dramas, perhaps, but it was drama nevertheless. For him this meeting did not merely bring about a few stolen bonds, or money fraudulently extracted from her bank, or furniture humped laboriously down difficult stairs on its way to his Clichy garage. It began an association which was to be significant for both of them until the end of their separate lives.

They went boating on the lake in the Bois de Boulogne, and strolled in the woods which had echoed to the sound of the hunting horn in the days of the Valois kings, which has been the scene of assassinations, suicides and the despoliation by the detachments of British and Russian troops encamped there after the Battle of Waterloo and the abdication of Napoleon. Indeed, Landru's father had committed suicide in the same park, from grief at his son's behaviour, but this did not inhibit Landru in paying fervent suit to his new girl-friend.

Fernande was with him fairly constantly from May 1917, onwards, and went to live with him in the rue Rochechouart. But there were gaps in their association, which are easily explained. Fernande, to whom he promised marriage, insisted on him meeting her family. From Fernande herself we have an interesting picture of Landru's dual disposition:

> We were all seated at family dinner. Grandfather was with us, and I could see from his happy smile how much he was enjoying Lucien's [Landru's] lively conversation and many polite attentions.

In the evening, Lucien, with his energy and humour, was brilliant. He joked, talked wittily, and even juggled with the napkin rings to keep us amused. The conversation veered to music-halls, and he seemed to know all about them, telling us about the stars of the past, and even breaking into song with the old favourite, '*Le Bal à l'Hôtel de Ville*'. Everybody took to him. He was the focus of everyone's attention.

Since Fernande owned no property, not even any furniture or the simplest pieces of jewellery to attract Landru's assessor's eye, one wonders why he went to such trouble and behaved in this way. Fernande Segret proved a reliable and objective witness, and one can only assume from her accounts that Landru could shake off completely all thoughts of guilt— assuming he ever had any—all thoughts of fear of the consequences implied in his innumerable crimes.

Landru found time for the sort of attentions that women like. He never appeared empty-handed. Somehow there was always a bottle of wine, a box of sweets, some expensive pastries, or munificent bunches of flowers.

All these blandishments did nothing to impress her mother.

'I can't see what you see in him,' Mme Segret complained. 'He's well past his prime and far too old for you. I don't think old goats should frisk about with young lambs.'

'Mother, I love him very much. Please don't speak slightingly of my Lucien.'

'I love you, too—I've spent nearly a quarter of a century looking after you—and I tell you, I don't want to see you snatched away by a man I consider an imposter.'

'An imposter!'

'Is he not? Where's this factory of his he talks about? What does it make in Rocroi? What's his firm called?'

'I haven't asked.'

'Well, I suggest you try asking, and remember what he says in reply.'

When Fernande and Landru lived together, Mme Segret urged her daughter to marry.

'If you've enough confidence to live with him, then you've enough in common to marry him. He says he wants to marry you, doesn't he?'

'Yes, but I don't know whether I want to marry him. I'm so happy with him, with things as they are.'

Mme Segret would shrug her shoulders and give up. But every time she met Landru, she made her hostility plain and asked pointed questions. Landru never lost his patience or his temper. 'Mama,' he would say, in that soothing, well-modulated voice of his, 'I only want Fernande's happiness.'

Once, when he gave a house-warming at their apartment in the rue de Rochechouart, an amazing spectacle greeted the guests:

> It was not a mere flat on which the door opened, it was a real green-house. The dining-room was nothing but an immense basket of flowers. I have never seen such a display, in size or variety. He had with careful taste mixed humble violets with the rarest gardenias, and everything was so well arranged, with such harmonies of colour, such taste in the bouquets, that mother and I looked as if we were paralysed. 'You must have robbed the Nice train,' I said at last.

This lavish display, the continual patience and gentle speech and the uncompromising loyalty of Fernande to her strange lover at last persuaded Mme Segret to accept the inevitable. She was still uneasy about the man, but did not know what to say when he declared that for the time being at least he could not marry her as it was impossible to prove his identity, the documents having been destroyed by war.

He invited her to Gambais. They hired a couple of bicycles and explored the countryside around, dismounting and wheeling their bicycles through the dense woods. Fernande loved Gambais, and could not understand why the generous gentleman would not agree with her suggestion that his country retreat would be a grand refuge from air raids for her family. The thought of grandfather, the ferocious Madame, the pert daughter and who knows who else, all trooping into Gambais just when he was in the mood to stoke up the stove was too much for him. To her annoyance, he rejected it out of hand.

There were other dangerous moments in their relationship. One day he had found her rummaging through a pile of documents in their flat. He flew into a rage—as well he might, for some of the documents were the stolen securities of some of his vanished fiancées. Was she in danger of her life at that time? She may well have been. But when she protested that they had no secrets from each other (as she fondly imagined) he had been soothed, and apologised for his temper.

1. Vernouillet, scene of Landru's first four murders. His villa is the whitewashed house on the right, with a tree in the front garden.
(*Radio Times Hulton Picture Library*)

2. Landru with his mistress Mlle Segret—'the one that got away'.
(*Radio Times*)

3. Landru's lonely villa at Gambais, where seven victims perished.
(Press Association)

4. The kitchen at Gambais. In the corner is the stove in which Landru's victims are said to have been incinerated.
(Press Association)

5. Mlle Marchadier, the brothel keeper who was the last of Landru's known victims. (*Radio Times*)

6. Landru's kitchen stove being taken away from the Gambais villa for examination by forensic experts. (*Press Association*)

7. Landru on the way to court, flanked by warders. (*Radio Times*)

8. The court at Versailles. Landru is in the dock (right). On the table in front of the judges (left) lies an assortment of victims' clothing.
(*Radio Times*)

9. A police photograph of Landru outside his cell.

10. Landru proclaiming his innocence during the trial.

11. Judge Gilbert, the presiding judge at the trial.

12. Landru in the dock.

13. Maître de Moro-Giafferi,
Landru's leading counsel.
(*Radio Times*)

14. M. Godefroy, the Avocat Général,
on his way to the courts.

15. 'I have no fiancées up my sleeve.' A contemporary cartoon from
L'Avenir, showing Landru's counsel in action.

16. Inspector Belin arriving at the court, with prisoner in tow.
(*Radio Times*)

17. Mme Collin takes the stand on behalf of her daughter Andrée, who was probably Landru's youngest victim. (*Radio Times*)

RÉPUBLIQUE FRANÇAISE

PRÉFECTURE DE POLICE

PARIS, LE 19 novembre 1971

Cher Monsieur Bardens,

En m'excusant du retard apporté à répondre à votre
lettre du 9 octobre dernier, j'ai l'honneur de vous faire
savoir que l'état de nos archives ne nous permet pas de savoir
quelle suite a été donnée à la découverte d'ossements humains
appartenant à deux corps différents exhumés en 1958 dans une
propriété voisine de celle louée naguère par Landru à Vernouillet.

S'agit-il des corps de Mme CUCHET et de son fils ?
Il est difficile de répondre affirmativement à cette question
car d'après le rapport établi alors par le médecin légiste,
les fragments d'ossements semblent correspondre à ceux d'une
femme de 30 ans et à ceux d'un adolescent d'une dizaine d'années.
Or Mme CUCHET avait 40 ans et son fils 17 ans ½ au moment de
leur disparition.

Avec mes regrets de ne pouvoir seconder davantage
vos recherches, je vous prie d'agréer, Cher Monsieur Bardens,
l'expression de mes sentiments les meilleurs.

L'Administrateur
Chef du Bureau des Archives
et du Musée

Imp. S T 101 12-65

Monsieur Dennis BARDENS
3 Horbury Mews
London W11 3NL

ENGLAND

18. The recent letter to the author from the Préfecture de Police
in Paris concerning the human bone fragments discovered in
1958 in the next-door property to Landru's at Vernouillet. The
remains were thought to be a woman of about thirty and a boy
of about ten, and could have been those of Mme Cuchet and
her son André.

Then there was a period in September 1917, when he had disappeared for months after promising marriage. At her mother's insistence, they took the train to Rocroi and sought the 'Lucien Guillet' who was supposed to have a factory there. They could find no factory, nor had anyone heard of Lucien Guillet. When next Landru did contact her, after acquiring and disposing of Mme Buisson's assets, he found to his dismay that the daughter was now as sceptical as her mother. Landru sat down with ink, pen and a lot of paper and wrote the following letter. It throws interesting light upon his literary style and his powers of persuasion:

Thursday evening.

I am, my pretty little friend, in such a sorry state that I must come near to your warm heart to find consolation and forgetfulness of my sorrow.

And, first of all, I must tell you about it, mustn't I? Don't worry, it's not your fault, you couldn't make me unhappy, I am the sole author of my troubles but I cannot yet tell you exactly what that trouble is. I saw yesterday in your beautiful eyes, so deep, veiled and disturbing, a shadow of distress. I had no doubt, since we were alone, that I was its cause.

But what is distressing you?

Have I said something—a word, a sentence which shocked you? Or is there something else, for which I have searched in vain?

And so my thoughts go round and I have been led to think of all sorts of reasons which, since I was so happy with you near me, I hadn't thought of at first when my impulsive heart was so full of you. Alas, reason is relentless and this dissection (of feelings) has made me see a thousand things which may be irrelevant or may, sadly enough, be near the truth.

Among them, I have discounted the idea that you were saddened because the love I brought you was not virginal. Certainly your lovely soul deserves such a love and would that I could have given it to you. But we promised to be frank with each other, and I will tell you about myself all that you may wish to know or that you should know, but, I beg of you, don't rush me. By nature, by the life I have led, by my loneliness—both in mundane and spiritual matters—I am a solitary, shut up in myself. In me you may still find some fresh and new things, more perhaps than you think. To you, who have had the good sense not to ask too much to begin with, I will try to make up for what harsh experience has taught me by my friendly concern, to protect you from what troubles you may have and that you may wish to confide in me.

The Ladykiller

Another of the harsh truths which I have had to learn and which may not be irrelevant, may even have contributed to your sorrow, is the realisation that I am no longer your age, an age so full of charm and hope. The years that have passed me over have been hard, in the full meaning of the word, and if my body is still supple and healthy, that is because I have lived to the strictest rules of hygiene and have avoided excess. It's true that I can still stand on my two feet—better, perhaps, than many a young townee of our day—but the years have marked me nevertheless and I would regard it as childish to try and discuss it. But with you, my little friend, whose prettiness is in each step, in each gesture, whose eyes and fresh smile entitle you to happiness, to dreams, may I be allowed to think of becoming a comrade-by-accident without being accused of wanting too much? As a woman of the world you don't protest? Don't worry, I know what I'm worth. If I have a few qualities, I have also many serious faults: in the balance I don't come out well.

But if this could prove sufficient for you, I have for you a great friendship, a feeling which is, I fear, more than affection, drawing me near to you and growing daily as I discover in you the precious treasures of your heart and soul. Such things as are, sad to say, little valued today.

Following on your pretty tracks, where shall I go, my pretty little friend, where will you lead me?

What shall I be to you?

What will you wish to be to me?

All these thoughts, all these reasons, as I was saying, have led me to seek the source of your little sorrow. Tell me what it is, my beloved friend, let your heart open up a little for me. You may find it a relief, and you will certainly find a friend who will be indulgent, affectionate and assiduous, whom you may use as you will. I feel that we hardly know each other as yet, but I foretell that we would gain much in getting to know each other better by being truly open with each other. Would you like that? It is not too much to ask?

There are still other questions that I have thought of, but they are of so delicate a nature that I could speak of them only, and will tell you of them, only, if I fail in finding out what motive, what cause, is behind your clouded eyes, one of these days when circumstances are more favourable.

Forgive my prosiness, my incoherence, but the very idea of having hurt you tortures me. You alone, by one word, can restore to me, along with my peace of mind, the tremendous happiness of seeing once again those deep, dreamy eyes whose memory haunts me both night and day. Adieu, don't leave me languishing; whatever your answer may be, it will be welcome and I will accept it without a murmur. You will still have my respect, my goodwill and, if you wish it, on your dear little hands, a thousand kisses from your

Lucien Guillet

The letter is deeply interesting. Landru's capacity for self-dramatisation comes through in every line. It also seems as though he is probing for the reason behind a change of attitude—had she hit upon something terrible in his past, and would this knowledge make her a danger if she were allowed to live? She had held herself aloof and given him no reason. With the memory of the complications and crimes behind him, this worried him considerably—yet he had no choice but to skirt around the subject, making no admissions which could damage him.

Even allowing for all that, some sense of being desperate at the thought of losing her does come through the wording. Since she had been with him to Gambais, he had had ample chance of disposing of her, had he been so inclined. The letter shows with what skill Landru could play on a woman's feelings.

Did Fernande Segret respond at once? It seems not. From the house he once described to her as 'my little paradise' (the villa at Gambais) he wrote, in well-simulated despair:

It is almost night. A silence, empty and absolute, has annihilated Nature after her day's work. Not a leaf on our trees stirs, and I think of you here, where we were so happy for a period, blessed and unforgettable by me, where, without promises or paths, and without troubling ourselves about the cares of the world, we tasted a complete happiness through the sole joy of living together in isolation. Did our love not smile like Nature in springtime? My pretty treasure, why have you left me? How do you think I can live without you, when all my thoughts and aspirations are turned towards you?

Further letters convinced Fernande Segret that Landru (Guillet) was reduced to suicidal despair by her obduracy. She met him, and was much troubled by his depressed and agitated demeanour. What did it mean? She reproached herself. Had she driven her lover to his doom? At all costs, she must ease her mind.

The Ladykiller

She made her way to the rue de Rochechouart in the evening. The door of his flat was open, and, anxiously feeling her way through the darkened flat, she called his name. There was silence. Terrified, she went quickly from room to room. In one of them she found his desk, on which were scattered pieces of poetry including various scraps indicative of melancholy:

Dieu, soutiens mon courage et chasse comme une ombre
Des biens que j'ai perdu le souvenir si doux.

Puzzled and trembling, she entered his room. A strange scene met her eyes. The entire floor was strewn with rose-petals! On the window-sill stood her photograph, festooned with black crepe and in front of it a chair placed in the position of a praying-stool. Theatrical and fantastic though the symbolism was, she was deeply disturbed by it. Had her criticisms of him (centred mainly on the vagueness of his background, and her discovery that he was in contact with innumerable other women) driven him to suicide?

Suddenly she screamed. Landru appeared from a cupboard in which he had been hiding and took her in his arms.

What a bizarre way to resolve a lover's quarrel! The more one considers Landru, the more mystified one becomes about the workings of his mind. However fantastic this strange exercise was, it achieved its intended purpose—to frighten her into loving him again.

That Landru was a good lover is something which we may accept, so far as Fernande Segret was concerned. She has described him as passionate, though normal. She seems to have been more accommodating than many women, in agreeing to absent herself from their love-nest while he 'interviewed' other women (correspondents who had seen his matrimonial advertisements). Of course, she knew that he did some genuine business in second-hand furniture. She had also, on her own insistence, visited his garage at Clichy and been supremely unimpressed by it. It did not fit at all with his stories of being an important business man.

However, she broke off relations with a young lover, a handsome youth who had been fighting at the Front, and to whom throughout the war she had been a *marraine de guerre*. It was the custom of these 'war godmothers' to write to soldiers at the Front, send them parcels and gifts, attend to any personal matters at home which they could not deal with themselves, and also entertain, sustain and accommodate—often in the broadest sense of the word—their protegés when they were on leave.

To Segret's annoyance and bewilderment, 'Lucien' had postponed their proposed marriage, at the time of the Armistice, on the feeble excuse that her 'godson' would be coming home. 'Youth calls to youth,' he wrote to her at the time. 'You have loved him very much. I fear that his return may be fatal to our marriage plans. If you prefer him, stay with him. If you accept me, in spite of my years, I hope never to see a look of regret in your eyes.' And on another occasion he wrote 'Fernande, think no more of me. All I desire is your happiness.'

Obedient to his insistence, she saw the youth on his return from the Front. He had hoped to marry her, and was deeply in love with her. She insisted that her association with Guillet was not a passing phase, no mere infatuation, but a deep relationship that could never be broken. The youth went his tearful way, and she to the flat on the rue Rochechouart, where Landru, no doubt confidently, was awaiting her decision.

'Lucien,' she said, 'I have chosen you.'

With tears in his eyes, he went down on his knees before her, kissing her hand passionately.

And now their love-nest was overrun by police and detectives, rummaging through every drawer, knocking on every wall, pulling up every carpet, floor covering or floorboard. The wickerwork basket crammed with letters from various women had been taken away.

Fernande Segret was alone. But at least she was alive.

8

Where Have All the Bodies Gone?

THE STORY of Landru had broken on the world. An army of journalists and photographers descended on hitherto unknown Gambais and the ordinary suburb of Vernouillet. The local inn at Gambais made a small fortune. Obscure cafés and bars found they hadn't an inch to spare. For there were the police, too, digging in the garden, banging on walls, digging up the paving in the basement, searching, searching, searching.

Journalists speculated hopefully, snatching at the scantiest information as tired prospectors awaken to hope at the mere glint of gold dust. 'Among the cinders in the garden were found calcined bones, portions of ribs, thigh-bones, elbows, a single tooth,' wrote the correspondent of the London *Times*. He was probably told that, for rumours were rife and even many of the police on the job had a very incomplete picture.

In fact, no thigh-bones or elbows were found. Not a single complete bone was discovered. 'Female hair has been discovered clinging to bloodstained sand in the cellar,' reported another correspondent. Urgh! Bloodstained sand *was* discovered, but tests revealed it to be animal blood.

It was with a sense almost of desperation that Riboulet, Dautel and Belin searched around. In Landru's wicker basket they had found references to 283 women. He had engaged in personal contact with 169 of these. He had slept with, and made love to, a considerable number. Every single case was followed up. Of the ten women (and André Cuchet, son of his first victim) mentioned in Landru's notebook, and who were known to have gone to stay with him at Vernouillet or Gambais, all had vanished totally. But where had all the bodies gone? It is no easy matter to dispose of even one body.

Belin learned from Mme Segret that Landru had repapered some of the villa walls at Gambais, to cover up stains.

Laboriously, all the paper was stripped. It revealed nothing.

The water reservoir in the garden was drained. The cesspool, the well and the pump were examined, also revealing nothing unusual. A canvas suit which Landru always wore at Gambais was discovered in an outhouse, but its 'suspicious' stains proved innocuous under forensic tests.

What about that great lake at Bruyères, the huge pond, known only to poachers and wild-duck hunters, on the edge of the Taravise Wood? Dr Monteilhet had come forward with his story of having seen Landru throw some package into the pond, and how firemen came from Paris to explore the bed of the lake. It was no easy matter, for although shallow at the borders, the lake descended to a depth of twenty feet in the centre, and its bed was deep, viscous mud choked with rushes and weeds. The smell was appalling, and rumour soon spread amongst the thousands who watched that decomposing remains lay in the fetid mud. Every scrap of the mud was examined. Nothing was discovered. Spectators jeered at the police and firemen. People came in—or on—every kind of vehicle—farm carts, limousines, bicycles. Even an aeroplane circled overhead, a rare enough thing in those days.

What of the three women who had been picking lilies by the side of the Étang Neuf in July 1918, and had seen a large canvas bag, slumped strangely as though it contained a corpse, floating in the water about thirty yards from the bank? 'It looks like a body,' one of them had said, 'perhaps it's somebody drowning.' If they had entertained the last hypothesis, the occasion had not seemed to be urgent to them, for they had done nothing except to return the following day to see how the somebody 'drowning' was getting on. On that and subsequent days the bag, and whatever it contained, sank lower and lower in the water until it disappeared from view.

The pond was on the estate of the Duchesse d'Uzès and had not been dredged since 1914. Belin thought that perhaps Landru, picking the lock that moored it to the bank, had borrowed a boat at the water's side and taken a corpse to the centre and dumped it. Yet there was nothing to support such a theory—only those uneasy entries in Landru's diary, written between 1916 and 1917, in which he wrote of the difficulty experienced by authorities in the matter of identifying corpses. He quoted an example of a woman who was unable to identify her own child which had been drowned, and the instance of a woman murdered who was at first identified by people who had known her, but who had afterwards admitted that they were mistaken.

And what of the unhappy fisherman, Marguin, who while fishing with friends near the Villa Tric one day had 'landed' a piece of putrescent flesh?

Apart from the strong suspicion—let us say, assumption— that the ten women mentioned in Landru's diary, and who had all disappeared after staying with him, had been murdered, there could have been other victims. One of Landru's correspondents had been a Mme Benoist, a well-to-do widow and proprietress of the 'Palmarium Concert', a music-hall. She had disappeared at Tarascon, and the police believed that it was her body which was found later in the Canal de Craponne, bearing signs of strangulation. Apart, however, from the fact that she had been a friend of Landru's (a sinister enough prospect for anyone) there was only scrappy circumstantial evidence that he might have caused her death.

Somebody fishing in a flooded sandpit at Gennevilliers in June 1919 hooked what looked like a mass of flesh with human hair attached to it. Another man said that several months before he had seen a sack there containing flesh which he assumed to be diseased meat discarded by a butcher. Other witnesses said that they had seen a motorcar pull up there one night and dump something in the pit.

And there was M. Bernard, an architect who stayed near Landru's earlier villa at Vernouillet. During the last month of Landru's residence he was aroused from his sleep every night by dull sounds which seemed to come from 'Bluebeard's' cellar. Supposing that burglars were at work, M. Bernard took his shot gun and, accompanied by his dog, went into his garden. The sounds became more distinct, and came from Landru's cellar. There was no mistaking the sound—somebody was at work in Landru's cellar, striking some hard substance with a pick. 'Why should Landru, who does almost nothing during the day, be working at night?' Bernard asked himself.

Commissioner Tanguy, one of the detectives in charge of the case, took Landru with him to search the little flat in the rue Rochechouart. It must have been a poignant return for him since here at least he had known something approaching harmony, if he could be said to have been happy anywhere. He watched impassively as the police parcelled up linen, bearing various initials, and made no comment as they scooped up a pile of ashes in the cellar.

'Why did you not throw these out, Landru?' asked Tanguy. 'You knew well enough that it was the custom of the tenants here to place their ashes in a box in the courtyard for the dust-man to clear away in the morning.'

Word had got around among the neighbours that 'Blue-beard' was in the building, and as he was led handcuffed down to the police taxi the people tried to close in round him. One red-faced woman with a basket of groceries shouted 'Death to the assassin!' and the cry was taken up by others. They probably meant it. Landru looked at them with cold disdain.

One curious discovery in Gambais (Belin found it) was a period costume from the reign of Louis XV. What on earth could Landru have wanted it for? It didn't seem the sort of merchandise he normally bought and sold. Did he like dressing up? Apparently, yes, for he once donned evening clothes and told Mme. Segret that he was off to—of all things!—a reunion of his comrades in the Sûreté. The costly and ornate trappings were those of a gentleman of fashion in the days when the Marquis de Sade lived his evil life and bequeathed to the world, by his excesses, the word 'Sadism'. An interesting thought, except that nowhere in anything Landru said or wrote is there one word of praise for pain, or power, or death. The love of tormenting others, the twisted sensuality of the typical sadist, is nowhere to be discerned.

One discovery at Gambais which interested detectives was the variety of handsaws. There was also a billhook. For what purpose, Landru was asked, did he need so many saws? What was the billhook for? He had no answer, or at least made none. Belin looked gloomily at a huge slab of stone in the cellar. It bore signs of use, yet was unstained. This hardly supported his theory—which he never abandoned—that Landru had cut up his mistresses upon it.

The stove, with its lofty metal chimney, was of particular interest. Belin was convinced that it had been used to consume the human bodies once these had been dismembered. Landru had bought this stove specially and seen it installed before he set up in residence in the Villa Tric. He had paid particular care to the chimney, so that it would ensure a powerful draught. He had used coal, instead of the local wood, and his consignments of coal had coincided with the arrival of, and shortly afterwards the disappearance of, a new lady guest.

Well and good, but what about proof?

Belin tried the experiment of filling the stove with good quality coal, lighting it, and placing a sheep's head in the fire. Within fifteen minutes it had been consumed completely, except for the blackened and calcined teeth. A leg of mutton was subjected to the same treatment and within an hour and a quarter all trace of it had disappeared.

But could the skulls of the victims have been so completely consumed? It seemed unlikely. And how could this theory apply to Landru's villa at Vernouillet, which was so near to its neighbours? There had indeed been reports of foul-smelling smoke coming from the chimneys of that villa during his tenancy there, but would a murderer burn the corpses of four people under the very noses of his next-door neighbours? Of course, there were precedents in French criminal history, though none quite so spectacular as this. A watchmaker named Pel, of Montreuil, was sentenced to death in 1885 for poisoning his wife and servant. Their bodies were never found, and the authorities concluded that he must have incinerated them in the kitchen stove. But the police were convinced that Landru had done away with at least eleven people, and probably more. Disposing of such a number would be infinitely more difficult.

In the meantime, the Landru case was already having some unusual side-effects. Apart from an unexpected boom for the bars, cafés and inns in the affected localities, Mlle Segret found herself rather more in demand in concert halls and night clubs than had formerly been the case. Previously, she had been a furrier's assistant first and a lyric artist second. The notoriety attaching to her name was an easy passport to public appearances, but although she was not so sentimental in her references to their love affair as Landru himself, she uttered no word against him, and found in work an escape from the agony of suspecting that they might never be together again.

Landru's arrest proved a windfall for the barbers, particularly in Paris. His famous beard had suddenly become a symbol of lechery combined with butchery, and solid, sober citizens once proud of their hirsute adornment went rushing off to their

barbers and hairdressers to have their beards removed. Anybody late in doing so would find little boys running after him in
the street yelling 'Bluebeard! Bluebeard!', and there was
always the possibility that some excitable or naïve character
would take the cry seriously and exact an on-the-spot revenge.

Landru was a godsend for the comic men, songsters and
artists in the café-concerts and music-halls. The futile efforts
of detectives and magistrates to get anywhere with their enquiries were the butt of endless jokes. And Landru was the
main topic of conversation. There was a rumour in circulation
which is still solemnly repeated by some—that the whole *affaire
Landru* was a put-up job, a farce engineered by the Government to divert the attention of the populace from the peace
negotiations.

While it would be an offence in Britain to reveal anything of a
suspect's past whilst the case was still *sub judice*, no such
inhibitions applied to the French press. Landru's criminal
career, and suspicions regarding his latest, albeit alleged, crimes,
were voiced openly. The *Journal* had the bright idea of getting a
reading of Landru's physiognomy from M. Pactat, a disciple
of Franz Joseph Gall (1758–1828) the anatomist, physiologist
and founder of phrenology. The basis of his teaching was that
the character and capacities of every individual could be inferred with precision from a detailed examination of the skull.

M. Pactat (assuming, with a fair degree of safety, that Landru
would not be acquitted and thus would not be able to sue him
for libel) declared that if Landru's victims had possessed even
an elementary knowledge of physiognomy they would have
been filled with suspicion right away. His verdict was:

> The osteology of the skull of *l'homme aux finances* is significant.
> Its form is clearly conoidal, which indicates sanguinary and brutal
> instincts, but of a practical nature withal, a man of strongly
> developed business talent, active and enterprising. Were it not
> for a protruberance which is very marked on the forehead, the
> head would show a perfectly balanced brain, but the forehead is
> receding, and this indicates a far from strong intelligence. It
> also shows idealism and obstinacy. The man might have died
> for an ideal, but he has no generous instincts. The eyes are re-
> markably fixed, showing a very strong will. The bushy eyebrows
> show determination and decision and indicate a domineering,
> irascible and unsociable character. The profile of the nose shows

courage. The open nostrils are excessively sensual and lascivious. So is the mouth.

M. Pactat thought that it was Landru's strange eyes that attracted his victims. Shown photographs of the missing women, he waved them away as 'defenceless women, credulous, round-visaged, therefore easy to deceive'. The logic of his reasoning would hardly convince anybody nowadays. Some of the victims were women-of-the-world and in the accepted sense far from defenceless. They did, however, all have one thing in common; they were lonely. Of Mme Buisson's rather determined features Pactat commented, 'Here is one that ought to have resisted. She has a square face. She ought to have downed Landru.'

Although the police had put seals on the villa at Gambais after their detailed search, a party of men arrived and broke in, within full sight of villagers, who assumed that the men were acting with authority. There was nothing for them to take away, as by then all the necessary evidence had been removed. Landru, told of the breaking-in, was indignant. 'What behaviour!' he said. 'Property is no longer respected.'

The authorities were still baffled at the lack of real clues. What had Landru done with the bodies? Where had all the bodies gone? Landru waited in jail as the files grew and grew. He had been assigned a brilliant, mercurial advocate to defend him, Maître de Moro-Giafferi and seemed actually to enjoy the prospect of his long questioning by the examining magistrate. He was not to wait long for this, as the Gambais police had by now produced a document that makes chilling reading:

PREFECTURE DE POLICE　　　　　　　*Paris, le 2 Mai 1919*

　　　—o—
DIRECTION
de la
Police Judiciare
　　　—o—
No. A 8.705
PARQUET

Soit transmise à Monsieur BONIN
Juge d'Instruction
la copie du rapport fourni par l'Inspec-
teur Principal NICOLE et le sous-
brigadier RIBOULET, de mon
service, au sujet de l'affaire LANDRU

　　　SOMMAIRE
Enquête à Gambais
lors du transport
de Justice

LE COMMISSIONAIRE DE
POLICE.

RAPPORT

We have the honour to report to Police Commissioner TANGUY, attached to Judicial Police Headquarters, that, during the official enquiry carried out on April 29 last at Gambais, in connection with the case against LANDRU, accused of murder, we carried out an investigation in the region which gave the following results:

Mme DAVID, née GOLTIER, Sidonie, aged 40, of no profession, stated:

'At the end of 1917, one day during the winter, which I cannot place more precisely, as I was returning from washing my linen, with a neighbour, Mme AUCHET, we passed LANDRU'S villa, at nightfall, around five o'clock. There was thick smoke coming from the kitchen chimney, with the smell of burning meat.

'The shutters of the windows giving on to the road were closed, as was usual, by the way, so that you could only know that the tenant was in the house when you saw him going off to do his shopping.

'I have also heard schoolchildren, whom I could not name, saying that they had already noticed this smell of roasting meat several times.'

Mme DAVID added that she had only seen Landru come once by car to the house.

Her son, René DAVID, aged 17, a wheelwright, said that he had several times seen the accused riding a lady's bicycle around the countryside...

Mme Auchet had also seen Landru riding on a bicycle....

The report goes on to state that Mme Auchet confirmed Mme David's statement, and adds that Mme David had also said, 'He must be burning horsemeat.' The French word used in the report is '*carne*', which can mean rotten meat, but it is also used to describe a 'bad-tempered bitch' or 'good-for-nothing slut', though it is doubtful if this was an intentional play on words.

Mlle Cecile Bournerias, 28, a schoolteacher at Gambais, declared:

I twice had the occasion to travel in the same compartment as LANDRU, when he came to Gambais.

The first time was when he was taking over the villa; he was accompanied by a woman whom I quite definitely recognise in the photograph of Mme COLLOMB.

The second time another woman, who is none other than Mme PASCAL, whose photograph you have shown me, was travelling with him. That was about a year ago.

The Ladykiller

I remember that Mme PASCAL had a basket with her. She seemed to be unwell, and LANDRU took most affectionate care of her; he arranged the rug she had round her, and asked her frequently whether she was cold.

The report gives details of an interview with the village shoemaker, M. Pierre Vallet, 51, who was responsible for keeping an eye on, and maintaining, the villa before it had been let to Landru, and with whom Landru first entered into discussion before renting it. When 'consulted' by the police, he said:

The villa belonged to M. TRIC, and had been unoccupied since 1911, when the previous tenant, M. RAVETON, had left to live at Meudon [a Paris suburb].

M. TRIC, who intended to sell his property, had put up a notice to this effect.

On January 13 or 15, 1916, LANDRU, whom I had never met before, came to ask me if he could rent the villa. I gave him M. TRIC's address . . . and the letting was fixed up several days later.

After that, at first, LANDRU lived continuously in the house, but for how long exactly I don't quite know, in the company of a woman; then he went away, and only came to Gambais from time to time at irregular intervals, staying only for two or three days. Often he was accompanied by different women.

Sometimes he would come to see me, but our conversations were about the most ordinary matters.

On January 13 or 15 last, he came to see me at nightfall.

I heard that he had come about a week before his arrest, in a motor-car.

When LANDRU came to live in the villa, he bought a cooking-stove at M. GOHIER's, at Houdan. He installed it himself—the same one that is there now—and, at the same time, he had the chimney-stack repaired. I have heard it said that LANDRU brought his own coal, but I know nothing precise about this.

The piles of dry leaves which were under the [open] shed and more or less all over the garden were not there when he took possession of the villa. As for the pile of cinders which is in the shed, that was not there either, I think, but I'm not sure.

The mason who repaired the chimney, Clovis Mauguin, 35, said that when he visited the villa, Landru never left him for a minute all the time he was doing the repairs. It had struck him as curious that he would lock every door on leaving a room, and had to unlock every room they visited together. He also said that he had seen him in a car the last time he came to

Gambais and that, two years earlier, he had seen, while some way away, an open four-seater in front of the house.

The plumber, Paul Schmit, 18, who helped M. Mauguin with the repairs, said that he had to do other repairs later. He stated:

> During the month of June 1917, my father, the zinc-merchant, received a letter from M. TRIC, asking him to get in touch with the tenant of the villa for the repair of a gutter.
>
> We knew, as everyone did around, that LANDRU was not there most of the time and that even when he was there very often we did not know, as he never opened the shutters; so we decided to wait until he got in touch with us.
>
> A few days later, LANDRU came to ask my father whether he had heard from M. TRIC about the repair in question.
>
> He replied in the affirmative, and the tenant of the villa asked us to come with him immediately to see what work had to be done.
>
> I went there a few moments later on my bicycle.
>
> LANDRU himself came to open the door of the [high iron] fence which separated the garden from the road. He insisted I bring the bicycle into the garden, and locked the door again behind him.
>
> We went together to the back of the house; he led me into the kitchen, where he showed me marks where water had run along the wall, and then into the room next door on the ground floor, where we found the same thing; finally, we went outside to see where the gutter was faulty. As we left each of the rooms I have mentioned, Landru locked the doors with keys which he put into his pocket.
>
> I thought this was very odd, and even remarked on it to my father when I got back.
>
> Following M. LANDRU's orders, a few days later, to be precise, June 22, according to our books, I went to M. VALLET's [the shoemaker] to get the key for the fence door which he had left for this purpose, and I carried out the repair.
>
> I did not have to go into the house for this, and I noticed nothing of interest.

The police then interrogated the local shopkeepers, so as to find out how long and how often Landru was at Gambais, and also to find out what he bought. The baker, M. Auchet—no doubt the husband of the first witness's friend, Mme Auchet—said that he had served Landru up to about eighteen months before, when, for some unknown reason, Landru ceased to buy his bread there. He would come three or four days a week at around seven in the morning, and buy one kilo of bread. M. Auchet had offered to deliver it for him, but Landru had refused the offer. The second baker, to whom Landru went after ceasing to buy from Auchet, was Mme Debras, who said he only came very irregularly. Sometimes she would not see him for a week or a fortnight, then he would come back again and stay for from two to six days, during which he would buy every day either a pound or a kilo of bread. She said she had often seen him on a bicycle, but never in a car. She remembered 'very well' Mme Buisson.

Landru had also been a customer at the pork-butcher's, Mme Joséphine Auchet, 60, and used to buy pâté from her at the beginning, but later stopped coming to her shop. He had also been a customer, though not a frequent one, of M. Gustave Andrieu, butcher. M. Andrieu said that Landru sometimes went for a whole month without coming to him, and then he would come two or three days running, invariably buying a fillet steak.

The grocer, Mme Quignon, said Landru only came to the villa for a day or two at a time, except 'last' January [i.e. January 1919], when he stayed for about a week. Each time he would come and buy wine, sugar, chocolate, coffee and potatoes. She added that he was always 'exquisitely polite' [*d'une correction parfaite*] to her, and that he either came alone or with one of his 'successive companions', and she reckoned having seen about seven of these, indicating Mme Collomb, Mme Buisson, Mlle Segret, and another older woman whom she presumed to be her mother.

The report suggested that a photograph of Mme Benoît should be showed to Mme Quignon—At this point in the investigations, Landru was suspected of having murdered, in addition to the eleven named victims, a Mme Benoît, a friend who disappeared at Tarascon, and whose body was found floating in the Canal de Craponne bearing signs of strangulation.

Other people had testified that they had seen Landru going around in workman's overalls. 'As he arrived in Gambais in town clothes,' the report states, 'it may be supposed that these clothes were kept in the villa.'

The report continues: 'The presence of a certain quantity of coal having been noticed inside the villa, enquiries were made as to where it had come from. There is no coal merchant in

Gambais, where all the inhabitants burn only wood, which is abundant in the region.'

It was learned from M. Bournerias, Secretary to the Town Hall, that Landru brought this coal from Paris; that he had recenty brought 200 kilos (about one fifth of a ton) coming to Gambais, and that this load had been transported from the station at Houdan to Gambais by the local transport merchant. The report suggested that the police should find out how much coal this man had delivered altogether to Landru's villa.

'Regarding the bad smells from the villa chimney,' it concludes, 'it would seem useful to point out that, in the opinion of M. Andrieu, the aforementioned butcher, it was not surprising that these had not been noticed by many people, because the south-west wind which generally blows in the area would take the smell away from the village across the fields.'

The report which M. Bonin examined was enough to raise profound suspicions—it contained enough circumstantial evidence to justify the murder charges; and in any event Landru could now be charged with, and sentenced for, the offences committed in 1914 prior to his wartime 'career'.

Yet the absence of a body was a great handicap to the investigators. Not even a skull could be found. No identifiable part of any particular body could be certified. The village chit-chat, and dated gossip about Landru's comings and goings, were not enough.

The most damnatory evidence was Landru's *carnet*, but where, oh where, were the bodies? The authorities did not really believe that he had cremated all eleven bodies in a stove. The facilities for murdering the first four victims at Vernouillet were surely inadequate; could he have dismembered and burned the bodies under the noses of his near neighbours? As for the others, the seven who disappeared from Gambais, the *milieu* was infinitely more in his favour, if the hypothesis of murder were accepted. There was that cemetery at the bottom of the garden. Might he have opened a grave at the dead of night and deposited another tenant? Did some vault there contain more corpses than were originally buried there? And who could search every part of the vast forest of Rambouillet? Was one to dig up every part of its twenty-five-mile expanse?

One of the most baffling problems was how Landru could

E

possibly have dismembered seven corpses in the Villa Tric without making the most terrible and gruesome mess. Apart from the calcined remains, which were not very extensive, there was no evidence of such wholesale slaughter.

A heavy task lay ahead for M. Bonin, the examining magistrate, whose eventual report would provide the basis for Landru's trial. In all interviews with Landru, he had kept his nerve, revealed nothing, shown a memory better than those of his questioners, so that mere repetition of a question at irregular and unpredictable intervals would not floor him. Whenever it suited him, he lapsed into silence.

It was commonly accepted at the time that Clemenceau, the 'Tiger', who had become wartime leader at the age of seventy-six and had before then clamoured continually, like Churchill, about the German menace, had issued a directive to 'play up' the Landru case—some say in order that people might realise that law and order ruled again, others that he wanted to divert public attention from the peace negotiations, from the Treaty of Versailles. Its preparation involved immense work and delicate diplomacy. France, having fought her enemies, now found herself at loggerheads with her friends on many vital post-war issues, and the pattern of her future destiny was being drawn by measures whose future implications few ordinary people could foresee. Clemenceau had to cope with President Wilson and Mr Lloyd George. Clemenceau's political enemies, and a considerable portion of the French public too, felt that the old war leader was keeping too many secrets to himself and keeping out of the negotiations any who did not agree with him.

The French system of justice differs in many respects from that in Britain and in many other countries. In Landru's case the system had its advantages and disadvantages. Much of his insolence under questioning would not have been tolerated in Britain, still less in Central Europe, or Latin America, or the U.S.A. Landru was questioned rigorously, but not brutally. For one thing, the eyes of the world were now upon him. There were hordes of reporters and photographers present at every appearance before the magistrate. If he had appeared with black eyes, or contusion, or shock, or scratches and abrasions, or bruises, no amount of talk by the authorities about him trying to escape, or getting violent with his captors, would have been believed.

When a prisoner is to face a serious charge and is awaiting trial, he is placed in the hands of a *juge d'instruction* whom, having no equivalent in Britain, we describe as an 'examining magistrate'. The analogy is unfair as no magistrate possesses comparable powers in Britain. The *juge d'instruction* may examine the prisoner at length, and in whatever detail and for whatever time he pleases. He can do this in private, examining documents, receiving reports from police and detectives and basing his questions to the prisoner on any of the allegations or facts such reports contain. He may even produce witnesses to confront the prisoner with accusations and statements.

By the time the prisoner is sent for trial, most of the basic information the court requires is already assembled. But even the composition of the court itself, when the trial takes place, has no exact counterpart in British legal procedure. There is a bench of several judges, with a presiding judge. There are no individual directions to the jury, as occurs in British trials ('You may think that the defendant is a scoundrel ... it may be your view that he is certainly a murderer,' etc., etc.) There is the usual verbal, gladiatorial contest between defending and prosecuting counsel. So far as the pre-trial interrogations are concerned, a prisoner is not bound to make a reply. Nor can he prevent any inferences being drawn from the fact that he chooses to remain silent on particular issues.

Once Boswell commented to Dr Johnson that he did not believe that the confessions of a man who was to be hanged publicly, and which were being sold as a broadsheet at his execution, were genuine. Dr Johnson replied that he saw no reason why the prisoner should not have written them. Did not the prospect of imminent execution sharpen his wits wonderfully?

Landru was on a capital charge, as his interrogators constantly reminded him. He seems to have been a naturally crafty man—as well as a very foolish man, in that he kept, unnecessarily, so much documentary evidence of his frauds—but there is no doubt that the peril of his situation sharpened his already sharp wits. Never before, in the annals of French criminal law, had the authorities had to deal with a criminal so adroit, so secretive, so tireless and so audacious. A long tussle stretched ahead for all of them, which includes, of course, Landru himself.

9

Preparing the Case

WHILE HUNDREDS of police and detectives tried to piece together the complicated story of Landru's activities, M. Bonin, the examining magistrate, began one of the longest and most exhaustive examinations in French criminal history. It entailed following the often tenuous trail of the 283 women who had been in touch with Landru, and the 169 women selected from that number to be the recipient of Landru's amorous and commercial attentions. Many of these women, too, had disappeared, but is it not true that if one were to take at random a hundred names from any directory, and endeavour to trace them, the trail would be lost in many cases?

There was the endless list of witnesses to be seen, too, including those involved in Landru's frauds, the concierges of the innumerable addresses he had used, the numerous furniture stores which he rented from time to time.

The police had hoped that Landru, a man with a long record of petty crime, would see the hopelessness of attempting any innocent explanation of the sinister disappearances. Here they grossly underrated their man. Cajolery, bullying, vicarious pressure through the questioning of his wife and children and of Mlle Segret, the production of witnesses or of victims of his frauds, all failed to induce him to make the slightest damaging admission. As his questioning lasted from April 13, 1919 to November 1921, it is almost incredible that a man with so much on his conscience could have kept his nerve through it all.

Furthermore, aided by Maître de Moro-Giafferi, a brilliant and histrionic lawyer, he lost no chance of frustrating or obstructing either the examining magistrate or the authorities in general. Any illusion that they had in their hands a frightened little crook who would try to purchase leniency by making a full confession was soon dispelled. It was as though, by what he said and did, Landru was saying, in effect: 'You'll try and get me, but I'll make it as hard for you as I can.' This he certainly did. The whole thing became a game of legal chess in which he would observe no rules.

Already M. Bonin was plagued by a superabundance of documents. As the police enquiries continued these increased. Many of them were repetitive, or added only a sentence or small fact to previous references. The sheer deadweight of the paperwork would have discouraged the most experienced bureaucrat. Landru's obduracy made it worse. The whole thing would have been simpler if there were one real clue, something pointing unquestioningly to *one* provable murder. There were a few scraps of bone, alleged to be human, but the forensic basis of this assumption was dubious. None of the scraps was larger than a bean, and these so badly charred or calcined that real proof was impossible.

Bonin, then, faced a formidable task, but at least in this contest he did not stand to lose his head.

Landru was brought from the Santé prison by police car to M. Bonin's office in the Palais de Justice, a solid, heavy room whose solemnity was only partly mitigated by a few, vaguely erotic, Rodin-style statuettes (the work of a man who once made casts for Rodin).

'M. Landru,' Bonin began, with punctilious courtesy, 'my first question, in this first interrogation of you, arises from the preliminary investigations of the police and detectives. You know the charges against you. You knew Mmes Cuchet, Buisson, and Anne Collomb, and Mlles Marchadier and Annette Pascal, Mme Jaume, Mme Guillin, Mme Heon and Andrée Babelay. They all disappeared after telling their friends they were going away with you.'

Landru stroked his beard gravely as Bonin finished the catalogue of names. 'It is true,' he said, 'that I knew the ladies in question, but I am *un homme galant* and cannot allow you to ask me questions concerning them. If they have disappeared it is nothing to do with me. It is not for me to say what has become of them. It is for you to make the necessary search. I am innocent, I swear. When you can produce proof of what you claim, I will discuss it.'

M. Bonin sighed. Then, suddenly, he sprang a surprise on Landru, who could have expected, in the normal course of things, that Bonin would attempt to deal with the disappearances *seriatim.*

'Let us take the case of Mlle Marchadier. At the beginning of January 1918, you were without funds. You made Mlle Marchadier's acquaintance and in the middle of January you took her and her two dogs to Gambais. You spent two days there. Witnesses have deposed that they saw strange gleams of light coming from the kitchen of the Villa Tric. Then you left for Paris—alone. Mlle Marchadier had disappeared. You went to her lodgings in the rue St Jacques and removed her furniture and sold it. Then you paid your most pressing debts. What has happened to Mlle Marchadier? What has happened to those other women?'

'I will not reply.'

'Very well. Let us take one instance. Here in front of me are letters addressed to you by Marchadier. You saw her often. The letters speak of journeys you made with her. These journeys suddenly ceased. Why?'

Landru maintained his air of utter indifference.

'I repeat, Monsieur le Juge, I will not reply to questions which are of a private nature.'

'What became of Mlle Marchadier?'

'I have nothing to say.'

'Let me now acquaint you with the first results of the expert findings to which the accusation attaches extreme importance. During the search made at Gambais and subsequent investigations, heaps of ashes have been found under an outhouse and in the grate of the kitchen stove. A great number of bone fragments and teeth, partially calcined, were discovered. Dr Paul, and Professors Anthony and Sauvez, to whom they have been submitted for examination, have confirmed that they are human remains. Perhaps some of them are the remains of Mlle Marchadier? You killed her, didn't you, on January 13, and burnt her body on the 18th? Well?'

'You accuse me of crimes. Prove them.'

'Today, Landru, we are dealing with a lady who has disappeared, and whose name must be familiar to you—Mme Benoît.'

'I know nothing about her.'

'She was proprietress of a variety hall—the "Palmerium

Concert" in the rue Montmartre. You were seen with her in Paris. You were with her in Tarascon when she disappeared....'

'I have never heard of her.'

'Well now, we have a witness who saw you frequently with her.'

M. Dilham, a variety singer often engaged by the vanished Mme Benoît, came into the magistrate's room. His real name, he told the magistrate, was Durand. He had only seen Mme Benoît and 'M. Dubois' for about eight minutes in Marseilles, and afterwards at Tarascon and Avignon.

'In the latter town,' he said, 'we talked together for about an hour. Dubois was as thin as Landru, but his beard was less bushy and more peaked. Mme Benoît called him Désiré [Landru's forename].'

Bonin turned to Landru and asked him if he had been to the South of France in May 1918. 'I must admit,' he said, 'that your notebook makes no mention of such a journey.'

On this occasion Landru found his tongue.

'I have never been to the South of France, and never mixed with theatrical or café concert artists. I have never seen the witness before. I have always protested my innocence.'

Dilham, hearing Landru speak, declared that his voice was different from that of the 'M. Dubois' whom he had met, and who knew the missing Mme Benoît. Bonin looked crestfallen. If the police suspicion that the body found floating in the Canal de Craponne was that of Mme Benoît, who had disappeared whilst at Tarascon, an identification of Landru as the man who had been with her in three different towns, including the town from which she disappeared, would have been crucial. Irritably, Bonin dismissed Dilham.

Alone again with Landru, he tried hard to make him confess.

'You look as if a secret weighed heavily on your conscience,' he said, 'confide in me. What is it?'

Landru sighed. 'M. le Juge,' he said, gravely, 'I am heartbroken to think that, thanks to all this scandal, my wife knows that I have been unfaithful to her.' Once again, he fell into silence.

The case of Mme Benoît was still pursued, however. On another occasion Landru was confronted with M. Soyer, the manager of Mme Benoît's show in Montmartre, who declared that he had seen Landru on two occasions with Mme Benoît.

While Soyer was speaking, Landru fixed him with a piercing, unwavering look, and the moment his statement ended spoke firmly and quietly to M. Bonin:

'I must congratulate this gentleman. He has an astonishing memory. He identifies me after a lapse of time. Hundreds of people pass into his concert hall every evening. Among the frequenters of the establishment, doubtless there were some who paid homage to Madame Benoît. I would be the last man to disapprove of that, for I am among those who know how to render the homage that is due to a woman, but I repeat that I do not know Madame Benoît.

'I have never attended a concert in the rue Montmartre. Since this gentleman has such a good memory, let him give dates. I also have a good memory, and I shall be able to say where I was and what I did on the dates he gives.'

Landru turned to Bonin, his eyes glowing with triumph. He received a cold look in return.

'I will make note of your declaration when the time comes to question *you*.'

'As you wish,' said Landru, quietly, 'but I must ask you to finish with this business. You have all my papers. I am a man of order, and you yourself have said so. Now tell me, have you found the name of Madame Benoît in them? No! Then why speak to me of her disappearance? I know nothing about it.'

As Landru left, he turned once more to Monsieur Bonin.

'I shall be obliged,' he said, in his most dignified manner, 'if you will refrain in future from confrontations of this kind.'

It will be gathered that Landru was not easily intimidated. Indeed, at this time (the summer of 1919) he wrote to M. Bonin asking for a holiday! 'The prison régime,' he wrote on a note of decently restrained indignation, 'is contrary to my temperament. I have a great need of fresh air, and I ask that you will liberate me provisionally. I shall go to my house at Gambais, if possible, and I give my word of honour to remain at your disposition, for I am ready to justify myself regarding the flimsy accusations brought against me.'

Landru had been looking ill at this time, but his request for parole was never seriously considered. To have done so would have brought upon authority the contempt and abuse of the nation.

There was no respite for him. Witness after witness was produced. In every case he kept his head, either scoring off the magistrate or the witness, or else loftily ignoring them and their questions. At no point did he seem nervous or ruffled. Indeed, when confronted with the relatives of Mme Cuchet, his first victim at Vernouillet, he seemed actually sprightly, and had taken considerable trouble with the grooming and cutting of his beard, and the pressing of his clothes.

Mme Cuchet's concierge was heard. 'She told me that she was going to marry an engineer called Diard, but later told me that he had deceived her, and that his real name was Landru. Even so, in January 1915, she removed her furniture and left with Landru and her son, begging me not to give her address to anyone. Once Landru came with two little fair-haired girls. He said they were his daughters.'

Landru stared at the concierge with incredulity.

'They could not possibly have been my daughters, who are much older—and I do not remember ever going to your house with two little girls.'

There was a dramatic moment, however, when Mme Cuchet's relatives appeared. It was they who had discovered Landru's deception and real identity, and warned her that he was an imposter. Probably her request to the concierge where she lived, not to mention where she was going, had been made on Landru's prompting, so that relatives and enquirers might be kept in ignorance.

Landru's disdain caused an uproar when Mme Cuchet's relatives were giving evidence. They claimed that Mme Cuchet possessed furniture, jewels and securities worth 30,000 francs (then worth about £1,200). They accused Landru of making use of papers belonging to their family, and when Landru, questioned about this, said that he would account for them only to their rightful owners, and furthermore he did not know the witnesses, one of them sprang at Landru, and the pair were separated only with difficulty.

'Where is Mme Cuchet now?' asked M. Bonin.

'Mme Cuchet's hiding-place is a secret known only to her and to me,' he replied. 'I am a man of honour, and though I understand the accusation which has been brought against me, I will not reveal it. I have given my word.'

For weeks Bonin reverted to the subject of Mme Cuchet, but

Landru would never let himself be drawn. He only admitted to negotiating several securities of Mme Cuchet.

He was asked why he gave the name of Cuchet at Vernouillet when proceedings were taken against him for travelling without a railway ticket.

'Why, that is what everyone does when proceedings are taken against him! I gave the name of Cuchet just as I would give yours tomorrow. There is nothing in it.'

Maurice Landru was called for questioning. He admitted to having helped his father move furniture from the garage at Neuilly, where some of Madame Cuchet's effects had been stored. Landru was quick to defend his son against any suspicion:

'When I give an order to my children,' he said, interrupting his son's evidence and addressing M. Bonin directly, 'they execute it. That's how I bring up *my* children. I don't know how you bring up yours.'

Bonin enquired into a sinister aspect of the whole Cuchet affair—how, one by one, she was estranged from all who knew her. Why had she severed relations with relatives and friends?

'Madame Cuchet was heartbroken by the hypocrisy of the world, like myself.'

'You were to have married her?'

'Damnation! Does a man have to marry every woman he flirts with?'

'But witnesses have sworn that you promised to marry her.'

'Does a judge believe witnesses?'

'But you allege that Mme Cuchet went to England—how is it that you retained documents belonging to her, which would be indispensable to a woman travelling to another country?'

'It was much less difficult than you imagine to travel at that moment, but [*in an intense voice*] it is a secret which I cannot, and will not, lay bare.'

Bonin looked intently at Landru, who on that day was suffering from a raging toothache:

'This mystery, Landru, which you alone pretend to know, and which you coddle in yourself—the law will relieve you of it sooner or later.'

'I would rather it relieved me now, of my abscess and toothache,' was the reply.

The enquiry, still in its early stages, had dragged on into late August 1919, and Landru's continuous obstruction held things up at every point. There were still no corpses—only a mounting list of circumstantial evidence. While the questioning continued, day after day, week after week, strange things were constantly happening outside. In the flooded gravel pit where fishermen had found their lines embedded in decomposing flesh, a wreath of everlasting flowers was found, with the inscription 'To my betrothed'. Landru, of course, denied all knowledge of this strange discovery. 'Am I to be custodian of every corpse in France?' he asked irritably.

A sad exhibition of relics found in Landru's home and garages was put on show in Paris, and relatives and friends were called up to identify them. Simple objects like combs, thimbles and scissors were enough to reduce some visitors to tears, and many were identified as having belonged to one or other of the missing women.

One very odd fact emerged when furniture was taken from Landru's garages at Clinchy and Neuilly to the Law Courts. There were various pieces of furniture identified as having belonged to one or other of Landru's vanished 'fiancées', including an oil painting of the virgin and child, with the Madonna's eyes pierced by revolver shots. Landru was asked if he had used the painting for target practice.

'I know nothing about it' was all he would say.

The question of Landru's mental balance was investigated, with rather interesting results. No less than two prison doctors, over a period of three years, had expressed serious doubts as to Landru's sanity. The first report, dated April 30, 1904, and signed by Dr Ullon, read:

> Landru, who seems to be suffering from personal and hereditary taints, was, during two months of his imprisonment at La Santé Prison, in a condition bordering on mental prostration, and is still in a state of depression, sadness and weakness which is likely to decrease his sense of responsibility.

While a second report, dated May 15, 1906 and signed by Dr Dubuisson, stated:

> Landru is mentally unbalanced, and has grave personal and hereditary taints from the pathological point of view. He has been for some years, as the result of mental overstrain and prolonged

mental sufferings, in a state which, without being madness, is no longer a normal state.

From his prison cell, Landru took up the subject of his sanity with M. Bonin:

I am mad and I do not hide it. Why this lack of confidence towards me? Whether I am mad or not, I am accused of terrible crimes, of having murdered women—I, whose whole life attests the delicate respect I have always professed for woman, an exquisite being of perfect grace and sensibility.

The last sentence was, perhaps, too kind a description of his unlucky fiancées. He concluded his letter by asking for an examination, and M. Bonin thereupon instructed three doctors to examine him and report upon his mental condition.

Bonin was a gentleman of courtesy, but he was also an official. Landru had forgotten that there is one thing officialdom never forgives—being ridiculed. Perhaps he instinctively played for time, on whatever pretext. Perhaps he was over-confident that the absence of a body would preclude his sentence for murder. Or was he really mad—a Jekyll-and-Hyde personality? While doctors examined Landru over a period, he continued to stall on important questions.

Convinced that Landru's wife and sons were involved in the frauds, Bonin ordered the arrest of Mme Landru and Maurice on December 17, 1919. What had caught Bonin's attention was one entry in Landru's *carnet* which said 'Visit No. 1'. 'No. 1' was a euphemism for Mme Landru. His children, too, were numbered. The movements of Mme Landru as revealed in his notes fitted in with visits to bankers and a money-changer for the transfer of a bond belonging to Mme Buisson. The papers were signed 'Veuve (widow) Buisson, *née* Lavie.' The handwriting on the documents was that of Mme Landru, while others were signed 'Fremyet'. Mme Landru must therefore have helped her husband obtain his victim's money, Bonin reasoned. Similar operations were traced in the obtaining of 500 francs which had stood to the credit of Mme Collomb, as well as that of another 'fiancée'.

There was the fact, too, that furniture, jewellery and other property of the missing women was found in Mme Landru's possession, and the examining magistrate was not satisfied with her explanation of how she came to be entrusted with them.

Maurice, the eldest son, came naturally under suspicion because Landru had commissioned him to sell some of Mme Guillin's jewellery. His explanation of how his father came to do it was most improbable. It was also noted by the police that Maurice had been sent by his father to tell friends of Mme Collomb that he had dined at the same *table d'hôte* with her at Aix, and that she appeared to be in first-class health and spirits. He had also driven his father to Gambais with Mlle Segret.

Under interrogation, Mme Landru confessed to having impersonated two of Landru's missing mistresses. She could not deny that the entry in Landru's notebook, 'Bus No. 1 30 centimes, 15 September '17', related to Landru's visit to a banker's office in the Boulevard Voltaire, and that on the following day she had accompanied him to the money-changers, where she impersonated Mme Buisson and signed the missing woman's name in order to get possession of a three per cent *rente*, and that she signed a receipt for 2,500 francs in Mme Buisson's maiden name, 'Lavie'. When she was identified by two bank employees she burst into tears. 'I have suffered. I have brought up my children, and have always done my duty. If I have done wrong, it was done unwittingly. I am a martyr, not a criminal. My misfortune has been to love my husband too well.'

After questioning the bank employees away from the hearing of Mme Landru, Bonin questioned her again, and she confessed in these terms:

'I have thought about it. It is true that, at a period I cannot determine exactly, he asked me to do him a service, and sign for a woman who was in hospital. But I swear that my husband did not receive any money in my presence.'

Bonin motioned to an assistant. 'Bring the prisoner in.'

Landru entered, looked briefly at his wife and son, and addressed the examining magistrate with cold hauteur.

'I have drawn up a note which is the expression of my thoughts, and I stand by it without adding or subtracting one iota.'

He took a piece of paper from his pocket and read, calmly, and clearly:

'I received from Madame Buisson, for use for a purpose which I will not explain here, various deeds and securities as my property. When I desired to cash the money represented by the nominal stock, Mme Buisson's signature was necessary. She was away in the country, so I asked my wife to sign for her. If it is a punishable offence, I alone am responsible. My wife merely acted under my orders. She was an unconscious instrument. So was my son.'

Landru then handed the piece of paper to Bonin, who began to ask questions. Landru interrupted him curtly. 'I have nothing more to say. I have signed my note. That is all.' Landru refused to sign the clerk's minutes as a correct record, or say anything more.

Landru had protected his wife and son, accepting any blame that might be involved in the transactions complained of, yet admitting no culpable motive or action himself. The authorities found it difficult not to believe Mme Landru's assertion that she was dominated by her husband. His imperviousness to questioning, his utter callous indifference in face of the tragic disappearance of all the eleven victims in question, the fascination he appeared to be able to assert with women of every kind, all pointed to the basic innocence of his wife and son. 'He is a monster!' Mme Landru stormed, through her tears. 'He would have allowed me to be sentenced to death!'

Mme Landru seemed not merely frightened by the predicament in which she found herself. She appeared to be genuinely astonished at the ramifications of Landru's private life. We have no reason to doubt that she loved him, as she had remained loyal to him through the long, penurious, lonely years. Now, beset by doubts as to the fate of the missing women, the thought of being his wife was suddenly intolerable. In mid-November 1919, she instituted proceedings for divorce. By April 1920, when M. Bonin supposed—fondly—that his examination of Landru was nearing the end, Mme Landru and her son Maurice were released. The Civil Tribunal granted Mme Landru a divorce from her husband, who allowed the case to go by default, giving her the custody of the children of their marriage.

If Landru felt any emotion at all these things, he did not show it. He discussed nothing with the warders in prison. He made no comment on his wife's action in divorcing him. Sometimes he would be deep in thought, but even if jolted out of a brown study he was ever on his guard.

'You seem preoccupied, Landru,' Bonin had said, at the end

of a fruitless and tedious investigation. Landru was silent, even pensive. ('It may have been this wistful streak in his nature that appealed to the feminine mind,' Inspector Belin, who arrested Landru, once declared.)

'True, true sir, I am,' said Landru, sighing deeply, 'and who could help being so? Alas! My thoughts are engrossed by the electoral situation in this unhappy country.'

Landru was sobered considerably by the report of the doctors on his mental state (a copy of the report was supplied to him). It disposed effectually of any hope he might have entertained of pleading insanity. The committee of three doctors decided that he was entirely responsible for his actions.

The evidence of his many frauds was irrefutable. The forensic evidence was far more involved. In April 1920 one of the experts became ill and the research was held up. By July the report was available at last, a lengthy document of 300 pages setting forth in the most minute detail the scraps and oddments on which the real evidence of murder rested. The report was signed by Dr Paul, a medical jurist; M. Sauvez, whose illness had held up the enquiry and who was Professor of the Dental College; M. Kling, Director of the Police Laboratory; M. Beyle, Director of the Legal Identity Department; and M. Anthony, Director of the School of Anthropology. In effect, it concluded that the scraps of bones found in Landru's villa were from three separate corpses of human beings. The fragments were too small and too badly burnt to dogmatise as to sex.

A report was handed to Landru, who made no comment. But in his prison cell he studied it with the detailed detachment of a lawyer. His letter to Bonin, from La Santé Prison, dated August 14, 1920, is too long to quote in full, but bears all the imprint of an acute and alert mind. He protested at the searches made during his absence, pointed out that no bones had been identified as female bones, and that nothing incriminating whatsoever had been discovered at Vernouillet, where he was accused of having committed four murders. As to Gambais, 'three-quarters of the bones had, at any rate, an animal origin. The remainder, not even one kilogramme in weight, even though asserted by the experts to be of human origin, for the most part cannot be really identified, and in no case is it certain that they are the bones of women. Other investigations are equally weak. The blood found in the cellar has not been proved to be human blood, nor has any sign of human blood been found on the linen, furniture or tools. The sum total of these reports is sufficiently conclusive (naturally in his defence) for me to consider it unnecessary to protest against the accusations of theft, murder and so on, which I have constantly denied.'

In the course of his endless sessions with M. Bonin, a strange relationship had been established between the two. The judge (or examining magistrate, as his role is sometimes translated) inwardly loathed the man whom he was convinced was a mass murderer, yet the prisoner's spirit under constant questioning and imprisonment was rather extraordinary, and his concern to establish the innocence of his wife and son and of his mistress, Mlle Segret, won him secret admiration.

Landru, for his part, would alternate between badinage, ridicule and concern for his hard-worked questioner. His expressed concern may have been irony, but if so he was so good an actor that it sounded genuine.

As the enquiry drew to a close, M. Bonin had been hard-worked on a sensational murder case of another kind. One morning the chauffeur of a wealthy Paris merchant named Bessarabo informed the police that his employer, after depositing 200,000 francs in a bank three days before, had failed to turn up at a rendezvous they had made for the next day, a Saturday, and had not been seen since. He added that Mme Bessarabo had surprised him by saying that her husband had gone away until Monday—which was not in line with what his employer had told him—and he became really suspicious when refusing his services, which would have been the usual and obvious thing to do, Mme Bessarabo and her daughter left in a taxi for the station taking with them a large and heavy trunk. Knowing that husband and wife led a cat-and-dog life, he became alarmed and informed the police.

Mme Bessarabo told the police that her husband had been obliged to go away on business and that she had accompanied him on Friday afternoon to the Gare du Nord. Later in the day, she said, she had, at his request, taken a large trunk containing certain compromising papers and despatched them to Nancy from the Gare de l'Est. Telegrams were sent by the police to Nancy, where a trunk was found lying unclaimed at the station. Inside the trunk was the strangled body of Bessarabo.

Landru had, of course, read of the case. Mme Bessarabo had been charged with murder, and the enquiries were a heavy burden on Bonin, worn down even more than Landru by the endless enquiries into the disappearances of Landru's many mistresses.

'Don't you think you can manage to have a holiday this year?' Landru asked, in a kindly voice. The unfortunate Bonin, weary from his exertions to get Landru to the guillotine, sighed. 'We all have our cares, I think, Landru,' he answered.

Weary or not, at every session Bonin read out to Landru every report which was to form part of the mounting indictment. However obstructive Landru might be, however defiant or taciturn, the letter of the law was kept and every statement made available to him. The talk, longer than a very long novel, went on and on, every statement being read at length while Landru stood or sat, impassive and bored. The *Interrogatoire Définitif* bears witness to Bonin's infinite patience and Landru's indifference—or seeming indifference.

10

Hiatus

IN LA SANTE Landru was the star prisoner, a favourite with the Governor for his unshakeable courtesy and extraordinary air of keeping a certain distance from those with whom he must perforce mix, but could never accept as equals. Maître Navières du Treuil, assistant to the chief defence counsel, came frequently to see him. Usually, all contact with Landru whilst in prison was through du Treuil. When he had first called on Landru, the latter had been cold and uncooperative, until du Treuil said firmly: 'Landru, I have fought at the Front. I am here to help you, but I am not easily bullied.'

Landru took the point without further ado. Du Treuil was a valuable contact with the outside world, bringing the newspapers with him, showing Landru the numerous press references to himself and his impending trial. The prisoner would ask about his family, and clicked his tongue with disapproval when told that sometimes trespassers invaded the privacy of his villa at Gambais. He received an enormous 'fan mail', including many love letters from total strangers, offering all they might be permitted to give him, however uninviting the place of assignation might be.

On December 8, 1920, the preliminary court committed Landru for trial before the Assizes of the Seine. Playing for time, Landru appealed to the Cour de Cassation (equivalent of the Supreme Court of Appeal) on the grounds that certain necessary procedures had not been observed in the course of his examination.

To the disgust of M. Bonin and all who had worked so hard on the case, this appeal was upheld. Some of the forensic witnesses had failed to take the oath as required by law, and their evidence was, for the time being, inadmissible. The trial was to have begun on March 1, but the 7,000 documents were not in Landru's hands until February 15, and he complained that this was insufficient time in which to examine them. M. Lescouve, the Public Prosecutor, accepted the justice of this protest. To have kept to the original date would have pre-supposed Landru's ability to absorb the content of 500 documents a day!

The affair was remitted to the authorities at Rouen to decide if there was a case against Landru. On May 20 they decided that there was, and committed him for trial.

When Landru heard that he would leave soon for the prison at Versailles, he went on a hunger-strike. He threw himself on his bed, crying in his rage, 'Why do they want me to leave here, where I have been so happy and nicely cared for?'

'Your case,' Navières du Treuil explained to him, 'is to be heard in the court of the Palais de Justice at Versailles, and for convenience you will be lodged in the adjacent Saint Pierre prison. But there's been a further postponement of the trial itself, and you probably won't be moved for a month or so.'

For technical reasons there had been a further postponement of the trial, and Landru had ample opportunity, assisted by a new pair of spectacles made for him at the expense of the authorities, to study the mountain of documents on which his fate depended. In the meantime, he read with interest of the sale of his effects, held in May. A rusty old bicycle with green mould on the saddle—he had used it to explore the countryside at Gambais, and often wheeled it through the forest of Ram-bouillet—fetched over thirty francs. A shabby old writing table with a heart pierced in it fetched the equivalent of a pound.

On June 14, the warders awakened him with the news that he was to be taken by car to Versailles. He took a courteous leave of them all, shook the governor by the hand and thanked him for his many courtesies.

Through the window of the car he watched the busy Paris scene for the last time. The car sped through familiar streets, and along roads he had often used when going by car himself to Gambais, past familiar inns, farms and woods. But at Versailles, when he was handed over to the prison governor, he learned that he was to be lodged in the condemned cell.

'I haven't been tried yet,' he said, politely. 'Isn't it rushing things a bit?'

'We are short of accommodation here,' said the Governor,

like a hotelier making apologies in the height of the holiday season, 'and it's all we could find.'

The daily deliveries of mail grew enormously. Landru had asked for a pack of cards, a privilege usually accorded to a condemned man. 'I know I'm not condemned, and could never be, as I am innocent,' he told the warders, 'but since I'm in the condemned cell, surely I ought to have the privileges?'

The governor was not so amenable as his counterpart in Paris, and curtly refused the request. Landru made a pack for himself from picture postcards sent to him from well-wishers from all over Europe. With these he told the fortunes of the warders. He also read, as he imagined, his own fate in the cut-out scraps of brightly coloured card. When the chief warder came to him late in September and told him that his trial had been fixed to start on November 7, he said that the cards had told him this already. He added that the cards revealed to him that he would be found guilty and condemned to a long term of imprisonment, but that before he could finish his sentence his complete innocence would be triumphantly vindicated.

Landru's distress at being moved from Paris to Versailles shows how much careful thought he had given to his struggle for acquittal, remote though his prospects were. In France such a trial is played out as a drama, and emotionalism plays a greater part than in some countries. But Versailles juries were noted for their stern and dour approach to law and order, and, in those days at least, the mere appearance of a suspect in the dock was taken to imply automatically some measure of guilt. Landru was too shrewd a man not to recognise that the choice of Versailles as the place of trial, and the allocation of the condemned cell to him for accommodation, showed, for all their patience in face of Landru's obstinacy and delaying tactics, that the authorities were convinced of his guilt and determined to make the charge stick.

Preparations for the trial involved, beyond the usual judicial administrative steps, all the work usual to a public event. Special trains—they came to be known as 'Landru specials'— were run from Paris to arrive in time for the opening. The reporters of the world began to converge on Versailles. The authorities were driven to distraction by the invidious choice of allocating special tickets. Twelve new telephone boxes were installed, so that the dénouement to this long serial story could be rushed to the press.

A van containing what are called the *pièces à conviction* arrived at the Palais de Justice, and included all the exhibits from Landru's villa and homes, or from his garages and stores, which would figure in the case. They included a dining table, an armchair, a wardrobe containing linen with various marks, a number of cases and travelling bags, a box of ashes and—of course—the famous stove in which, it was to be alleged he had incinerated his mistresses. Landru, informed of the arrival of the goods, followed the list with interest. 'All we need now,' he said, smiling, 'is the pothanger.'

II

Interrogation

You were born in the 19th arrondissement of Paris on April 12, 1869, of Julien-Alexandre Sylvain (father) and Flore (née Henriquel, mother). Your father was first employed as a stoker at the Forges de Vulcain... Your mother died in 1912... Your father committed suicide on August 25 or 26 of that year... You went to school up to the age of about sixteen....

Landru inspected his fingernails, glanced around the room, regarding the faked statuettes with ill-disguised distaste, yawned ostentatiously, looked through notes. But the letter of the law had to be observed. On and on droned the voice, delving back into the past, raking out every tiny detail of family life, school, past employment, army service, and the long record of petty crime...

... you were guilty of false pretences... Have you any observations to make regarding the information collected regarding yourself and your history?'

Landru did not reply.

Back to the cell, to sessions with his defending counsel, de Moro-Giafferi, and the deadly dull prison meals. Back to his tremendous files and notebooks, which grew larger and bulkier every day as he made notes on every point that affected his chance of living. For he had a good sense of discrimination between the trivial and the vital. He answered promptly any accusation that was not proven or inadequately based. He remained silent on any issue that might commit him unfavourably.

It has been established that you took possession of all the belongings of the eleven persons who disappeared while they were living with you, and that the entire activity of the numerous matrimonial projects you made was aimed at getting money. You have in no way wished to give a precise reply as to the origins of your means of existence from the time you left the Central Prison at Loos. Have you decided today to give an explanation on the subject?

The accused, says the police report, monotonously, did not reply.
Nor did the authorities tire.

When you left the Central Prison at Loos ... your personal resources were insignificant. Your wife has stated that you inherited a sum of 10,000 francs in shares which you sold when you came out of prison... There is nothing to support this statement. It is clear that these resources must have been rapidly exhausted, for you committed a whole series of frauds from August 1913 to April 1914... [Then followed an endless series of details of payments received and paid into various accounts, a list of fifteen names dating from August 23, 1913 to April 21, 1914, a total of 35,600 francs.] This fraudulent misuse of funds [continued Bonin, in his relentless monotone] seems to have been your sole means of subsistence during these years. In any case, you made a final withdrawal of money on July 28, 1914; you must have come to the aid of your family at Malakoff, settled your accounts, paid your expenses and your journey so that logically there could not have been much money left for yourself. What were your means of subsistence during the last months of 1914?

No reply.

Was it because of your difficult financial situation that you lived with Mme Cuchet and her son at Vernouillet? This seems very probable, particularly when one knows that this lady had such confidence in you that she had earlier given you, or let you take, some of her jewellery, which you later gave as a present to your wife. Probably before March 16, 1915, André Cuchet and his mother had disappeared, because on that date you were thinking of carrying out fresh projects, by inserting a marriage advertisement in the *Echo de Paris* and by renting a few days later a room at 152, Faubourg Saint Martin. You have claimed they owed you money and that, in general settlement, you paid them 4,500 francs, for which they agreed to hand over their belongings, but it is not possible that your own resources could have permitted such an arrangement; once again, can you tell us where came the money you had at that moment?

No reply.

The investigation has established that from the beginning of 1915 until April, 1919, you lived almost completely from the profits arising from the disappearance of André Cuchet, Mesdames Cuchet, Laborde-Line, Guillin, Heon, Collomb, Babelay, Buisson, Jaume, Pascal and Mlle Marchadier...

No reply.

The police have followed up the cases of no less than 169 of the women with whom you were in contact. You were, in fact, in correspondence with 283 women, but these 169 are those to whom you wrote letters expressing interest, asked for photographs, enclosed your own photograph, and so on. But the advertisements you put in the newspapers seeming insufficient to you, you also contacted a number of marriage agencies, certain intermediaries—five marriage brokers whose names I shall read to you... Now of these replies from women, statements from certain of these are of particular interest if we refer to your notebook, where you have made very precise and most significant comments—whether they have close relations or children, and above all you note carefully the information they gave regarding their financial means... certain of your correspondents thought such curiosity strange, and we cannot refrain from mentioning that only those who had some small savings and few, or no relations had your particular attention. The question of the financial situation was your main concern, and the notes in your notebooks are an unquestionable witness to this. You note 'eaten up her legacy,' '*situation* 4000–500 francs [presumably per annum] plus 2,000 francs savings,' and, again, 'no money,' 'has some possessions,' 'Keeping her mother' and 'suspect to have f' by which you probably meant 'fric' [slang for 'cash'].

Have you any statement to make?

Silence again. Landru fixed Bonin with that bored, yet penetrating look, the look which scores of women had found repulsive, scores more fascinating. The ancient clock ticked loudly. Bonin looked vacantly at Landru and pushed the deposition towards him, for signature.

... All the disappearances have the same preparatory circumstances ... all the women who disappeared were supposed to marry you in the near future, under the different names you had adopted (Diard, Cuchet, Fremyet, Guillet, Petit) and the different situations you invented (postman, consulate clerk, engineer, manufacturer)... Practically all concealed the name of the place where they were supposed to be staying with you. Some of them separated themselves from their relations, or broke off with their families ... and yet all of them, without exception, at the moment they were leaving Paris, stated that they would return to see their friends, mother, sisters or relatives with whom they had continued to keep in contact. Several of them even fixed the precise date of their return, and all promised to write to give their news.

Not one of them sold their jewellery, so as to have ready money for a journey. It is impossible to find anything, in their acts and in what they did and in what they said, ... which could lead anybody to think that they were preparing to go abroad shortly, or that they were leaving Paris never to return.

It must also be noted that none of these women, any more than André Cuchet, could possibly have considered going abroad, where they had no relatives, no money, and knew no foreign language, while for most of them, in view of their age and their health, it would have been almost impossible for them to find employment by which they could subsist...

Bonin listed, at great length, the plans which all the vanished women had for the future, as expressed in letters to or conversations with their friends and relatives. Then he listed Landru's unlikely stories of the strange new lives they had chosen for themselves.

Then there were the disturbing entries in the notebooks.

It is not possible to date exactly the disappearances of Mme Cuchet and André, but those of Mme Laborde-Line and Mme Guillin, and all those at Gambais, are in identical circumstances. With the exception of Mlle Marchadier, for whom there is no entry in the notebooks, their last journeys were all made in your company, and each time you carefully took one single ticket and one return, as if, on leaving, it was understood that only one person would be coming back to Paris. . . .
What was it that happened then, on the dates we have just quoted, dates which are of capital importance, since they fix the last moment when we have proof from your notebooks that certain of these women were still in existence?

Landru yawned. Did they imagine that all this was new to him? Or that he would confirm, from his own mouth, their elaborately worded suspicions? He sat with glazed eyes as they intoned the story of the women of Gambais.

The Ladykiller

The extreme care you took to see that your trail could not be picked up was apparently sufficient to keep you protected from legal proceedings if they had complained to the police about you, and yet, not one of the eleven persons you noted in your notebooks has been found, despite exceptionally thorough investigations and an unusual amount of publicity; we methodically worked out a system by which, if any of the eleven people had still been alive, or if they had died in any town whatsoever, we should have been able to find them.

Here Bonin read at length the report of all the elaborate steps taken by the authorities, including the distribution of photographs and details to police in all the affected regions, to commissariats throughout France, the checking of all hotel and boarding-house registers, checking with the passport services, frontier posts, railway stations, ports, all the shipping countries and even all the personnel of the then numerous bordels and everyone associated with the white slave traffic. The police had obtained official proof from the British Army that André Cuchet had not joined up there. Reports of all unidentified dead persons were investigated and photographs shown to the relatives of the eleven dead people.

Everything [M. Bonin continued] was in vain. The eleven people whom you had so carefully noted in this special way have never been found. Before giving you the result of the medico-legal reports which we called for on everything found in Vernouillet and Gambais, have you any precise statements which can be verified to make?

The accused did not reply.

... fragments of burnt bone which seemed to have come from human skeletons in the heap of cinders somewhat hidden under dry leaves in the furthermost garden shed, the enquiry was immediately switched to the kitchen, where the medical expert [Dr Paul] himself brushed out bits of bone from the stove itself and in the ashcan, of which the origin was not in the slightest doubt. A few moments later other bone fragments were found in the little shed near the wash house, while inside the wall surrounding the property other ash was found, with clinker and slag, in which bone fragments were found.

After the cinders had been separately sifted, 4 kilos 176 grammes of calcined bone fragments were extracted, together with 47 teeth or fragments of teeth. Of this total, some of the bones were from animals, but more than 1,500 grammes had belonged to human bodies and of this 996 grammes were from human skulls. . . .

In these circumstances, the experts established that:

1)—These human bone fragments came unquestionably from three skulls, six hands, and five feet, while it seemed quite clear to them that there were also the remains of a fourth corpse.

2)—The 47 teeth or tooth fragments proved on careful examination to be of human origin.

The experts, Bonin explained to Landru, had shown great care in seeking to establish the sex of the people from whom these bone fragments came. Although they were personally convinced that the fragments were feminine (how, Bonin did not say), the lack of the clearly defined and identifiable bones of the pelvis made them limit their assertions on this subject to the fact that it was one skull and the teeth which were of undoubted feminine origin.

The bones came from 'mature human beings between twenty-six and fifty years of age', one of them being small (say about four foot seven inches). The human skull bones bore traces of cutting instruments, such as a meat hatchet, while other bones not directly identifiable, but all long bones, being limb bones, had been dismembered, probably with a metal saw, a fragment of which was found among the ashes.

The soot had been analysed, but had revealed nothing unusual.

The ashes revealed 'interesting results' in the presence of metal fasteners, press-studs, a safety-pin, a hairpin, glass and mother-of-pearl buttons and six metallic fragments which had come from clothing, and two complete fastenings from corset suspenders. All these remains had been subject to intense heat.

But if the victims were incinerated, it seemed that the pretty young Mlle Babelay had been the exception.

We must note that you do not seem to have had any coal at the villa at that time, but that you took the trouble to get in a supply of wood. When you returned to Gambais, a week after *her* disappearance, you were in the company of Mme Buisson. If a crime had been committed (e.g. in the case of Mlle Babelay) all hypothesis of incineration must be excluded, therefore, and some other method of getting rid of the proof (the body) must be considered, such as burial.

Bonin handed the enormous dossier to Landru.

'These, generally speaking, are a summary of the charges against you. You have many times affirmed that you are absolutely innocent of the accusation of murder of these eleven people. You have categorically affirmed that these people are still alive, and that you know where they are.

'Do you persist in not making the slightest disclosure regarding them, despite the fact that, if we are to believe you, a few words from you could dissipate these most serious suspicions which hang over you, and thus you could escape indictments whose importance and possible consequences you perfectly well know?'

'*Possible consequences*'. It was Bonin's polite euphemism for the guillotine. Landru, although he looked a little pale after his long ordeal, seemed otherwise indifferent. Making no reply, he gathered up his file and left, with his escort, for the prison.

Landru On Trial

THE COURT in which France's most celebrated crime case was heard lacked any sense of visual drama. Shabby, dingy, poorly lit and painted in green, its focal points of interest were the bench where the judges sat, presided over by Conseiller Gilbert; the jury box, where the *petite bourgeoisie*—middle-aged and elderly—sat grimly listening, the public gallery packed with a heterogeneous crowd of midinettes, sober tradesmen, prostitutes, and aristocrats; and, of course, the dock. The dock was a long one, allowing ample room for the prisoner and his two guards, soldiers in uniform.

On a table in front of the judges was scattered a clutter of old garments and linen, giving a curious appearance of a pawn-broker's counter or a secondhand shop. In the well of the court, photographers set up their cameras, and moved around with a freedom unknown in Britain where, in any case, photographs cannot be taken inside a court.

Outside it was bitterly cold, several degrees below freezing. Sensation hunters had cheerfully risked pneumonia to be first in on a trial which had become a major topic of conversation for the last two and a half years. Everyone wanted to see 'Old Bluebeard', 'The Red Man of Gambais' and 'The Lady-killer' as he was described, amiably, in many night-club songs. The press gallery was crowded with some of France's most famous journalists and cartoonists, besides the cream of the world's reporting staff. America, Britain, Germany, Spain, Italy were all represented. Judge Gilbert had issued printed invitations strategically, but the organisation broke down under sheer pressure of demand, and even the darlings of Paris social life had to elbow their way through crowds to claim their seats at the most popular show in France. Mistinguette and Maurice Chevalier—then joint stars at the Casino de Paris—were there.

So was Colette, the famous novelist. Outside, astute opportunists were hawking seats for sale. Some fetched as much as a Cup Final ticket.

At French Assizes the presiding judge is given the title of President and with two assessors, who sit on either side, directs the proceedings. He has before him the papers in the case, including, of course, the *Interrogatoire*—in this instance the tremendous files built up by M. Bonin on the basis of the original police enquiries. The jury of twelve consisted of citizens of known respectability, whose names had first been included in the jurors list by magistrates or local mayors, and who had been selected by draw from a list of thirty-six names taken at random from the main lists.

The Presiding Judge can interrogate the prisoner on any or every point, something that occurs only rarely in Britain. He does this on the basis of the previous interrogation by the examining magistrate, and has invariably studied the papers long before he finds himself in court. Landru's trial could hardly have proceeded if the judge had not done this, as such a mass of material could not be assimilated in a hurry.

At the beginning of a trial, an Act of Accusation is read—a statement of the case against the accused. It includes anything that is known of the prisoner's previous convictions, if any, and these are disclosed at the beginning of the trial. It is inevitable that such disclosures colour, to some degree, the attitude of prosecuting counsel, jury and, perhaps, even of witnesses. In England such information cannot be disclosed until the case has been heard and the verdict given, although the judge himself knows from the very outset of the trial.

Witnesses are called after the examination of the prisoner, or when their evidence is being reviewed. Both counsel for the defence and prosecution may question witnesses—asking their questions through the President—and so may members of the jury. Counsel for the defence have the right to the final question. Witnesses are entitled to quote hearsay, which is not acceptable evidence in some countries.

After the witnesses, speeches for the prosecution and defence follow, but there is no summing up or direction to the jury of the sort one gets in an English trial, and which so often indicates which way the verdict is likely to go. The jury retire, and make their decision of guilty or not guilty by secret ballot.

They return to court, state their verdict, and the Presiding Judge, in consultation with his two fellow-judges, decides upon the sentence.

The President of the Court was a man in his fifties, sober, painstaking, fair, and dignified. His red robes provided the only touch of colour in the otherwise sombre court. His assessors, or fellow adviser-judges, were Judge Schuler, counsellor of the Court of Appeal of Paris, and Judge Gloria, of the Civil Tribunal of Versailles. The prosecution was entrusted to the Avocat Général, Maître Godefroy, whose urbanity and genial smile belied an icy determination. He was assisted by M. Brouchot, Assistant Judge of the Civil Tribunal of Versailles.

Most colourful of all was Landru's counsel, Maître de Moro-Giafferi, the fiery Corsican who had already featured in many famous cases, including the celebrated treason trials of Caillaux and Humbert, and who was as famous at the French bar as Sir Edward Marshall-Hall and Lord Birkett were at the English bar. He had also defended the infamous Bonnot gang, whose leader, chief of a gang of anarchists whose murders and violence terrorised Paris in the twenties, was killed by police at the 'siege' of Choisy-le-Roi. De Moro-Giafferi's vigour, quick thinking, eloquence and histrionic gestures made any place light up with vitality the moment he entered it. As we have seen Navières du Treuil, the Assistant Defence Counsel, had been in constant touch with Landru since his arrest. Maître Legrand and Maître Legasse represented (for the purposes of a civil claim for the return of stolen property) the families of Mme Pascal and Mme Fauchet.

The journalists regarded the iron stove curiously. Could Landru possibly have incinerated eight corpses in that poky little thing? It just didn't seem possible. One journalist, Fauvergne, told his colleagues that he had *proved* such a stove would be useless. He had bought its duplicate and put in a kilo (about 2lb) of meat to see how long it would take to burn to cinders. 'I burnt the coal up all right,' he declared, 'but not the meat! Maybe the court may decide that Landru dissolved heads, hands, feet and so on chopped off from his victims to prevent them being identified . . . They may. We'll see.'

The previous day Landru had spent a long session with M. Papillion, the barber, giving him the most explicit instructions on the grooming of his beard. After all, the whole world had heard of it. It should be seen to best advantage. Furthermore, there were other bearded participants whose whiskers must not be permitted to dominate the proceedings—Judge Gilbert, Godefroy, the Avocat Général, even the press photographer who sat behind his plate camera, set on a tripod, the lens pointed straight at the dock.

Landru ate well and heartily on the morning of November 7, 1921, the day the trial opened. He wore the putty-coloured military-style topcoat with outside pockets, which had always been a favourite garment of his, and was admirably suited as a general-purpose or motoring coat.

The court was assembled, except for the Judge and the adjudged-to-be, M. Landru. A hush of expectancy fell upon the chattering public as the soldiers in full uniform presented arms, and the President took his seat. An enormous number of witnesses, mostly sisters, mothers, aunts, friends, tradesmen or concierges of the missing women, or women who had been in correspondence or association with Landru as a result of his matrimonial advertisements, were present. They looked sad and drab and lost, a reluctant army of nonentities thrust unwittingly into prominence by a sordid tragedy. Mme Collin, whose pretty young daughter once she had met Landru, had disappeared into oblivion after running away from home, waited, pale and angry, for the confrontation. She was in full mourning.

The bell rang, and the court was in session. Landru had been waiting in an anteroom. At a given signal a door to the side of the dock opened and Landru found himself guided, almost pushed, into his place between the two armed soldiers. Immediately all eyes were upon him. He looked so *respectable*, so much at ease. He glanced around the court, taking in every detail—almost, it seemed, every face. Maître de Moro-Giafferi had given him a comforting pat on the shoulder, out of sight of the court, before Landru had made his entry, as good as to say: 'This is it, but I'm with you.' He looked pale, but the scissors and curling-irons of the barber of Saint Pierre prison had given him the well-kempt air he sought.

The jurors were sworn in. They undertook, every one of them, 'to betray neither the interests of the accused nor those of the society which accuses him; nor to communicate with anyone until after the verdict is declared; to give ear neither to hatred, nor malice, nor fear, nor affection; to decide according to the charges and the means of defence, following their conscience and their intimate conviction with the impartiality and the firmness which becomes an upright and free man'. As they did so, Landru looked down into the well of the court, surveying them with his sombre, deep-set eyes. Whatever else one might expect of the jury members, it could not be affection.

He sat down on the cold iron bench, and nodded briefly as the President read out his name in order to establish his identity:

'Your name is Landru, Henri Désiré, son of Julien-Alexandre and of Flore (Henriquel), born in Paris on April 12, 1869, and your last residence was 76 rue de Rochechouart?'

Landru nodded, then answered, 'Yes.'

Journalists watched the scene for 'colour', hardly bothering to make notes for the moment. The Act of Indictment, which the Clerk of the Court began reading—a long, tedious document which by now Landru knew almost by heart—was equally of no interest to the press, for they had long possessed, and published, its text. It was merely a necessary preliminary to the hearing that would follow. Even so, Landru himself followed it carefully, pausing occasionally to make a note, or to stroke his ample beard gravely with his large, sensitive hands. Perhaps he was not happy with the spectacles provided for him by the prison authorities, for he tended more frequently to use them as a magnifying glass, than to wear them.

On and on went the statement, and the attention of most people in the court drifted, for the monotone voice continued for over two hours. The gendarmes, conscious of their important charge and the fact that so many eyes were on them, tried hard not to doze off. The prosecuting counsel, a huge man, heavy with many lunches, slumped deep into his armchair, a ray of sunlight from the window highlighting his red robe like a danger signal. The witnesses exchanged quiet words with each other.

It was difficult for the jury, too. The details of Landru's various moves through the different courts was read out, and a summary of the twenty-six accusations given, all of M. Bonin's prose getting full value. Landru looked the clerk full in the face, as though not to seem discourteous to the man who was taking the trouble to address him personally.

By ten past four the reading was finished. The Avocat Général motioned to an usher, whispered to him, and instructed him to request the novelist Colette, who was making copious notes, to move farther away from the jury box. The only light touch in the whole proceedings was a reference to Landru having had relations with 283 women. Many a woman looked towards the gentlemanly figure of Landru, ostensibly the perfect French *paterfamilias*, and roared with laughter. Landru seemed almost to approve of this, but then few men would be insulted at the suggestion that, in their middle fifties, they were acceptable to so great a range of women, and physically capable of keeping a great number of them content.

The list of witnesses, nearly 150 of them, was then read, each indicating his presence in the manner of a roll call. Necks were craned when the name of Mlle Fernande Segret was called. Everyone wanted a glimpse of Landru's 'dear friend'. She looked composed, though serious.

One curious development was that a Désirée Guillin had been found alive. She had answered Landru's advertisement, had been in correspondence with him. The head juryman, M. Martin, a ruddy-faced farmer with a permanent, cheerful smile, looked suddenly alert. But no. By a coincidence, Landru had known two Mme Guillins, one of them still alive, the other missing, presumed dead. The Avocat Général exchanged a few polite words with de Moro-Giafferi and then, turning to Landru, said, with great deliberation:

'Landru, if you have anything to say, say it. Any precise details to give, give them! I have no fear of anything you may say, because I have the deep and unshakeable conviction that I shall demolish any defence you may give!'

De Moro-Giafferi was quickly on his feet. After a courteous exchange with his opponent he stressed the curious coincidence of the two Mesdames Guillin.

'There is not only *one* coincidence,' he continued. 'I am sure that Madame Désirée Guillin has nothing in common with the widow Guillin who has disappeared. But reflect, gentlemen of the jury, on these troubling and numerous coincidences, and you will see whether the death penalty can be demanded for a man who is defending himself, who affirms his innocence, and who swears to you that he has no drop of blood on his hands.'

At last it was Landru's turn. He had little to say, but every word seemed carefully considered, and was delivered in an unfaltering, clear voice.

'I simply want to say a few words, to protest my innocence. From the very first day I have held to my protest. I have asked for proof, and have had but words proffered to me, never any proof. I acknowledge the eloquence of the Public Prosecutor, but I am also aware of the great impartiality of the Judge, and that I can count on the devotion of my defending counsel. Thus, I trust that these discussions will finally prove my innocence.'

The next day Landru had to listen, as he had so many times before, to a reconstruction of his early life.

'You were educated at the École des Frères in the rue de Bretonvilliers. You were a clever boy, and earned high praise from your schoolmasters. You were admitted a subdeacon at the religious establishment of St Louis-en-l'Ile.'

'Only for a short time.'

'Perhaps,' continued Judge Gilbert, imperturbably, 'it was there that you learned that gentle and unctuous manner which has been one of your chief means of seduction, and has helped you to capture the confidence of so many women. But then you took up more profane occupations....'

The London *Times,* whose representative attended the trial, commented on Landru's appearance and demeanour: 'The prisoner seemed to have grown weary under the strain, but he was as calm, as courteous, as indomitable and as ready with his answers, as ever. The strange, powerful head, too big for a man of his height, and the deep eyes, now tired, now glittering with curious brilliance, give him an enigmatic air that masks completely what is in his mind.'

It was really Landru's demeanour and personality that dominated the proceedings from start to finish, for it was impossible for people who saw him day after day, observed him under all conditions and at close quarters, to form any conclusions as to the key motivations of his character. Was it possible that a man of this calm manner, quick repartee and dignified exterior could have murdered and dismembered so many people? The artists sketched away with pen and pencil. Sometimes Landru, noting that an artist had him in gaze and was applying his charcoal or pencil or pen swiftly, as though anxious to capture the angle and expression before it was lost, would hold his position long enough to let the artist finish—but with no actual gesture to indicate that this was deliberate.

The Judge questioned him on his origins, his father, his illegitimate child, the time he spent in the army, and something that happened when he came out, which might have affected the whole course of his life:

'Your wife has told us that when you entered the service of one firm you had to pay a deposit, and your employer disappeared without returning the deposit. Was it this that gave you the idea of practising robbery?'

Landru replied: 'That is right. But my acts had nothing in common with the robbery of this old employer, who went to America, taking with him money given as security by his employees and workpeople.'

The Judge mentioned that enquiries had failed to trace one of Landru's previous employers.

'This indicates, your honour, the value of police investigations. Yet they can find so many things when it pleases them.'

'You are accusing the police?'

'Oh, no. I am merely stating the position!'

Later Landru reminded Judge Gilbert that the police had not found a single one of his supposed victims: 'There's not a single one who has come to accuse me!'

'That,' commented the Judge, severely, 'is hardly surprising.'

The only sign of anger which Landru showed was when his list of seven previous convictions was read to him:

'Does that prove today that I am a murderer, because I sinned earlier on? I was sentenced. I have served my sentence. I have paid my debt to society and to justice, and I am still being asked to pay. All my past now becomes a ground of complaint against me. I am even criticised for changing my profession several times. Nevertheless, I remained in industry until 1919. Since then, I have remained in prison.' Landru smiled, feeling he had scored a point. The Judge gave him tit for tat.

'Your record reveals you as one who lives by his wits, a *chevalier d'industrie.*'

'Chivalry no longer exists in our day,' replied Landru, with detachment.

Landru tried to argue the merits of some of the sentences passed upon him for fraud.

'Your convictions are a closed case,' the Judge told him, 'it if for you to acknowledge, not to dispute them.'

It was mentioned that, having been arrested for attempting to withdraw money belonging to another from the Comptoir d'Escompte, he feigned suicide in prison by putting his head into a noose at the moment a warden opened the door of his prison cell.

Landru denied indignantly that the attempt had been a fake. 'I was tired of my unhappy life, of being continually arrested, and my suicide attempt was genuine. It was my full intention to end a life so full of anguish and torment.'

'It was seven o'clock in the morning when you made your attempt, an hour at which, as you well knew, the cells were regularly visited.'

When his frauds were again referred to, Landru, emboldened by the smiles and laughs from the public at some of his sallies, said: 'That's the correct thing to do in business. If you succeed, you become a big man. If you don't succeed, as Victor Hugo said, you are simply *un misérable*.'

When it was mentioned that he was continually 'on the run' after his last sentence *in absentia*, Landru said triumphantly: 'The police were always looking for me, but they never caught up with me. Ah, the police never have any luck with their investigations.'

The Judge continued with Landru's swindling of a widow named Izoret, to whom he got engaged in 1910 before making off with her cash-box containing 20,000 francs, and then went on to his final arrest, the searches made in the different houses, where the furniture was carefully listed, and the correspondence with various women so carefully filed away. Finally, he came to the famous—and fatal—notebook with its list of eleven names ('Like an epitaph in a mausoleum,' Judge Gilbert remarked).

'What,' enquired the Judge, 'is the reason for the eleven names on this page?'

'It is the list of a dealer who notes down the names of the people with whom he is doing business,' Landru answered. 'I knew some of these people so little that I had to use words like "Havre", "Brésil" and "Crozatier" to designate them. The list is of no importance, but the police, who see evil everywhere, have seen, instead of a dealer's notes, a criminal's list of his victims. A wholly gratuitous supposition. And besides, the list is not signed 'I, Landru, Désiré, certify having murdered the persons mentioned above.'

Now nobody in court was smiling. The cold facetiousness in face of an enquiry into the fate of eleven vanished people was too grotesquely out of place to be seen as anything but callousness. And there was a new, ominous, defiant note in Landru's next comment:

'This list limits the number of my crimes. Eleven names in the notebook, so eleven crimes. And who can prove to you that I have not committed more?"

The Judge continued:

'Explain to us, Landru, why you corresponded with so many women, whom you got to know through your matrimonial advertisements, and why you kept the letters from all these women, annotated, classified and listed?'

Landru: 'That is very simple. It was at the beginning of the war. I considered that all these women, living alone and without much money, in Paris, would be finding themselves faced with great financial difficulties, and that many of them would want, sensibly enough, to retire to the provinces. I considered that, under such circumstances, they would sell their furniture. I decided to buy this furniture under the best possible conditions, so as to sell it later when the peace had been signed, in the area devastated by the war. This was how the idea of trading came to me. And in order to get into contact with these women, who would eventually become my customers, I put advertisements into the papers. . . .'

'But these were advertisements for *marriage?*'

'Certainly. But you realize, your honour, that there is no business today without publicity, and that any publicity is only of value insofar as it brings results. Yes, my advertisements were of matrimony. I spoke of marriage! What a crime! Indeed, I did speak of marriage with my clients . . . a pretext to get into closer relations with them, a ruse of a businessman who wants to be better informed of his customers' secret intentions. A very innocent little ruse. I did not think that there was anything reprehensible at all in that, all the more in that they were all adults, and, once I had got in touch with them, there was no question of marriage. I may have sometimes become their lover, but I was never their fiancé.'

This was the clue for which the Judge was waiting. 'Usher,' he instructed, 'call Mme Izoret.' Women in the public gallery craned their necks. The word 'lover' had made them all wake up.

A lady, more determined than beautiful, but clearly upset by the publicity, swept in. She winced as the photographers trained their cameras on her. 'But I have no wish for anyone to take my picture! I am an honest woman. I am married.'

There was no time to examine the logic of the last two sentences. The Judge reassured her, and at his request she related details of how Landru had swindled her before the War.

'And did the accused promise to marry you?'

'Oh, yes, sir. And it was the very day that we were to sign the [marriage] contract that he made off with my savings.'

This time, Landru said nothing.

Two witnesses, Commissioner Dautel and Inspector Belin (who arrested Landru), gave evidence of Landru's arrest, and of the search of his various premises. Belin claimed that no search had ever been made without Landru having been present. This claim, although accepted by the court, was patently ludicrous, since Belin himself made it plain years later that he searched the flat in rue de Rochechouart *after* Landru had been taken away.

Landru then told the court: 'We went in a cab along the rue de Rochechouart, rue de Chateaudun, Boulevard Ney, and others. In the carriage were Dautel, Belin, a third inspector Braunberger, and myself. The carriage stopped before my home, and you all went up, leaving me alone. I accuse this man [pointing to Belin] of having arrested me illegally, in violation of the law, inside my house, without a warrant and of entering by surprise aided by subterfuge.'

Well, Landru had a point there. He did not bother to mention that if the police had *not* surprised him he would never have been available for arrest, and that the dismal catalogue of female disappearances would have grown larger and larger. In later years Belin confessed, without apology, to obtaining access to Landru's flat in the rue de Rochechouart by means of a trick.

To the delight of the public, Landru's protest sparked off a fierce verbal duel between de Moro-Giafferi and the Prosecuting Counsel, the fiery Corsican banging his desk and moving, in his black gown, like an angry outsized bat in full flight. He glared at Judge Gilbert. 'Are you the President of this court, or aren't you? It's your job to protect me from these intolerable interruptions!'

The queues outside the court grew longer and longer. The élite of Paris, as well as a generous portion of the solid bourgeoisie and the underworld, and prominent people from a dozen countries, clamoured for admission or pulled every influential string they might have to secure a seat at the trial.

As it progressed, the courtroom looked more and more like some pawnbroker's shop in a very poor area that had decided to hold a clearance sale of unclaimed pledges. There were furniture, mattresses, drab, well-worn linen, miscellaneous clothes, boxes and even umbrellas.

Yet all these were the tangible remains of two human lives—of Mme Cuchet and her son. These, and a few documents.

Landru knew that this would be a difficult day. He polished his spectacles continually, laid out his documents and notes carefully and listened attentively. The indictment described his version, given during interrogation, of how he met Mme Cuchet and her son. André, he had declared, then working as a delivery-boy for a grocer, came to his garage at Malakoff and asked for work. He came again, said Landru, and introduced his mother.

'And you offered to marry Mme Cuchet?' Judge Gilbert interposed.

'There couldn't be any question of marriage, because she knew my real situation [i.e. that he was already married].'

'On the contrary, she did not know, because you introduced yourself as Raymond Diard.'

'Oh, excuse me she knew me under the name of Landru. It was only later, after I had been condemned *in absentia*, in July 1914, that I admitted my trouble with the police to her, and, to escape the police, I called myself Diard.' (This was later disproved, as was his version of how he came to meet Mme Cuchet.)

Landru was never at a loss for a reply—or, on the infrequent occasions when he felt himself to be, he gave none. With the pained air of a wrongfully accused man, he denied that Madame Cuchet had been his mistress. When it was pointed out to him that they lived in the same apartment, he said, 'She sublet me one room only.'

Then the court heard how, during August, 1914, Mme Cuchet, feeling dubious of Landru's character, had rummaged in a trunk with the aid of her brother-in-law, M. Friedmann, finding Landru's marriage certificate and military papers. She told her family about it, and broke with Landru, but was talked into resuming relations with him and went to live with him in the villa at Vernouillet, where, Landru claimed, he rented two rooms.

'Mme Cuchet was forty, she knew her own mind, and whether she wanted to break off relations with her relatives. As far as the villa was concerned, it is true that I looked for one and chose one. The most elementary politeness demanded that I should have avoided a woman having to do this sort of thing.' Landru glanced around the court as he said this, as though to say, 'can't everyone see that I'm a *gentleman*? Do I look the sort of man who would allow a woman to do things that any gentleman should do for her?'

The Judge asked: 'Landru, how do you explain the disappearance of Mme Cuchet and her son? And how is it that, after this disappearance, the furniture and identity papers of this woman and her son were found on your premises?'

Landru clenched the dock rail tightly.

'Mme Cuchet and her son left me one day, when it pleased them. Before they left, we settled our accounts and made certain arrangements [he was covering himself for the furniture and identity papers]. Since then, I have not seen them any more. The arrangements were private ones between Mme Cuchet and myself. Neither she nor I did anything which is illegal or immoral. We did what we thought fit. We both had the right to do this, as a question of individual liberty.'

'You refuse to give us details of the arrangements with Mme Cuchet?'

'Precisely!'

'And the identity papers?'

'If Mme Cuchet left her identity papers with me, it was perhaps because she wanted to travel incognito.'

'Why this incognito?'

'Oh,' replied Landru, airily, 'I have quite enough on my hands answering for myself, without having to concern myself with what other people do.'

Prosecutor Godefroy loomed up before Landru.

'You persist in refusing to say what agreement you entered into with Mme Cuchet?'

Landru pulled himself erect, lifted his head back so that he seemed to be looking down on his threatening opponent. 'Mme Cuchet's actions and mine in private only concern ourselves!'

'You persist in this line of action, even when your head is at stake?'

'Yes!'

The witnesses gave their evidence, one by one. Mme Bazire, a friend of Mme Cuchet. Landru was introduced to her as 'Monsieur Diard', she recalled. She considered him 'well brought up'. M. Lovaric, Mme Cuchet's employer, said she would certainly have written to him, had she been alive. Her brother-in-law, M. Friedmann, told of discovering the documents that proved 'M. Diard' an imposter and of his sister-in-law's grief and disillusion, followed by an incurable infatuation for the man who had deceived her. The surprising reconciliation caused an estrangement with her family. 'I called several times afterwards at the home of Mme Cuchet,' Friedmann told the court, 'but was always refused admittance, so I made no further attempt, and the rupture was complete.'

Mme Friedmann wept as she surveyed the melancholy bits and pieces of furniture and belongings. When 'Diard' had been introduced to her, she had told her sister that she didn't think much of him. However, her sister went to live with him.

Judge: 'He lived completely with your sister, didn't he? There was complete intimacy between them?'

'Oh, yes. They were going to get married.'

'You do not quite follow me, madame. Do you believe your sister was Landru's mistress?'

'Oh, that could well be, your honour,' replied Mme Friedmann, very cheerfully.

She described her unavailing efforts to write to her sister. Even a registered letter sent to Vernouillet had been returned 'Gone, no address'. She added that she was convinced that her sister was murdered.

'On what,' demanded Landru, 'does she base her conviction?'

The sad, middle-aged woman looked towards Landru. She was trembling with emotion. She motioned towards the miserable sticks of furniture and jaded bric-à-brac. 'If my sister was living,' she said, struggling to keep her voice steady, 'she would never have left behind her treasured belongings.'

Landru: 'I have not been properly understood. I repeat my question.'

'If my sister had not been murdered, she would have been in touch with me when she was ill! She felt for people, my sister did!'

Her emotion had no effect on Landru, but his counsel sensed the court's sympathy for Mme Cuchet's sister. Suddenly the tragedy of the missing widow and her son seemed terribly real, and the cynical composure of the prisoner terribly cruel. Something must be done, thought de Moro-Giafferi, to stop the drift:

'Might not your long story of your sister's disappearance have been a mere dream?' he asked.

She looked, it seemed, blankly, at counsel.

'A dream,' he repeated, 'remember? The dream you mentioned to the examining magistrate.'

A strange tension pervaded the court. A typist stopped in the act of rouging her lips. Colette looked towards her, startled. Mme Friedmann seemed to be going into a sort of trance. Her voice assumed a kind of sepulchral monotone, her eyes had a glazed, faraway look, as though the court and its occupants had disappeared altogether for her, and she was looking at something else.

'Yes ... I had a dream! In this dream my sister came to me, deathly pale and with her throat cut. "Landru has done this," she told me, "he killed me, the *misérable*." "Did you suffer much?" I asked. "No! No! I was asleep," she replied. Yes, she said that in a dream.'

De Moro-Giafferi looked around the court, hoping his point was made. If the lady had dreamed of one thing, might she not dream of another? Was she not an hysterical woman, impressed, convinced even, by unrealities?

The looks he received in return can have done little to reassure him on the progress of the case. Everyone was quiet, as though in the face of truth.

Mme Friedmann spoke of her sister's love of sky-blue as a colour, and of the sky-blue dressing-gown she had. 'Well, your honour,' she told the judge, 'they found that blue dressing-gown at Mlle Segret's. That—bandit—had given it to *her*!'

The 'bandit' smirked disdainfully and gave the witness a 'thank you' nod.

The sister of the dead woman saw it, and returned his look, her eyes blazing with hatred.

'If you were not the murderer of my sister, she would be here to stop you being condemned. She loved you to the point of abandoning her family for you!'

At this, she sobbed so pitifully that no further business could be done. Hastily, Judge Gilbert adjourned the court.

13

A Procession of Ghosts

THE PROSECUTION'S CASE for the murder of the Cuchets seemed unarguable. The vagueness, the deception, the insolent indifference displayed by Landru, coupled with his devious disposal of all that was valuable, and his unlikely stories of where they had gone, all pointed to their death. Would Mme Cuchet have vanished, with no word to her friends and relatives, with no money or possessions of value with her, to a country whose language she could not speak? Would any woman leave behind her marriage certificate, her dead husband's army book, the photograph of her baby, the certificate of her husband's first communion, her own birth certificate and two savings-bank books?

The prosecution moved on to the case of 'Brésil', or Mme Laborde-Line. The President tried to squeeze from Landru some clue as to her fate: Mme Laborde-Line had advertised that she was looking for work.

'This advertisement proved to me,' said Landru, 'that this lady was in need of money. This gave me the idea of buying her furniture. That was why I got in touch with her.'

'Under what name?'

'I don't remember.'

'Under the name of Cuchet, probably, because you had taken on the name of the deceased husband of your first fiancée. Was there any question of marriage between Mme Laborde-Line and yourself?'

'The short time I was in contact with her proves that we did not have the time to sketch out the most elementary idyll.'

'Yet Mme Laborde-Line confided to witnesses how bothered she was not to be able to marry you right away because her [identity] papers were in Argentina, adding that in the meantime she intended setting up house with you.'

'Oh, I should never have set up house with her.'

On June 28, 1915, Landru had taken away her furniture and left with her.

'To Vernouillet?' asked the Judge.

'Never!'

'And yet she was seen there!'

'She was visiting.'

'But she was seen gathering flowers.'

'Gathering flowers! Every Parisian woman does so.'

'But she no longer had a home, or any furniture.'

'I did not concern myself about her private affairs.'

'Do you know what became of her?'

'I do not know....'

'You refuse to tell us?'

'I do not know ... or, rather, I do not want to know. I am a furniture dealer and did business with Mme Laborde-Line as with Mme Cuchet. Do not deprive me of my job.'

'So here is Mme Laborde-Line, without a home, without any furniture, without money, since she had moved from the rue de Patay, since you had her furniture, since you cashed her valuables. What could have become of her?'

'How do you expect me to know?'

Maître Godefroy, sick of all this prevarication, was on his feet, waving an accusing finger at Landru, fixing him with an angry look.

'Landru! Your head is at stake. What became of Mme Laborde-Line?'

'I do not wish to reply. All that concerns my private life.'

If Landru was not speaking the truth—and nobody accepted that he was speaking the truth—he was certainly a consummate actor. He looked at Godefroy with such indignation, such outraged dignity that it was hard to imagine him dismembering a corpse, burning it in an oven and burying or throwing the ashes to the winds, which was what the prosecution was all about. The dapper little man talking of furniture deals, and holding fast to strict precepts of gallantry that forbore mention of his personal relationships, did not look at all like the popular conception of a mass killer.

He addressed the court in general: 'When a crime is committed the first idea is to get rid of all evidence of it. The fact that I kept in my villas all the furniture found in them which I bought, proves that my conscience is clear.'

Godefroy changed his tactics. Suddenly he became ingratiating, soft-voiced, courteous. The tactic seemed to disconcert Landru (as well it might) more than obvious aggression. Why, asked Godefroy, had Landru not told the examining magistrate so many of the facts now adduced in court?

'Bonin had threatened to send me to the Assizes if I did not answer his questions. Having a police record, and sure that I would be presumed guilty if sent for trial, I refused to reply further to him. Then again, at the cantonal elections in 1919, M. Bonin was a candidate for the post of consul-general of Corrèze, his home area. Some jokers put my name down instead of his in a number of voting papers.'

The court rocked with laughter at this. Even Godefroy's dour, accusing visage relaxed into a smile. But Landru did not join in the merriment. He turned accusingly to the jury, public and press gallery. 'There is nothing to laugh at! I am innocent! I have never stained my hands with blood. M. Bonin, not having secured the necessary number of votes, blamed me for it. He resented me from that day on, arrested my wife, my son.'

Now Godefroy was serious again. 'Landru, reply to these serious charges which may make your head fall—what has become of Mme Laborde-Line?'

'I refuse to reply to you.'

'Will you say nothing to save your head?'

'No.'

Mme Laborde-Line's son, whose wife had quarrelled with her, described how he sent his mother money by registered post, which she never acknowledged. The reason for that seemingly ungrateful, and so uncharacteristic silence, was now obvious to him; somebody to whom she entrusted her letter for posting had decided to suppress it. This proved his mother had been murdered, for she had loved him very much and certainly would have answered him.

The 'Landru Special' left Paris every day, arriving at Versailles with its strange mixture of characters—the journalists, cartoonists, artists, immaculate 'toffs', street girls, bourgeoisie and others. The train became a sort of club. The same destination, the same train at the same time, meant proximity and the excitement of discussing the previous day's evidence and speculation as to what the day's proceedings would bring forth.

The weather was cold. Vacuum flasks were produced, pies, bottles of wine, fruit. The air of the carriage became thick with tobacco fog, sweat and perfume. Newspapers were eagerly exchanged, for variations in the accounts to be noticed. Somebody tried to open the window to let in some air, but then gave it up. The leather straps which manipulated the heavy window had long since been cut away to provide shoe-leather during the war years, and had not yet been replaced.

Now all the characters were as familiar to France as the actors in a play. Their characteristics, too, were by now familiar. The explosive, volatile de Moro-Giafferi could be relied upon for sparks and light relief; Godefroy could be depended upon for stern, unrelenting intervention, ponderous threats about the prisoner's eventual fate, frowning, thunderous denunciations and relentless logic. Judge Gilbert sometimes listened for a long time whilst the verbal gladiators engaged in bitter fighting, or perhaps he chipped in with a telling comment or rapier-like question just when Landru was holding forth like a leading actor in a Shakespearean drama.

So the trial, at each session, was like a variation on a familiar theme. The principal actors had established their identities, the dingy courtroom was as familiar as a stage set. But the situations, the dialogue and repartee, the walk-on parts and the exhibits changed all the time. And the procession of ghosts changed too. Last time it was Mme Laborde-Line, but they could not produce her body. 'Produce the corpse!' Landru said, whenever an accusation of murder was made against him. It was clear that he knew they could not. Why was he so sure? Well, that was what the trial was about. Yet at this stage of the trial, everyone was talking about what happened at his villa at Vernouillet. How, hedged in on each side by neighbours, could four people have disappeared totally?

It was the fifth day of the trial—Armistice Day. The soldiers guarding Landru proudly displayed their medals, black ties were in evidence in memory of France's dead. A huge line of limousines now converged on the court, for the interest in the Landru case had gathered momentum. Landru had been swamped with 'fan' mail but had had little time to read it, for at night, when he returned to the condemned cell, he read the prolific notes he had made in court, and studied with care the enormous files on which his life depended.

The exhibits in court seemed an odd introduction to a drama. Some well-worn underwear of the solid, unerotic sort, reminiscent of what might be given away by a charity association to some female vagrant; a few scraps of tasteless jewellery; false hair-pieces. There was a long, coral necklace. These were the relics of the strong-jawed, shrewd, determined widow Guillin, whom Landru, in his more affectionate moments, liked to call 'my little baggage'. Such language had emptied her pockets of her employer's legacy of 20,000 francs, which he had intended as a reward for long and faithful service. If he had proved generous in death, he had been pretty demanding in life, and to invest the legacy in belated romance—and, of course, the respectable security of married life—had been an attractive, if short-lived, idea.

There was the glamour of her fiancé's new office as Consul in Australia. Australia! Far, far away from war and Gothas and rationing and endless housekeeping chores. A consul was important. He would have a car, and chauffeur and, of course, servants. Australia had sunshine and space, and something called the Great Barrier Reef, and something called the Outback where, of course, consuls didn't go.

And now these rags and unwanted hair-pieces and bits and pieces of pathetic adornment were all that remained of Mme Guillin's dreams. The fashionable women in the public gallery —and women vastly outnumbered the men—surveyed the relics with disdain, hilarity or distaste.

Now the door to the side of the dock opened, and Landru, dapper and pale and bright-eyed, entered with his burly soldier guards, his shirt pristine, his polka-dot tie neatly tied.

The story was told of his advertisement, her replies, of his pretence to be M. Petit, whom the grateful town of Lille had rewarded with the honour of appointing him consul. The choice of Lille, as the court observed, could be due to the fact that it was, in 1915, in the war zone and it would have been impossible to have checked his claims.

Witnesses described how often Mme Guillin had gone to Vernouillet, her infatuation with the charming M. Petit, and how she came back loaded with cherries. Another told of how she was surprised and crestfallen to have earned a rebuke from her fiancé, who had caught her looking through a keyhole, speculating on the origin of the woman's slippers and underwear that she had seen strewn about the floor of the locked room. Landru had been cross with his 'little baggage' that day! He had wiped from his eye an invisible tear. 'That is the room my beloved mother died in. I have left it exactly as it was, as a sort of shrine, a *pieux sanctuaire*.' How Mme Guillin had admired so worthy a son!

Landru sought to demolish the evidence.

'Oh, it's quite true, Mme Guillin was very inquisitive ... but do not let us exaggerate. You must be careful of legends, you know, gentlemen of the jury. So much has been written and talked of in my unfortunate affair, that a legend has grown up which must be carefully distinguished from the truth.

'To tell the truth, there were no feminine objects left around the villa. You have recognised, your honour, and I am grateful to you for it, my qualities of orderliness; under these circumstances, how could I have left around objects that could have compromised me?'

Evidence was given that, since she owed rent which she could not pay, Mme Guillin could not move her furniture out of her flat, and had to go off with Landru to Vernouillet with no luggage, setting herself up in the villa.

'Excuse me,' Landru interrupted, 'she came as a guest.'

Surely, it was argued, she must have expected marriage? Landru denied it. Her daughter, Mme Coquet, declared that she received a letter from her on August 2, 1915 to which 'Monsieur Petit' had added a postscript: 'Your mother is very happy in the country and we should be pleased to have you here [on a visit].' Since then—nothing.

The Judge was interested in the fact that, on that same day, Landru entered in his notebook a list of all Mme Guillin's jewellery.

'What does this signify?' asked the Judge.

'I no longer remember.'

Prosecutor Godefroy glowered at Landru's complacency. Oh for an inquisition, something to break his stubborn, insolent spirit!

Two months later, it was said, on October 15, 1915, Landru— who was no longer the tenant of the villa at Vernouillet—

appeared at 35, rue Crozatier, settled Madame Guillin's debts, removed her furniture, and told the puzzled concierge that he was doing it 'to save her the worry.'

A few days later Landru was selling her bonds.

'Where was Madame Guillin then?' asked Judge Gilbert.

'Ah,' said Landru ruminatively, stroking his beard and looking at the judge with mild reproach, 'it is not for me to say. It is for the police to find out. They took six years to find me again, six years to find an innocent man, yet they cannot find my vanished clients!'

'They found Landru because he existed,' commented the Judge, quietly. 'They did not find Mme Guillin because she is no longer alive.'

The examination turned to the forgeries committed by Landru to secure Mme Guillin's money. He had presented a demand, allegedly signed by Mme Guillin but in reality signed by himself. 'I imagine the Banque de France would have examined the signature before accepting the instructions,' he replied. But Landru had taken a room in the name of Mme Guillin in the Avenue MacMahon, in order to give seeming authenticity to the demands made in her name. How was it that nobody ever saw her there?

But Landru was never lost for words. '. . . it was too high for her. She resided in a little apartment on the ground floor at 45, Avenue des Ternes, at the back of the courtyard. . .'

'In your garage at Neuilly police found all Madame Guillin's papers, and her false hair. How do you account for these being in your possession if Madame Guillin were alive?'

Once again the question: 'What has become of Madame Guillin?'

Landru seemed suddenly to lose patience and self-control. He had been defiant, impudent, satirical before, but never like this. His hands tightened on the bar, his knuckles gleaming bluish-white; he turned deathly pale, and his eyes seemed to project shafts of hatred and contempt. The whole court suddenly became tense, the public dead silent.

'What I have said for one of these women you call my victims, I shall say for all of them.' He turned to the Avocat Général. 'You know very well that I shall say nothing, either for this woman or for any of the others!'

Godefroy, sitting silent and sullen in a corner of the court, was on his feet in an instant.

'This is your last word, Landru? I will not repeat what I think of the gravity of such an attitude. It would be bad taste on my part.'

Landru was contemptuous. 'Always the same question! I fully realize, M. l'Avocat Général, that you are after my head. I regret that I have not got more than one head to offer.'

Immediately there was an uproar. Maître de Moro-Giafferi, distressed at his client's foolhardy insolence and contemptuous attitude for the court, tried hard to excuse his client: 'I have enough experience and respect for the jury to know that they do not judge an accused man by his attitude.'

Landru at this point came the nearest he ever did to apologising. 'I expressed myself badly . . .' he stuttered.

He persisted that he negotiated the shares, and sold the valuables and furniture as 'a friendly act'.

'And this false hair-piece,' said the Presiding Judge, 'which has been recognised as belonging to the missing woman. How did that come into your possession?'

Landru lifted his head back, as though some ill-favoured breeze might blow towards him, and with an expression of mixed boredom and nausea, said, 'I am rather surprised to see justice concerning itself with such details.'

The sixth day of the trial proved somewhat tedious. Landru was made to relive the move from Vernouillet to Gambais. Why, why, why, was the constant question, and always the response was a ludicrous and unlikely explanation, or a superior silence.

Judge Gilbert: 'I have established, Landru, that Madame Cuchet and her son, Mme Laborde-Line and the widow Guillin went to live at your villa at Vernouillet. I have also established that these are all women with whom you were in intimate relationship—you say it was merely commercial—and all of them have disappeared. The accusation maintains that you left Vernouillet because it was not sufficiently secluded. You chose a villa at Gambais. Why?'

Landru was quick to explain. The new home was half the rent. Unlike the previous house, it had sheds where 'industrial work' could be done. Vernouillet was cold—so cold that he had to keep his hat on for warmth. His pale, sweeping cranium made this explanation, at least, sound feasible.

Altogether an unpromising time of the year for poor Mme Heon, the widow from Le Havre ('Havre' in Landru's notebook) to come on a visit. Bereaved by the war, lonely, hardly able to make ends meet, she had taken a fancy to the little man in the putty-coloured coat. She had told her friends and neighbours, in Landru's presence, that they were to marry, said Judge Gilbert.

Landru denied it. 'That is possible. But I was not her fiancé. I know she very much *wanted* to remarry—the ambition kept her going. She was one of those who do not begin to count their age until after their First Communion.'

The court dissolved in laughter. The weird bonnets and hats, with their trailing strings, tassels, ribbons and taffeta flowers, perched on precarious hair-do's, waved like flowers in the wind.

Again the question: 'What has become of Mme Heon?'

'I have nothing to say.'

The enquiry switched, on the seventh day, to the missing Mme Collomb.

'Was Madame Collomb your mistress?'

'Never.'

'And yet you took her to Gambais, and she slept there?'

Silence.

'You also took her to the new flat you had rented in the rue de Chateaudun [quite near rue Rodier] in the name of Fremyet?'

'She went there a few times, but she never slept there.'

Yet Mme Collomb had finally gone to live in the rue de Chateaudun flat at the end of 1916, and on December 8 Landru and his son cleared out the furniture in the rue Rodier flat and stored it in Landru's garage, from where it was later sold.

Was Mme Collomb present at the removal? Landru said yes, she was; the concierge said no, she wasn't.

On December 24, Mme Collomb had invited friends to the flat and introduced Landru as her fiancé.

Judge Gilbert intervened: 'And you didn't protest when you were introduced as her fiancé?'

'Simply out of courtesy. I am not in the habit of interrupting ladies when they are speaking ... a scruple from my good upbringing.'

There was a momentary diversion, a sort of scuffle in the Press Gallery: M. Vital Darzac, special correspondent of the *Dépêche de Toulouse*, pushed roughly past his colleagues, almost knocking their pencils out of their hands. 'I can't stand any more of it,' they heard him say, 'it's too terrible.' Only when they got back to the hotel bar did they hear that he had blown out his brains.

The mournful witnesses, in heavy mourning, told their stories. A sister told the court, sobbing, 'When she was leaving for Gambais, she said, "I will be back for January 1 at the latest. I never miss spending that day with the family." And she was never seen again.' The sobbing grew louder. 'If she was living she would never have left us like that.'

And Mme Moreau, her mother, repeated the accusation.

'My daughter,' she said, 'was murdered.'

Of all Landru's victims, the next woman was the greatest mystery, because she possessed absolutely nothing of value. If Landru was wholly preoccupied with people's furniture, jewellery and valuables, and not wishing to be in intimate liaison with anybody, what did he want with poor Andrée Babelay?

And now, with the investigation into the disappearance of Landru's seventh fiancée, we may justifiably speak of Landru as 'Bluebeard'; there is an analogy with the legend of the seven wives of Bluebeard, each of whom was killed because she would pry into the secret of the locked room. Like them, Mlle Babelay rummaged in the belongings of Landru's former 'fiancées', and the court maintained that, like them, she was murdered.

Landru denied making the trip to Gambais on April 11 and April 12. 'The indictment always talks about that. It is an obsession. Why, on April 12, Andrée was no longer at Gambais.'

'But on that date your notebook indicates the purchase of provisions for two people.'

And what of the ominous note in his notebook, 'four o'clock in the evening', similar to that found when Mme Collomb disappeared?

'I do not remember such insignificant details. Anyway, it is not the time of what you choose to call, with your insinuations, my crime. On April 12, three people visited me at my villa; there was no one there.'

'Then where was Andrée Babelay on April 12?' persisted the Judge.

'Paris, probably.'

'Yet the concierge in the rue de Mauberge says that she has never seen her since the day she left for Gambais, March 25.'

'All the same, Andrée came back to the rue de Mauberge to get her clothes. She then went to an employment bureau, found a situation ... and I haven't seen her since.'

'In these circumstances,' the Judge insisted, 'how is it that, after your arrest, the photographs of her grandparents, and other personal papers, were found in your possession?'

'Well, in her new job, there were several other servants. As she thought they might pry, Andrée left her papers in my care.'

For the first time, Landru was indiscreet, against his interests: 'One day, like any inquisitive child, Andrée lifted the lid of the trunk in which I kept the papers left in my care by my clients, whom you call my victims. She asked me what they were, and I told her. This was when she gave me her papers to keep with the others.'

'Was it not this discovery,' asked the Public Prosecutor, 'that urged you to this crime?'

Landru rose, white with rage, the living embodiment of innocence outraged: 'You accuse me of crimes? It is your business to prove them!

Godefroy was not so easily pushed aside, 'You were very hospitable to Andrée?'

Landru relaxed. 'Well,' he said confidingly, as though he and Maître Godefroy must have shared the same habits and tastes, 'a room nine foot square...'

'Nonetheless, she rummaged in your papers. Mme Cuchet also, at La Chaussée in 1914, had rummaged in your papers, and she died because of it. Was it not because Mlle Babelay, like Mme Cuchet, discovered the secret of your real identity or of your crimes, that you killed her?'

There was a complete silence. Landru seemed to have been taken off his guard. He drew himself up to face his accuser, and also to play for time. But there was not time enough. The arguments were not so glib, his manner less assured, the stream of thought confused.

'Madame Cuchet rummaged in my trunk in August, 1914, but it wasn't until 1915, according to you, that I killed her. I took my time. . .'

'Yes, the time it took you to win back her confidence and get her to break with her family.'

The Avocat Général pressed home his attack: 'Did you see Andrée Babelay again afterwards?'

'She came to pay me back some of the money she owed me.'

'And you didn't give her back her papers?'

'That is a question of no importance.'

'You wish to tell us nothing of what happened to Andrée Babelay?'

'I shall reply as for the others.'

'Yes, the "wall" of your private life?'

'Bring me the proof, and I will defend myself.'

'Landru! One of your judges,' and the Prosecutor pointed to the chief juryman, 'has asked you the same question. *What became of Mlle Babelay? Answer me!*'

Landru studied the court ceiling: 'I have nothing to say.'

Later, in heavy mourning, a sad Mme Collin, mother of Andrée Babelay, told the court: 'My daughter is dead. She has been murdered. She would never have left us with no news of herself for four years. She loved her little sister, Adrienne, too much for that. All that Landru has said is a tissue of lies.' She turned to Landru and looked him straight in the face: 'Yes. Murdered by you.'

A girl of fifteen, who was eleven when she met Andrée Babelay at Gambais, told of her missing friend's bubbling eulogies of her darling 'Lulu'—the kind gentleman with whom she was staying. She had shared the sweets so kindly given to Andrée by her 'Lulu', but soon afterwards Andrée had disappeared completely.

Another day completed. Another twenty-four hours nearer to the verdict. Landru looked as though he realised he had blundered. It was ominous that in the case of all these people with whom he had intimate associations, and whose property he managed to acquire, he should have had no trace of them at all, or was unwilling to answer questions concerning their whereabouts. But the biggest slip of all was to have admitted that Andrée

Babelay rummaged in his trunk and found the personal papers of his former 'fiancées', and so discovered his true identity.

The journalists scattered to write their articles. Cameras and tripods were gathered up. The cartoonists packed their folding stools and sketchbooks and crayons. The 'Landru special' rattled on its way back to Paris, carrying Mistinguette, Maurice Chevalier, Colette, the famous actress Jane Renouardt and somebody unnamed but described as 'a niece of Lloyd George'. For the railway guards it was the highlight of their day. They got the news first.

On the ninth day the court was concerned with the forty-four-old widow, Celestine Buisson, who had an illegitimate son, and had been living at 42, rue du Banquier, enjoying the security of some passable sticks of furniture and 10,000 francs in bonds. She had answered one of his advertisements in May, 1915. He had given her sweets and chocolates and even scraps of inexpensive jewellery obtained—the court would have said 'stolen'—from other women. Then he had disappeared for a year, Mme Buisson telling friends that he had gone away on urgent business to Tunisia.

'Yes,' Landru said, as the indictment reached this stage, 'my relations were interrupted the day I realized that she was more concerned with getting married than with selling her furniture.'

'And then,' added the Judge, understandingly, 'you were also very busy with Mesdames Laborde-Line, Heon and Guillin, who were going to disappear one after the other, at this time.'

'Oh,' Landru replied, airily, 'my concern with those you claim I murdered so easily did not take up all that much time.'

He had resumed relations with Mme Buisson at the beginning of 1916 and been introduced to her two sisters, Mlle Lacoste and Mme Paulet, as her fiancé.

'You were very attentive,' remarked Judge Gilbert, drily.

'Simply worldly politeness,' was the lofty answer. 'Madame Buisson also introduced me to her son.'

'In other words, you were behaving like a man who is soon to be a member of the family. And your relations were already very intimate with Mme Buisson. Was she your mistress?'

There were smiles all round as Landru replied that they had been like 'brother and sister'.

A trail of witnesses was heard: her brother-in-law, who testified that her son had gone blind, and that she would never have deserted him had she been alive; concierges, the dressmaker, bank clerks, and finally Mlle Lacoste, Mme Buisson's sister, whose original letter to the Mayor of Gambais had led to Landru's arrest.

Mlle Lacoste's eyes were brimming with tears as she re-lived it all.

Mlle Lacoste told of her suspicions of Landru coming with news of her sister. 'When my sister wants my news, she can come herself,' she told him. The story of Landru using his wife to forge Mme Buisson's signature in order to cash a bond was then told.

Landru, as usual during these demonstrations of personal grief, looked bored and detached.

The tenth day. Now the ghost of Mme Jaume. Landru had written in his notebook: '39, looks younger. Separated from her husband, who is in Italy. Lived with him "fraternally". Talkative. Very strong Catholic. Afraid of divorce.'

The court heard of their courtship—i.e., her initial reluctance, but eventual willingness, to get a divorce—of how they went to Mass together, sometimes in Paris, sometimes in the lonely forest church near Gambais.

'You became pious to suit the circumstances,' observed Judge Gilbert.

'I have always respected individual freedom and freedom of conscience,' said Landru gravely.

'And yet, once at Gambais, you suggested to Madame Jaume that you could spend the night together. She was very scandalised.'

Landru bristled with Puritan indignation. 'Oh! Oh!' He looked straight at the judge. 'I would never have allowed myself to do such a thing!'

The eleventh day of the trial, November 18, began on a note of expectancy. At the previous hearing, Landru, told that he could not produce the address of a single one of the eleven people who had disappeared, had accepted a challenge from Maître Godefroy to produce one.

'Here is my reply, Monsieur l'Avocat Général. It concerns Madame Heon who on October 6 or 8, was seen for the last time ... *eh bien!* when the widow left, and while a search was being made for her, Madame Heon had retired not far from her old home in the same street to a room at no. 159, the Hotel du Mans, where she occupied a room on the second or third floor. I could, if you wish, draw a little plan of this room... You can now deal with the matter.'

'We will investigate without delay,' Godefroy promised.

Now for the tenth ghost—Mme Anna Pascal, tall, dark, with elegantly waved hair, fond of pleasure, without embarrassing principles, divorced, thirty-three years old, no children, several lovers, dressmaker, had lived in the villa Stendhal. No savings, but her own furniture.

Landru had noted in his famous *carnet*: 'Widow for five years, young appearance, without children, 2 Villa Stendhal, Paris (20e), wearing a tailor-made costume and sombrero hat.'

Mme Pascal was not seen after April 5. The prosecution claimed that the time noted in Landru's *carnet* indicated the time of her death at his hands.

'What became of Madame Pascal?' asked the Judge. 'On the 5th of April you returned to Paris alone, and the unfortunate woman was never seen again. What have you to say to that?'

'She stayed on in the country.'

'And perhaps she is still there, enveloped in silence—the silence of death.'

'Oh,' said Landru airily, 'you don't have to make a tragedy out of it. Madame Pascal stayed on in Gambais. I went to fetch her on April 10th, and we went off together to Gambais on the 18th. Look in my notebook; for the date April 18, you will see "two return tickets".'

The Judge intervened: 'But what is there to prove that it was Madame Pascal you were accompanying?'

'And what is there to prove it was she who was with me on the 5th?'

Witnesses testified to the removal of her furniture by Landru and his son the day before her disappearance. Within days these few possessions, including an umbrella and her false teeth, were being sold.

Landru protested, 'The dental plate I sold belonged to my father. Madame Pascal's plate had five teeth mounted in gold, and was worth over 30 francs. I should not have sold it for 16 francs, you know that.'

Judge Gilbert looked hard and perceptively at Landru, perhaps thinking, what manner of lover is this, who, instead of gazing into his mistress's eyes, stared instead into her mouth, estimating the value of her dental plate and noting the number of teeth mounted in gold, with the care and accuracy of an actuary?

Mme Pascal's personal papers were found in Landru's possession. Why?

'A sacred trust.'

It was strange how the composition of the crowds of spectators seemed to change subtly from day to day. One day there were mink coats and flashing diamonds, and at refreshment time—not unlike the interval in a theatre—pâté and cheese and steaming coffee from vacuum flasks were consumed. On another day there were dowdy, durable dresses, imitation jewellery, dyed hair revealing its true colour at the roots; and at lunch break it was garlic sausage and hunks of bread, washed down with the cheapest wine. But whether the actors were playing to the stalls or the gallery, the shabby little court was to all appearances a sort of theatre.

For the case of Mlle Marchadier, the underworld of Paris turned up in force. The soldiers on guard, and the court ushers had tremendous difficulty in controlling the impatient throng. Before the case opened everyone was waving tickets, pushing and shoving and shouting their claims to priority. Outside the doors, which were pressed shut at last, there was an overflow of indignant and excluded people, muttering darkly about nepotism and social inequality. There was scarcely room to move in the court. There were crowds of witnesses; the press gallery was so crowded that the journalists were elbow to elbow, and people were even packed into the aisles.

On January 13 Landru and Mlle Marchadier, with her two dogs and a dog she was looking after for a friend, had gone to

Gambais. The coach-driver from Houdan told the court of the arrival of the elderly man, the not-so-young prostitute, the three dogs and three sacks of coal.

Of course, Mlle Marchadier was never seen again, and Landru, pleading gallantry, decent reticence and unwillingness to discuss his or anybody else's private affairs, did not know what had happened to her.

And the dogs? Their skeletons had been found in Landru's garden. Landru claimed Mlle Marchadier could not afford to keep them.

But, said the Judge, assuming that the court was disposed to accept Landru's explanation, assuming that Landru had, with Marchadier's consent, 'put down' her two dogs, what of the third, which did not belong to her?

'She asked me to destroy the three dogs,' Landru replied, 'I know nothing more about it.'

But Landru had lied in the first place. At first he had said, when taken to the villa in company with Belin and other detectives, that the dogs had been his, and that he had killed them to save the expense of feeding them. Only when a local resident revealed that the dogs had been brought to the villa by one of his lady friends had he altered his story, when he declared that he had strangled the dogs because it was *'la plus douce des morts'*.

Judge Gilbert asked: 'Do you know why this tenth ... client ... never gave any further sign of herself, although she had promised to return soon when she left with you for Gambais?'

Landru: 'Oh, when one is leaving, what promises one makes, what *"au revoirs"* one says!'

14

Landru's Only Friend

THE DISAPPEARANCES, accounted as murders, of ten women in succession had by now established Landru's rubber-stamp formula for oblivion. Each was identically conceived. A matrimonial advertisement, whether in the name of Diard, Fremyet, Guillet, Forest or Petit, had more or less the same wording, drew the same type of victim, led to the usual type of introduction, courtship, engagement, removal of the furniture from the victim's house, and a visit to the lonely villa at Gambais. The victim disappeared. From that moment Landru observed with fidelity the 'sacred trust' of acting as custodian —indefinite custodian—of their treasures, from birth certificates to bonds, from jewellery to hair-pieces and dentures. Chairs, commodes, books, curling-tongs, cupboards, dressing tables, crockery and everything incidental to middle-class living changed hands for cash or collected the dust in one of his many garages. Nothing was thrown away. One never knows. The unlikeliest piece of property may one day fetch a few francs and, if only a few sous, well then, better than nothing.

There was much talk about Landru's method, or methods, of despatching his victims. Press and public speculated endlessly. There were some who said that, whatever the mode employed, it was probably the same for each. There was a remorseless tidiness about Landru that not even death would alter.

In his private office, between sessions, Judge Gilbert struggled manfully with his huge, mad mail. Letters poured in from all over the world. They must all be read, for any might contain a clue relevant to the guilt or innocence of the accused. Letters constantly arrived from people claiming to be the missing victims, and enquiry invariably proved that they were merely a hoax.

Yet so many bore the mark of authenticity. Here was one on good quality stationery, the grey envelope tissue-lined in brown. The writing was graceful and delicate: *'Je suis une des fiancées de Landru.'* She went on to say, not only that she was one of Landru's fiancées, but that, perforce she wrote under a pseudonym because she was prominent in the theatrical world and feared the adverse publicity that would result from an admission that she had been one of Landru's very numerous mistresses. Amazingly, the letter was signed, *'Votre toute dévouée,* Andrée Babelay.'

And here was a vicious-looking orange envelope, with florid, large, illiterate handwriting. '... *a l'honneur vous écrire au sujet du Monstre Landru ... un repris de justice, un relégable bagnard ... on ne va remettre en public un tel bandit?'* He was one of those who believed in lynch-law. Certainly he would have liked to see Landru handed over to the less-than-tender mercies of the mob. No doubt he would equally have approved of public executions. Well, if he was patient, he might yet have his wish, for Godefroy, the prosecuting counsel, never lost a chance of reminding Landru that his head was at stake.

There was a strange letter in English from a Miss J. W. Holloway, of 23 Oxford Street, Caversham, England:

> Dear and honoured gentlemen of the magisterial community in France. I am sending you one of my very special spiritual messages:
> SPIRITUAL MESSAGE FROM THE MURDERED LADY, MADAME MARCHADIER
> I met this murderer on January 14, 1919. It was in this way. He came to see a woman where I lodged, and she was out at the time, so he said 'We will have a little conversation until she comes back...'.

It was hardly worth reading on, for the message from the 'murdered lady' was so wide of the mark. Mlle Marchadier disappeared the day before she claimed—or her ghost is alleged to claim—she met Landru.

It transpired in court that Landru's claim that Mme Heon was alive, and staying in a hotel, after her alleged disappearance, was false.

Opinion was hardening against Landru. His witty ripostes and nonchalent or defiant bearing no longer camouflaged the sinister background picture. Even the cynical, who said that if the photographs were anything to go by, the gaiety of Parisian life had not lost much by the disappearance of most of Landru's victims, recoiled at the strangling of three dogs. If he had killed their owners (in fact the owner of one dog was safe and remote in Paris) he would have naturally followed through and destroyed their pets.

Witnesses came and went, but they added little of substance. But there was a stir in court as the cry went up: 'Usher, call Mademoiselle Segret.' They had read a lot about her. Only a day or so before, a correspondent of *Éclair* had interviewed her. 'I have not a single reproach against him,' she declared, thereby becoming his only vocal friend. She had gone on to say that possibly the court would be cleared of the public during a portion of her evidence. 'I think they want to put rather delicate questions to me on the physiology of Landru. Landru is a very normal man who goes to bed early and sleeps like a child. I shall wait till Monday to tell them in court that I love him very dearly and that I still keep all my affection for him.'

Landru never blinked an eyelid, but heads were craning in court to catch a glimpse of the only one of Landru's lovers to have escaped. She was very pale. She wore a heavy black coat, and a hat trimmed with black lace. She looked lost and very lonely. She came up to the bar. 'Usher,' said Judge Gilbert, 'give the lady a chair.'

It was too late. Her legs gave under her. She tottered backwards, fell into the arms of the usher who caught her just in time, and half carried, half dragged her out of court, her eyes turned back, her breath coming in short gasps and her golden ringlets in disorder.

Landru ignored the whole episode, rummaging in his folder of documents.

He ignored her, too, the following day. But his opal pallor made it clear that the long ordeal was telling on him, and that much sleep had been lost in his cell, poring over documents and notes on which his life depended.

Fernande Segret commanded considerable respect. It takes courage to stand by a man when the world has turned against him, or to believe implicitly in him when so many women who did the same have disappeared with clockwork regularity.

She was dressed neatly and with taste, a fur coat over a pink blouse. Her beige hat was trimmed with jet. She accepted the chair put in front of her and began her evidence in a voice almost choked with emotion.

'I met him in a tram. He stared at me for a long time, and then spoke to me, very politely.'

They arranged a first meeting in the Bois de Boulogne.

Her eyes veered round the court for a second, moving past the man in the dock swiftly, as though to fix a gaze would be too painful. 'I didn't want to go, and yet, in spite of everything I went. He was very correct and respectful. We talked of the weather, the theatre, of literature. He paid for a canoe ride on the lake.'

And then they began to meet every day. This was in 1917. Landru was then M. Lucien Guillet, a rich refugee from Rocroi. He spoke of marriage, and she did not reject him, even though she was engaged to a soldier who was a prisoner of war in Germany.

M. Guillet was introduced to Fernande's mother. He was charming. The engagement dinner was fixed for Easter Sunday, 1918. Everybody was there—except the romantic M. Guillet, who sent his apologies.

Fernande's mother, a protective tigress by no means satisfied with her pretty daughter's choice of beau, became frankly suspicious, and wrote to the Mayor of Rocroi enquiring about 'the industrialist named Guillet'. The Mayor hadn't heard of him. They went to see him, just to make sure. There was no doubt about it; Lucien Guillet was quite unknown in the town.

'This was a terrible blow to me,' Fernande told the court, and so expressive was her voice that her grief struck home. 'I had for this *garçon* very great sympathy and sincere affection.' Some days afterwards Landru returned, and made explanations that seemed to be true. The rupture was avoided.

The following month Landru arranged a fabulous engagement dinner in his flat in the rue de Rochechouart. The party was followed by a visit to the Opéra Comique. . .

Fernande glanced towards the pale, balding man in the dock, who was staring into space and clutching his notes. Suddenly the awful contrast between these two meetings came home to her, and she looked faint. An usher waved smelling salts under her nose, but ammonia is no cure for grief. Her head fell back, her arms flailed wildly, she seemed to choke with sobs, between which her words were barely distinguishable, 'I can't go on. I can't go on.'

There was an interval while she was led away, and a doctor was called.

Ten minutes later she picked up the threads of her story again:

'We decided to marry at the end of the year. When the Armistice came Landru said, *"The war is finishing too soon for me."*'

She told how her young lover returned from the Front, but she discovered that her heart was with Landru, with whom she now went to live permanently, with little further thought of marriage. The two lovers went several times to Gambais by car: 'The villa was not what you would call well furnished. In one room there was a revolver, a rifle and a lot of cartridges, which he was expert in using.' Her evidence was given so innocently that she did not notice the Avocat Général tensing himself like a cat about to spring, or Judge Gilbert's quietly appraising look. Landru had given evidence that he had strangled the dogs, a difficult and disagreeable alternative to the easy and quick method of shooting them.

What, asked the Judge, did her lover live on?

Mlle Segret understood his income to be derived from his garages, although, visiting one of them, she was very disappointed, as he had obviously given her a more impressive picture of his business. She described how Landru found her looking through some of his papers, and of how he flew into an ungovernable rage. It puzzled her, as she had never any compunction in letting him see all her letters and papers.

The court heard that Fernande liked cooking for him, and prepared many a delicious meal on the stove which, the prosecution maintained, was the means by which he reduced to ashes some portions of his victims.

Maître de Moro-Giafferi intervened: 'Did you see no skull or bones in the fire?'

Fernande was appalled by the question. 'Oh, Maître! Nothing like that! I would rake out the cinders and light the fire without seeing anything like that!'

Landru's counsel made the most of this point. If ashes were discovered in the stove in April 1919, they must have been there when Fernande cooked their delicious meals on or in the self-same stove.

Delicately, the Judge raised the question of their personal relationship. In her testimony before the *juge d'instruction* (in the course of the pre-trial investigations) she had said that Landru was ardent and passionate as a lover, but quite normal. Was that correct?

'Oh, yes, your honour. Passionate, but quite normal.' And then, with a mixture of courage and defiance, she added emphatically: 'I was very, very, very happy with him.'

Ever since his arrest she had uttered no word of reproach, given no hint of criticism of any kind. The court looked at her with a mixture of pity and puzzlement. Could she not have suspected that Landru's personal life was ... well ... unusual? His constant absences, his frenetic flittings from one address to another, his voluminous correspondence with other women, his rather useless collection of worn underwear and odd documents—did none of these things arouse in her any misgivings? Seemingly, not. There could be no doubting her sincerity, her affection, her loyalty—and her absolute faith in him.

Her testimony ended. Deliberately, judge and jury mitigated her sad lot as best they could, consistent with their duty, by limiting their questions. Shaking and deathly pale, casting a sad backward glance at the man she loved, she left the court. She was followed by the eyes of almost everybody—except Landru, who blinked behind his pebbly glasses as though lost in thought.

Fernande Segret, referred to as 'No. 7' in Landru's secret notebook, was the one that got away. Other women could disappear, while she cooked at that solid, business-like stove and comforted her bald, middle-aged lover in bed. But now the court heard the testimony of yet another who got away—a Mme Falque, who had got to know Landru through a matrimonial agency, under the name of Lucien Guillet. There was the usual talk of marriage. They went several times to Gambais, where Mme Falque remarked that she found the cooking stove a bit small. 'That may be,' Landru replied, 'but it is very good, and you can burn what you like in it.'

Mme Falque was comfortably placed financially. This interested Landru greatly. Several times he had painted a glowing picture of the benefits that would accrue to her if she but placed her property in his expert care. But Mme Falque had every faith in her own expert care. However, romantic overtures with their usual commercial undercurrent induced her to make him several loans.

The demands, she told the court, were so persistent that she became suspicious of Landru and employed a private detective to investigate his background. The self-employed sleuth reported to her that M. Lucien Guillet called himself Dupont in Gambais, Fremyet in Clichy, that he was married and the father of several children.

At Gambais she confronted him with this information the moment he tried to get another loan. He was taken aback, became confused with his explanations, left in a temper, and returned after a short absence, saying 'Oh well, I'll raise the money somewhere else.'

He did. Mme Falque, clutching her bank book tightly, left in haste, to be succeeded by the once-shrewd Mlle Marchadier on January 13, 1919. Mlle Marchadier never left Gambais nor was seen again. On January 15th, Landru paid back Mme Falque the money he owed her.

The stove was inspected. It was typical of those in use throughout France—two openings at the top to put in the coal, and for the saucepans, a boiler, a pipe. In the front, the ash-can, the roasting-oven and the drying-oven.

The journalists reporting the trial were in trouble. The hordes of women had invaded their box and stolen their seats. and they themselves were exiles, perching their books awkwardly on their knees while the women chattered and lunched, pointed and sneered. Judge Gilbert called their behaviour 'disgusting', but neither he nor the gendarmes seemed capable of controlling them.

There was interest in the psychological experts. Would they say that Landru was sane or insane? It was clear that Landru was listening attentively. He had a habit of drawing his head backwards when concentrating. There were three doctors, Vallon, Roques de Fursac and Roubinovitch.

Said Doctor Vallon: 'I already had to examine the accused in 1904, when he was being charged with obtaining money by false pretences. I found him then in a state bordering on lypemania, but he was not mad. Perhaps he was on the borderline, but not beyond it. I find now that Landru is perfectly lucid, perfectly conscious of what he is doing. He is quick and alert in his mind. He is easy and facile in repartee. In short, he must be considered responsible for the acts he is accused of.'

Dr Roques de Fursac added: 'There is no trace of an obsession. In examining Landru's personality, we have found him normal at every point.'

Doctor Roubinovitch: 'We were struck by his subtlety and presence of mind. His psychology is what might be called that of the "transportee". Transportation is always before his eyes as a nightmare which threatens him. They are all like this. The transportee has to live, and his past means that he cannot be choosy about the means he employs to keep himself alive. He will use any means to avoid being caught and sentenced afresh, to avoid transportation. Landru was in this situation in 1914, and it may be this which explains his conduct and the acts he is accused of.'

It did not look good for Landru. It added up to: 'This man is intelligent, resourceful, and cunning. He is also desperate and would stop at nothing.'

Landru was aware of his danger from this added evidence: 'The crimes of which I am accused could only be explained by the most marked insanity. They say I am sane—therefore I am innocent.'

Brigadier Riboulet added a little statistical information. From all of the eleven people Landru was said to have murdered, he obtained no more than 35,500 francs.

The trial entered an ominous new phase.

Judge Gilbert opened the fifteenth day with the direct question: 'Landru, how did you carry out your crimes?'

Landru adjusted his spectacles, said nothing, and made a vague sweeping gesture with his hand.

Judge Gilbert then advised the court that, in noting Landru's procedure in preparing the way for his crimes, it had, nevertheless, to restrict itself to hypotheses as to the actual mode of commission. In other words, the allegations of murder rested on circumstantial evidence.

The Judge ran over the various possibilities. *Did Landru use firearms?* Despite his claim not to have had any in the house, Mlle Segret (a truthful witness, and one predisposed to help,

183

rather than hinder, Landru) had seen revolvers, shotguns and rifles there. Did he use poison? During the police search several phials containing different chemicals had been found, as well as a list of antidotes to poisons and a book entitled *Les Grandes Empoisonneuses*. Did he hang or strangle his fiancées? Speaking of the dogs he had killed, Landru had said, 'It is the best way to die.' He had said that strangling was 'the gentlest of deaths'— permitting the inference that he was competent to assess the effectiveness of different modes of death.

'Oh yes, for *dogs*,' Landru chipped in. 'But the suspicious-looking phials contained nothing but photographic materials. As for the book on poisoners, does one poison people simply with books?'

The judge speculated as to the disposal of the victims, once they had been killed by means which must remain a matter of speculation. The prosecution said that Landru disposed of identifiable parts by burning, from which it could be inferred that Godefroy meant the heads, and any parts of the body having distinguishable marks. The rest of the bodies or parts of bodies, could be disposed easily enough in the various ponds, or in the thicknesses and thickets of nearby Rambouillet forest. Suspicious lights had been seen coming from the villas of Vernouillet and Gambais. There were witnesses a-plenty to testify to the evil smells that belched from the villa chimneys, and of Landru humping heavy and sinister-looking sacks and parcels around in darkness or semi-darkness, at curious times and in lonely places.

Landru interrupted again: 'Excuse me! When does smoke cease to be normal and become suspicious? Besides, all this is nothing but gossip by people who have been reading the newspapers.'

At the next session the forensic evidence was given. Commissioner Dautel spoke of finding the three skeletons of the dogs, and of the human bone fragments found later. De Moro-Giafferi was quick to challenge him. In the interval between finding the skeletons of the dogs and the bone fragments, a matter of twelve days, the villa was left unattended, and no seals were affixed until four days before the second investigation. What reliance could be put upon evidence of bone fragments which could have been planted there? But the prosecution pointed out that no pelvic bones were discovered, and it is these which make it possible to determine sex. A hoaxer wishing to pin the deaths of the missing women on Landru would surely have planted pelvic bones. 'Someone setting the scene in such a fashion would have to have been terribly stupid.'

But as the boxes containing the exhibits were seen in court, with their captions 'human teeth', 'skull fragments', and so on, Landru's customary defiance and composure appeared to have flagged. He looked utterly exhausted. Did he know that the trial was nearing its end, and that the verdict would be against him? For nearly three years, with every move and artifice his fertile mind could devise he had delayed and impeded the course of justice and, it would seem, assured himself that no guilt could ever be proven against him.

The court heard of the methodical researches made on the bone fragments found in a pile of cinders hidden by branches and dead leaves; and of the bone fragments found in the stove. The ashes had been found to contain 50 per cent of calcium phosphate, which could well be the ashes of bones, whereas the ashes of coal contain only one-half per cent. And there were the dress hooks, eyelets and other indestructible odds and ends of female clothing found among the ashes. The Judge asked Landru if he could account for them. Landru refused to do so, referring the question to de Moro-Giafferi. He said he would answer that when he made his defence speech. But Landru added his own comment regarding the proportion of calcium phosphate found. He was very fond of oysters, he told the court, and burnt the oyster shells. The jury look doubtful or puzzled. Whoever heard of anyone *burning* oyster shells?

The Avocat Général read a detailed report of the searches made and items found. M. Beyle, chief of the Identification Bureau, described experiments in which sheeps' heads were consumed in Landru's oven in a quarter of an hour. A five-pound leg of mutton took one hour and ten minutes to be totally consumed. Certain bone fragments showed evidence of a saw having been used. Skull fragments suggested that a hatchet had been employed. The Director of the Laboratory of Toxology gave evidence that sand found in Landru's cellar was impregnated with human blood. Dr Paul said that the skeletons of the dogs found showed clearest evidence of having been strangled. Ropes were tied tightly around their necks. The 150 skull-bone fragments weighed 996 grammes, whereas an adult skull weighed 400 grammes. The fragments must have come from three skulls at least.

The President of the court asked Landru to explain the saw marks on the bones, reminding him that his notebooks indicated the purchase of several saws. Landru refused to answer.

The President asked about the possibility of burning parts of a dismembered body in Landru's stove, and Dr Paul gave the court some gruesome statistics. Heads, limbs, feet and hands burn easily enough. Some parts of the trunk, and the thorax, are more difficult. Half a skull with the brains removed is consumed to ashes in thirty-six minutes, but a complete skull takes an hour and ten minutes.

A dentist gave specialised evidence on the teeth found. Some were carious and decayed. All were adult teeth. Some 'pretty teeth' had undoubtedly come from a young girl. Uneasily, thoughts turned to the missing Andrée Babelay.

Landru was showing signs of depression. His verve, his impudence, his confidence, seemed to have vanished before this array of expert evidence.

Did he notice that, among the fur-coated women in court, sipping their hot chocolate from flasks, nibbling at their sausage sandwiches, was Mlle Segret, who had once fainted in court, overcome by emotion, but who now looked as composed and interested as a spectator at the theatre?

But journalists and spectators who spotted her may have been oversimplifying her situation. The strain of giving evidence, and of trying to say only things likely to help her lover, was considerable. In fact, her honest though (from Landru's point of view) ill-considered reference to the firearms was fatal evidence. But now she was not giving evidence, merely watching the strange case unfold, learning things about her lover which she had never dreamed of when they lived so happily together in the rue de Rochechouart.

Counsel representing relatives of two of the missing women —Mme Cuchet and Mme Pascal—made impassioned speeches in defence of the good name of the missing women. Maître Surcouf, representing the family of Landru's first victim, Mme Cuchet, declared that her death was almost certainly due to her discovering Landru's secret identity.

'It is not my business how you murdered your victims,' Surcouf told Landru. 'If you cut them up in pieces and burnt them, it is not my business. I have nothing to do but to show that by lying promises of marriage you enticed Mme Cuchet and her son to your charnel-house... If Mme Cuchet were alive she would be sitting with her sister there [indicating Mme Friedmann] to defend you, for she loved you so much.'

Maître Lagasse, for the sister of Mme Pascal, had his say: 'I appear so that a grief-stricken woman can reveal her sorrow and demand ... the punishment of the offender. But if he can tell me where Mme Pascal is, I will shake hands with him and sit down.'

15

Red Dawn

A DRAMA is reaching its climax. It centres around a man now totally alone in the world. Fernande Segret can no longer comfort him. His wife and children, since Mme Landru divorced him, do not come to see him. His few pitiful bits and pieces of furniture have been sold, and even the setting for the trial on which his life depends is sordid and drab. The measly décor, the chaotic layout of the court, the grey-green and brown walls, the inadequate lighting from the seven electric lamps tied on to the old gas pendants, the army of sketchers and photographers moving around, encircling the jury-box, their pencils squeaking on the paper and the camera shutters clicking under Landru's very nose—it doesn't seem right that any man's life should draw to a close in such surroundings.

But then, were the cold and damp rooms of Gambais a fitting finale to the ebullience of Andrée Babelay?

The 'Landru Special', rattling along the lines from The Invalides station at eleven-forty every morning, is a non-stop with the odd peculiarity of having its second class carriages almost empty and the first class carriages full to overflowing. Judge Gilbert is on it, clutching tightly his huge brief-case with its heavy leather straps, warm and secure in a superbly-cut heavy overcoat. So is Maître Lagasse, appearing for her Pascal family, and keeping his companions in good humour with risqué judicial stories. There are special correspondents, enjoying a euphoria from good food and drink, so easily justified on their expense accounts when a really big story is being covered. There is a bevy of pretty Parisian women hoping that their looks, and a hint of future favours will prove effective with those influential enough to get them a *laissez-passer* for the day. The useful acquaintanceship must be struck up during the twenty-minutes journey. Some succeed.

Red Dawn

Raimu, Colette, Maurice Chevalier and Mistinguette are in court for the final stages of the drama. The hundred journalists are appallingly cramped. They wave over their heads the envelopes containing their latest batch of copy until some willing hand grasps it, passes it to another and so on, like a relay race, to the waiting messenger. One actress has even been permitted to sit on the judge's bench and—to ensure it gets a better view of Landru—has brought her dog with her! The dog, with other conceptions of contentment, looks supremely bored.

'You are not in the theatre!' Judge Gilbert warns the public, again and again. But what is the good of his protest? The public think they are. The dainty handbags, the fussy little powder puffs, the bags of sweets and rolls and sausage, the flasks of tea and chocolate, the surreptitious bottle of wine, the tittering and joking and whispering and exclamations—shut one's eyes, and one could easily imagine oneself at an important first night. The great influx of newcomers adds to the crowding. Chairs are put in the aisles, in corners, anywhere. Somehow, one expects programme-sellers suddenly to appear.

Landru looks deathly pale. He is so hemmed in that, crane and move as they may, nobody gets more than a fleeting glimpse of him through a sea of bodies and faces.

He remains impassive while prosecuting counsel hurls at him a cumulative volley of epithets: 'Bluebeard of Gambais', 'cruel monster', 'sinister assassin'.

Godefroy is at his most pungent, direct and deadly. In the past he has been sometimes almost persuasive with Landru, but now he is in at the kill. Landru has apologised for not having two heads to offer him, but Godefroy will be content with the one head he has.

He runs through the oft-repeated facts of Landru's life, his assignations, the network of petty fraud and the disappearance of his ten fiancées, together with the son of one of them. He touches on his psychology, goes over Landru's routine by which the women disappeared one after the other.

'This man Landru had relations with 283 women, and is now charged with having killed ten of them. Is such a crime possible? Public opinion was sceptical. It has even been suggested that this case has been got up to divert attention from the Peace Treaty, from which it was feared that all the hopes of victory might be dashed. But no. The crimes of Landru are all too real.'

He touches on past criminals with more than murder to their discredit. Delving in criminal annals, he mentions 'Jack the Ripper', the Dutch woman, Mrs Van der Zuiden, who was convicted of having given poison to more than a hundred people, and the French cases of Dumollard, Tropmann and Pel, the clockmaker. Landru, he says, in countries that revel in wit, is regarded as a sympathetic Guignol, getting the better of gendarmes and the police. But the truth is very different. Landru is a 'tracked beast'. It is true that no bodies can be produced, because the crimes took place in the midst of a war when the country itself was fighting for existence, and its better citizens engaged in fighting for freedom. Criminals, in such conditions, could be almost sure of escaping punishment. Landru was on the run. He murdered his victims to avoid denunciation, arrest and transportation for the suspended sentence. He turns to the jury, claiming that they are both, by now, old friends. 'I know that you have confidence in me, as I have confidence in you.'

The list of Landru's seventeen convictions, and the details of the disappearance of ten women, are old history, but everyone listens as Godefroy paints Landru's portrait in sombre colours. Landru is shown to be a meticulous man, a liar, a persuasive talker, a hypocrite, an opportunist, pitiless, impervious to and incapable of emotion. He swindled and robbed, and then murdered to ensure that the police got no track of him.

He turns towards Landru and addresses him directly:

'Landru, when you have pretended to know something I have implored you to speak, and each time you have answered in a sneering voice, "Seek".'

Landru says nothing, but the flicker of an ironic smile plays about his mouth.

The fashionable women in mink and sable cup their ears with their hands to get the full savour of Godefroy's denunciation of Landru's sexual exploitations. His flattery, his conquest of women, his pitless abuse of their affection, trust and love, were an invariable prelude to murder.

He turns, first to the bored Landru and then to the attentive jury. 'You have before you a murderer, callously cruel and ferocious. He kneels as a martyr in a church beside one of his fiancées, and a few hours afterwards he is bending over her dead body in the act of cutting it up. Afterwards he will go calm and serene to repose on the bosom of Mlle Fernande Segret.'

Mlle Segret, in the well of the court, listens impassively.

Godefroy retells the story of the visits to Gambais, the return and single tickets, the disappearance of Landru's victims, the sale of their furniture and the misappropriation of their money and securities.

'My conviction is deep and unshakeable: this man has killed eleven times with implacable cynicism, with horrifying composure. What destiny will you decide for him? My duty is to tell you to apply the law, however rigorous it may be. I have considered the question and I have no doubt in telling you that there is no risk of you committing a judicial error.

'With both my conviction and my conscience sure, I call for an affirmative verdict on all points, a verdict without attenuating circumstances, a verdict of death. No commiseration, no pity for him! He had none for them. Death is the sole punishment merited by his crimes. It is to the God of his youth alone from whom he may now demand a pardon that men find themselves unable to give him!

'It is good to raise the guillotine when it is necessary for the public safety! Voltaire and Rousseau have proclaimed it, and the great Montesquieu in *The Spirit of Laws,* wrote: "A citizen merits death when he has taken life. This punishment of death is the remedy for a suffering society." '

One thing Godefroy concedes. Nobody could say *how* Landru killed his victims, or how in each case he disposed of them. It is sufficient to say that he is a mass murderer and should die for it.

Now the time has come for the speech for the defence. The court has never been more quiet as Maître de Moro-Giafferi rises to defend the man who seems less troubled by this critical moment than his own brilliant faithful counsel.

De Moro-Giafferi has presence. He casts a quick, minatory look round the court, starting with the bench, sweeping onwards past the press gallery, then public gallery and finally fixing his gaze on the jury. The look carries its unmistakable message: 'A man's life is at stake, and you are cowards if you do not listen attentively.' Broadly speaking, Godefroy is respected, de Moro-Giafferi is admired.

The court is soon spellbound by the sheer oratory, passion and sincerity of a speech destined to pass into legal history as a classic defence speech. De Moro-Giafferi's memory is prodigious, his sense of priorities faultless. Many counsel would sink under the sheer dead-weight of paper, unable to see the wood for the trees. He makes his points tellingly, emphasizes the most important, moves swiftly to some sustaining or related fact. One moment he is roaring like an angry tiger, the next his voice has fallen to a whisper—a whisper he knows well enough, with his meticulous enunciation, will be strained for and heard perfectly. Within minutes his wisps of hair are falling about his face, and his ample gown flaps like the robe of a black angel mad with wrath.

He looks at his colleague, the Avocat Général: 'You called for a head, and I, who know you well as a man of sensibilities, I pity you! You have called for the death sentence, and there is death in your soul as a result. You have demanded the death sentence, yet I still do not know the basis of your accusation. You have said "There is no risk of possible judicial error in this case." All those who preceded you in your position said the same thing, and yet, there have been judicial errors. You know how many of their signatures I have found at the foot of the death warrants which, after an assurance such as yours, have afterwards been quashed as judicial errors—but quashed too late to redeem the error.

'Gentlemen of the jury, no proof of murder has been given. You must have *proof* on which your conviction must rest. I demand that you say, gentlemen of the jury, that you cannot come to a decision because the prosecution has not proven its case, and also because you are not convinced by him. What are they asking you to do, in effect? To punish a crime which they admit having no proof of. What have you been shown? A tight bundle of confused hypotheses held together only by the Avocat Général's talent.'

De Moro-Giafferi is withering about the prosecution's continual references to Landru's silence. 'That man has a right under our law to remain silent! Who shall deny him this right?'

He turns to Landru, perched like an alabaster bird of prey, motionless but observant: 'Eleven persons, Landru, have been seen with you. They passed through your hands. They were your companions, and you are asked to account for them. If you reply you will get absolution, but if you don't answer it is death which the Public Prosecutor holds out for you.'

The court is astounded by his vehemence. He turns again to Godefroy: 'The law forbids you to use towards this man the language you have used, for you have said "Speak! If not, you will be guillotined!"'

'If you admit that Landru can keep his silence, the prosecution is left with only a slight basis for its case. It is not true that the only possible supposition in Landru's case is murder; there are other more probable conjectures.'

De Moro-Giafferi turns now to a strange and sensational defence. Nobody can prove that the ten missing women are dead. It is not even legal to presume them dead. Article 115 of the Civil Code says that is dangerous to presume, except after a very long time, that a missing person is dead. He tells the jury that if Landru himself had died, the property of the missing women could not have passed by law to their relatives. The law presumes that they might turn up again to claim their property—and the duty of insisting upon their rights as living people would fall upon the Avocat Général, the very man who now says that Landru's ex-companions must be dead because they are missing. Nobody is legally dead until they have been missing for thirty years!

'We are thus drawn to the extraordinary conclusion that a public minister, who would be bound to give one decision in a civil court, is urging you to give an opposite decision here.'

Next, to the forensic evidence. One expert had said that 'ordinary' ashes contained only 10 per cent phosphate, whereas those found at Gambais contained 50 per cent. And what were 'ordinary' ashes? Ashes from wood could contain anything from 9 to 38 per cent. 'Has the expert ever bothered to ask if Landru burned wood? No? But Landru did burn wood.'

Now de Moro-Giafferi plays one of his strongest cards. He refuses to discuss the nature of the bone fragments found at Gambais, and which experts claim are human bones, because 'they were not found at the only moment when they should have been found'. An extremely important point, de Moro-Giafferi insists, is that when police searched the villa and grounds on April 13, 1919, they found none of these compromising fragments, that they did not seal the house after the search and that, therefore, their subsequent discovery of these fragments during their second search of April 29th proved nothing, as the house was open to anyone in the interval. In his most ironic tone, he says that the failure of the police to seal the house was 'regrettable'. '*Very* regrettable,' he adds, after a suitably dramatic pause.

Wasn't it possible that somebody, convinced of 'Bluebeard's' guilt, planted some false evidence in the interval? What of the false evidence adduced in the infamous Dreyfus case? What of the poor young French soldier only recently, at Verdun, shot for cowardice on the allegation that he had wounded himself—whereas the autopsy showed that the bullet which had wounded him was in fact a *German* bullet? What of the corpse of a 'young girl' washed up on the beach of St Malo in 1909, which proved to be the corpse of a chimpanzee thrown into the sea by a painter, Aimé Morot? If he hadn't reported what he had done the 'experts' ' misleading explanation would have been accepted.

As to whether the bones said to have been found at Gambais are human or not, it is irrelevant to the case, since the conditions under which they were found do not establish any connection with Landru whatever. They could have been planted when the house was under no supervision, and there was a cemetery near by. The evidence of the blood-soaked sand is equally unacceptable. It was not noticed on the first visit. The police had not seen it the first time, and as it was six feet long it certainly would have been seen. It must have been put there afterwards—and, anyway, it was not human blood.

He turns to the reports of the experts on the possibility of Landru having disposed of eleven corpses by means of a stove. He quotes cases of corpses being burned, to make his point that at the times at which Landru is said to have achieved an incineration, it would, in fact, be impossible. One murderer, Carrara, had taken twenty-four hours to burn the corpse of an office boy. M. Gillard, telling the story of the murder of the Czarist family, recorded that, even using 100 gallons of benzine and stakes of resinous wood, the bodies of the family had taken over three days to destroy. Was it conceivable that anyone could have consumed corpse after corpse in a fiddling little domestic stove, intended for little more ambitious than modest-sized joints and omelettes?

He is scathing about local witnesses. Must a man's life depend upon the idle chatter of village gossips? One witness had spoken of evil-smelling smoke borne by the wind on a dull and dark evening. The weather that night had been clear, and there had been a full moon.

So much for the old gossips of the village. 'There are no proofs, no witnesses, no evidence. Oh yes,' he adds, sarcastically, 'there is one witness, one dumb witness—Landru's notebook.

'Oh, this notebook of Landru is troubling. There are single and return tickets marked down there. Who is the single ticket for? For Landru, or for his companion? You say: for her. I say: for him. Which of us is right? Neither of us will ever know.

'Why does not one of the missing women come forward and say "I am alive?" For obvious reasons—what woman would jeopardise her reputation by coming forward? Each relies upon the other to save Landru. Then again, only a madman would keep so many documents of identification belonging to his victims if he was a murderer. Landru had kept them, and Landru was not mad; experts had said so. Therefore he was not a murderer.'

Now de Moro-Giafferi comes to a very strange part of his defence.

'Is Landru a white slave trafficker? Upon my soul and conscience, I know nothing about this, but it is a hypothesis, and a hypothesis which would explain why the women who have disappeared are silent, and have not shown themselves. It is, indeed, a hypothesis which could explain a number of things, including the entries in the notebooks.'

This wildly improbable hypothesis brings a fleeting smile to many a face in court. A white slave trafficker! It is difficult to conceive of large, elderly widows, minus their dentures, hairpieces and spectacles, being shipped off to the seraglios of the Middle East for the delight of tyrants who have a large choice of young and lithe Berber, Algerian, Tunisian and Arab girls.

However, de Moro-Giafferi is here to defend, and he is doing his passionate best.

Finally, his peroration: 'For the quiet of my spirit and my soul, and also for the quiet of your spirit and your soul, I must say to you: If one of these ten women came back tomorrow,

H

would you not fear to see, in your sleepless nights, a glassy-eyed mask which would murmur in your ear, *"You killed me!"* '

It is six o'clock. De Moro-Giafferi sits down to a hush that is a kind of silent applause.

Landru stands up. He is composed, but his pale face shows signs of cumulative strain: 'I affirm, on the love that I have for my wife and my children, feelings which have been testified to in these hearings, that I am innocent of the crimes that I am accused of.'

The jury leave to deliberate in private, to ask themselves these questions in respect of every one of the missing people:

1. Did Landru commit voluntary homicide on the person of Madame X [or in the case of young André Cuchet, of course, it was Monsieur Cuchet]?
2. Did he commit this homicide with premeditation?
3. Did he commit this homicide with intention to steal?
4. Did he steal?

There are also four supplementary questions relating to Madame Buisson, regarding the two forgeries carried out by Landru.

Landru is led down to his cell, for he can only hear his fate from Judge Gilbert himself, who must first, of course, receive the jury's verdict.

For two hours the jury argue among themselves. During the long interval spectators chat, joke, eat, drink and even, between couples, engage in ill-concealed and amorous horse-play. One man imitates farmyard noises. Photographers use the time to rig up an improvised floodlight to shine on Landru's face as he hears the verdict.

A bell rings. The jury is returning. Many try standing up, and are angrily ordered to sit down, or literally pulled back on to their seat by their shoulders. The jury give their verdict. All the questions put to them they answer in the affirmative, except those which concern little Andrée Babelay, who had nothing and from whom, therefore, Landru could steal nothing. They find no extenuating circumstances, and yet, strangely, add an appeal for clemency.

Tumult breaks out in the stifling, overcrowded courtroom. There are cheers for bets won, curses for bets lost, laughter, coarse jokes, repartee. It is too much for the Avocat Général, who draws himself up and literally shouts at the court: 'Be quiet, you filthy creatures!'

The Presiding Judge adds his protest in an attempt to restore order: 'This public clamour is disgraceful and cowardly! Have you no compassion in your hearts?'

The noise begins to subside, but too slowly for Maître Godefroy: 'Do you not realize that a man is going to be sentenced to death?'

The door in the side of the dock opens, and Landru appears. He looks quite composed, although his strange eyes glare in their deep recesses like shimmering black balls.

Maître de Moro-Giafferi looks agonised, as though it is he, and not Landru, who now stands at death's door. He grips his arm and whispers, quickly: 'Have courage. It is bad—very bad.'

'You may be at ease,' Landru assures him, almost genially, 'I have been expecting a death sentence.'

The clerk of the court reads the jury's findings. The Avocat Général demands the punishment provided under the Code. The lawyers for the families of Mme Cuchet and Mme Pascal ask for one franc damages and the restitution of objects which should belong to them, found in Landru's possession.

Landru, to everyone's amazement, actually looks relieved, buoyant almost. He is busy comforting Navières du Treuil, who has worked so hard for three years organising his defence, and his brilliant leading counsel, who is stricken with grief at the verdict. Landru tries hard to cheer him up.

Quickly, for there is no time to lose, de Moro-Giafferi goes round to the jury with a petition for mercy:

'The undersigned jury ... ask that the penalty of death shall not be executed, and appeal for the indulgence of the President of the Republic for the condemned.'

The jury sign. Even Mme Pascal's sister, weeping copiously, signs the appeal for mercy with trembling hand.

Judge Gilbert reads the sentence. 'In view of the fact that Landru, Henri Désiré, has been found guilty of voluntary homicide with premeditation, of theft and of forgery ... Landru is condemned to death. The execution shall take place in a public place in Versailles.' In the preamble the mode of death has been put in explicit terms. Landru's head will be cut off.'

The crowd has still not stopped its chatter.

The court gives the plaintiffs the damages they ask for.

Landru remains standing. His hands do not tremble. His bearing is dignified, almost imperious. He hears the sentence unmoved.

The instruction is given: 'Guards, take away the condemned man.'

The guards move to obey, and in an instant Landru raises his hand as if demanding silence. His gesture silences everyone, and his voice is heard loud and clear. Slowly, very calmly, he says:

'I have only one thing to say, your honour. I have never committed murder. This is my last protest.'

He waves to Navières du Treuil and to the tearful de Moro-Giafferi, puts on his natty bowler hat, and follows his guards to his doom.

16

Landru's Last Days

IN CELL No. 7 Landru lay on his bed, staring fixedly at the ceiling. He seemed, suddenly, to have lost all interest in the prison, its people, its staff, the world outside, his past, and the vanished army of fiancées. He refused to take exercise, and grew daily more thin and emaciated. He seemed, when he did shift, to drag himself rather than walk. The unvarying meals prescribed by the doctors—beefsteak and cheese for lunch, boiled or fried eggs and cheese for dinner—were often left untouched. His sons came to see him, briefly, but he had little to say to them, and they left him for the last time, pale, distressed and puzzled. Had this man, who had taken them for walks in the Bois de Boulogne, had bought them presents at Christmas, had sung scraps of opera to them in his more cheerful moments—had this man murdered eleven people, as the law said?

Mlle Segret was earning her 2500 francs a week as a star draw in a night club. Mme Landru, now divorced, had changed her name.

'The state of Landru's health,' reported the *Times*' Paris correspondent, 'is causing anxiety.'

Yes, the health of a condemned man always causes the authorities anxiety, the awful frustrating thought that their hard work and expense will not have achieved their intended purpose, the death of the accused, in their time and in their way.

The mail poured in from all over the world. No man ever had so many new friends and so little time in which to cultivate them, as Landru certainly would have done had he been free. There were offers of homes, of gifts, and of favours which women are sometimes, quixotically, disposed to offer to absolute strangers. One correspondent thought that, as he would almost certainly be sent to a penal colony, he should occupy himself by writing his memoirs. Judge Gilbert had his shower of 'fan mail,' too. One correspondent in Philadelphia declared that Landru must be innocent, 'since his victims are totally unknown in the astral!'

Another correspondent postulated that Landru must have been a spy, and that this accounted for the reluctance, indeed the impossibility, of the woman agents whom he recruited to appear and testify in his favour. One such statement was actually made by M. Henri Javal, a barrister, in a letter to *Oeuvre*, who declared that during the war Landru organised a wide network of espionage, of which his Gambais villa was his secret office. The women would naturally not appear during the trial because this would have revealed him as the arch-spy.

De Moro-Giafferi and Navières du Treuil managed to persuade Landru, rather against his will, to appeal to the High Court, on the grounds that there had been some minor irregularities of procedure.

By Christmas, Landru had thrown off his melancholy and seemed reconciled to his fate. But this did not stop correspondents from sending him sweets and fruit and wishing him a Happy New Year. Thoughtfully, the jailers kept back abusive letters, which were plentiful. An old lady in Lyons sent him a perfumed letter, asking plaintively, 'Why has not God willed that your ideal affections might be ours?'

A telegram from Montreal to the *Petit Journal* said that a Mme Heon, corresponding with the lady Landru was supposed to have murdered, had been living there. A Hector Vigoureux wrote to the authorities with a strange story which, he said, he related from conscience. Three days after the arrest of Landru, he was passing through Gambais at midnight and had reached a path skirting the low wall of the cemetery, when he noticed a light, and saw a man, whom he recognised, at the charnel house. Vigoureux was curious as to what the man might be about, and kept him in observation. He saw him take fragments of bones from the charnel house, which he examined by the light of a lantern and placed in a small box. Closing the charnel house, he leapt over the cemetery wall and followed the path which passed behind Landru's villa, scaled the fence, and vanished from sight.

Unfortunately, the man he had seen in the act, who was well known in the district and came from an honourable family, had since died.

Was de Moro-Giafferi right in thinking that the bones might have been planted in Landru's villa while it remained empty and unattended after the first abortive police search? He sent the letter to the Ministry of Justice, but it did not produce evidence conclusive enough to upset the verdict.

On February 1, 1922, Landru heard that his appeal against his sentence had been dismissed by the Cour de Cassation. Only one hope now remained, an appeal to the President of the Republic for clemency. Landru did not want to sign it. 'Why should an innocent man ask for pardon?' he demanded. But he decided that the jury's plea for clemency indicated a troubled conscience, and eventually the appeal went forward. It was examined by M. Barthou, Keeper of the Seals, and passed to President Millerand, who received Maître de Moro-Giafferi and Navières du Treuil at the Presidential Palace, heard their eloquent pleadings, promised to consider them and, having done so, announced his decision. The appeal for clemency could not be granted. Landru must die.

Now things moved swiftly. Anatole Deibler, the famous executioner, who had been holding himself in readiness pending the President's decision, had the guillotine in its wagon. There were two, one a larger one used for executions in Paris, the other a smaller version used in the provinces. Deibler, a permanent employee of the Ministry of Justice, drew a salary of £16 a month and travelling expenses. For every execution he would be paid £24, but out of this he had to pay his three assistants, all hefty, huge men well chosen for their task. One of them was Deibler's brother-in-law who, in his spare time, kept a bar. Deibler was a tall, mild-mannered man who brought to his sombre office the dignity and decorum so beloved by the Victorian executioner, Mr Berry, who tried vainly to comfort his victims by thrusting into their hands scraps of home-made poetry. Deibler always performed his office in a frock coat and hard black felt hat.

Caravans of motorcars made their way into Versailles. Trainloads of hopeful sightseers appeared. Hotels and boarding houses were crammed to capacity, but the authorities, shocked by the rowdy court scenes, were determined that this proceeding should be swift and salutary. Infantry, cavalry and hordes of policemen guarded the Place des Tribunaux outside the prison and, moving outwards, proceeded to eject all but residents from the streets nearby, even if the people were in bed. Strangers were ruthlessly evicted and the front of the prison was left absolutely free.

Except for officials of law and order, and about a hundred journalists with numbered green passes, nobody was to be allowed to witness Landru's execution.

Landru had been busy writing a last letter to Maître Godefroy, his merciless prosecutor:

'You were watching me during the trial, you noted how clear my answers were; and suddenly you doubted. You doubted, horribly, whether you could carry on with your accusation. I could see what you were thinking. You looked at that poor little stove, better suited to cook a little love-feast on. You saw it couldn't be the instrument of all the horrors you were expecting to accuse me of. You've been to Gambais. You know that there are only 100 yards between my house and the communal cemetery, so over-flowing with bones that children go there to pick them up for their games of knuckle-bones. The jury believed you. . . . Then why couldn't you bear to look me in the eye? Adieu, Monsieur. I go to my death innocent and at peace. May I hope, Monsieur, that when your turn comes, you will be in a similar state. . . .'

In the dim light of his cell, Landru signed the letter in his meticulous hand, and settled to rest. It was not easy, for the movement of the cavalry and soldiers, the arrival of cars and wagons, and the hammering of Deibler and his team setting up 'The Widow' awakened him.

Godefroy, to whom Landru had written, did not come to the execution. It fell to Maître Beguin, his deputy, to call on Landru at five in the morning and awaken him with the ill-chosen words: 'Landru, you must be brave.'

Landru looked very strange now, for his beard had been shaved off and he insisted on being clean-shaven 'to please the ladies.' He looked at his visitor with mild reproach. 'We haven't had the pleasure, Monsieur, of being introduced, and yet you insult me. You don't tell an innocent man to be brave. He is innocent, and that's enough.'

Beguin was formally introduced, and Landru was mollified.

He turned warmly, smiling to Maître de Moro-Giafferi and Maître Navières due Treuil. 'You have made desperate efforts to save me. Oh well, it is not the first time that an innocent man has been condemned.'

M. Beylot, the Procureur, asked: 'Have you any declaration you wish to make?'

Landru surveyed him haughtily. 'Such a question, addressed to an innocent man who is almost in the next world, is insulting.'

He rejected the traditional rum and cigarette.

'Do you wish to hear Mass?' asked the Abbé Loisel.

'I should be enchanted, but ...' and he motioned courteously to the executioner's assistants, 'I should hate to keep these gentlemen waiting.'

'Have you a last wish?'

'I would like to wash my feet.'

The wish was refused. At any moment the clock would strike six. Outside, in the dawn, the machine was waiting, with its wickerwork coffin at its side and a small wicker basket in front to receive the head. Guards were at the ready, reporters in place.

Landru was bound. They put the shears through his shirt to make his neck easily accessible. He was denied shoes and socks. He complained that they were pulling the ropes too tight but they said it was the regulations, and he fell silent. They led him to the huge double doors, one of which was open, and as he neared it, de Moro-Giafferi whispered in his ear: 'Landru, you've nothing to lose now. What is the truth, Landru?'

'I'm sorry, Maître,' Landru replied, 'my secret's my bit of hand-luggage.'

His hands strapped behind him, his bare feet silent on the freezing cobblestones, Landru was hurried, half carried, to the machine of death. Quickly they pushed him face downwards under the *lunette*, the crescent-shaped wooden block which would hold his neck in place beneath the heavy knife. In a split second, the knife fell. Landru's head dropped into the basket; his body was tilted sideways into the wickerwork coffin, his head placed with it, and the coffin was heaved hastily into a waiting horse van. There was the crack of a whip and the sturdy horses galloped away into the early morning mist.

Epilogue

Landru was not a commonplace man. He was courageous and intelligent, but misused both these gifts. What really led him from the altar-rails at St Louis-en-l'Île to the condemned cell at Versailles, he alone knew—and he took his secret to the grave.

We can only speculate on the manner of man he was. Was he cruel, in the sadistic sense, deriving pleasure from the sufferings of his victims? Or was he merely callous, indifferent to the pain and treachery which, so far as he was concerned, was a mere by-product of his swindling?

How was it that a man who could move and plan with such stealth and secrecy should, at the same time, throw caution to the winds—living with his mistress in the heart of Paris, shopping with her openly in one of its busiest thoroughfares? It was this last foolhardy act that brought him to the guillotine.

Why should a man of such callousness have so obvious an appeal to so many women? With the exception of pretty Mlle Babelay, most were of ample maturity and some, like Mme Marchadier, cynically world-wise. One would have expected them to see through him.

If Landru held human life in such contempt as to murder eleven people, why did he remain a fairly constant visitor to his family, and so keep their goodwill (or fear, or respect) that both his wife and sons helped him dispose of his victims' property?

To what extent, if any, was sex the bait that tempted his victims? It is easy to laugh, in retrospect, at the thought of this middle-aged, semi-educated and impecunious poseur playing the gallant with this procession of unprepossessing women, but there is evidence that some genuinely loved him.

To ask why somebody with a seemingly respectable home background should turn out a ne'er-do-well is pointless, because we know too little of the emotional background of his home. It was certainly unremarkable, but a good beginning does not guarantee a good end.

The greatest mystery of all is: how did Landru get rid of the bodies? What really happened to his victims?

Forensic medicine was in a poor state in France just after the First World War. Experts gave it as their opinion that the very small fragments of bone found in Landru's villa at Gambais were human, but I do not think this can be taken as proven.

It is remarkable that there were so few bloodstains about the villa at Gambais. If the authorities were right in assuming that Landru dismembered his victims and disposed of the pieces by incineration in his ordinary cooking-range and oven, what of the unspeakable carnage which this grisly process would involve? When 'Buck' Ruxton, the Indian doctor, murdered his wife and mistress in the thirties, the extent of the bloodstains about his home was indescribable, despite his incessant washing, scrubbing and re-papering. How, then, did Landru dispose of seven women at Gambais and leave virtually no trace?

In any case, what of the four people who disappeared from his earlier villa at Vernouillet between April or May and August 1915? It seems a lot of corpses to dispose of within a few months, in a house overlooked by neighbours. The only indication of murder at Vernouillet rests upon the evidence of neighbours who complained of the smoke. If Landru was really burning portions of his dismembered victims in this rather amateurish way, might he not have been disturbed by such complaints, and resorted to less risky methods? He does not seem to have done so. Having offended the nostrils of the *bourgeoisie* in Vernouillet, he persisted in even more offensive fashion in Gambais.

If Landru did dismember some or all of his victims, what happened to their bones and, in particular, their skulls? It may well be that, if this was Landru's method of disposal, he would first of all have destroyed the skulls, since these would be the likeliest means of identification in the event of discovery.

We have no guarantee, indeed, we have no right even to assume, that he disposed of every victim in the same way, or even that a single victim was disposed of in only one way. We know that Landru may have used poison on some occasions, or firearms. The evidence suggests that his women may have been first poisoned, strangled or shot, their bodies then dismembered and their parts either destroyed in the kitchen oven, or thrown into one of the numerous ponds in the Forest of Rambouillet, or buried in the forest.

Another possibility must be considered: Landru may have taken his victims on a walk through the forest, reaching it either by bicycle or car, and there shot them. It would have been simple for him to have dug a grave beforehand (though of course he would have despatched them well out of sight of it) so that, having shot them, they could be swiftly and secretly buried. The chances of being observed were so slight as to be hardly worth worrying about.

Not far from Gambais was a glassworks whose furnaces were kept going at night. There being nothing portable worth stealing, the furnaces were banked up and the premises left unattended all night. Did Landru somehow find an entry and put his victims into the furnace there? Somehow it seems unlikely. One feels that the simplest employee would have noticed calcified bones among the clinkers. But one can't be sure. The police considered this possibility, but no attempt was made to prove it during Landru's trial.

It was on going through a pile of letters addressed, during the trial, to M. Gilbert, the presiding judge, fifty years ago, that I came across a curious letter. '*You want to find the corpses? Search the cemetery!*' it suggested.

The cemetery at the bottom of Landru's garden at Gambais contains many family graves and vaults. Fifty years ago Gambais was a lonely spot, and except for a little life in the local *auberge* in the evenings, there wasn't much activity after late evening. Did Landru take any of the bodies into the cemetery and bury them there? Might he not have disposed of corpses, or parts of corpses, in one or other of the vaults?

The cemetery was not, in fact searched. How could it be? Who would have consented to an act of mass desecration?

Is this the reason why Landru was so defiant, so cocksure, so ready with his perpetual challenge: 'Produce the bodies!' He *knew* the police couldn't. Why was he so sure?

On balance, his assurance was more likely to be based on the secret knowledge that the bodies were destroyed, than that they could not be found. In this case, it is not unlikely that the stove he installed at Gambais (and he took special care to use firebricks to ensure a more-than-usual fierce draught) was used to destroy parts of his victims. A variety of saws were found at Gambais, and some of the bone scraps found bore signs of having been sawed.

The skeletons found at Vernouillet and St Denis years after his execution may be those of victims whose bodies he buried in houses adjoining his own. The authorities, after all this lapse of time, cannot be sure.

Was Landru impelled by sexual desire as well as the prospect of gain? Generally, no. The class of women he sought was usually of the kind who put security and companionship first, though there were occasional exceptions—women like Mlle Babelay and Mlle Segret. His sexual relations with his wife seemed to have been normal, and he remained on intimate, if sporadic, terms with her until his arrest.

The question of sanity is a more vexed one. If sanity implies an appreciation of the full implications of one's actions, then Landru was sane. Extreme evil and active intelligence are often found together. Plenty of mass killers were skilled organisers, able to appreciate the arts, often gregarious, making great show of affection, putting on a surface appearance of convincing respectability. Hitler, the mass murderer, wore black shoes that polished till they shone, and at social parties appeared gallant to the point of formality. Ivan the Terrible was a monster, yet his will was a detailed and masterly example of lucid thought. Himmler organised the deaths of millions of people—yet he was methodical, organised, and had some sort of family life. A mad person, as I see it, has a compulsion to kill but does not know what he is doing. The people I have mentioned, and there are scores of others, did know, and gloried in it.

However, two doctors who examined Landru early in his criminal career, and long before he turned his hand to murder, felt he was mentally abnormal. But perhaps he faked his suicide attempt in prison before World War One to make them think this. His behaviour after his arrest by Belin was adroit, cunning and self-possessed. Few men could maintain their composure under such a ceaseless barrage of questions.

I conclude from all I have learned about Landru that he was not mad, but merely bad. A psychiatrist would probably regard him as a psychopathic personality; his perpetual and polished lying; his fantasies—in which, however, he did not believe himself; his almost fetishistic collecting of useless objects connected with his killings, such as useless hair-pieces and unwanted dentures. Did he keep these things, including identity documents of no conceivable financial value, to remind himself of his misdeeds, to be able to gloat over them in secret? He would not have been the first murderer to do this.

Comparisons of one murderer with another are of limited use, because though they behave inhumanly, all murderers are human and individual. They are the product of genetics, environment, cultural influences and circumstances. However, there are points of similarity between the tawdry wickedness of Henri Désiré Landru and Dr Marcel Petiot, who was guillotined in May 1946 for the murder of twenty-seven people (although he admitted to killing as many as sixty-three in his house at 21 rue Lesueur in Paris).

Petiot, like Landru, owed his long run of immunity to the fact that France was convulsed by war, and because the forces of law and order were overworked. Petiot, like Landru, was an accomplished liar and a consummate actor. Like Landru, he often diverted suspicion by audacious lies thought up on the spur of the moment to meet some unexpected crisis. Like Landru, he specialised in people who would have a motive in keeping their movements secret (although many of Landru's victims told their friends and relatives where they were going).

There the comparison ends, for Petiot in some ways was far more evil than Landru. Petiot made a fortune by promising to help Jews to escape from France. When darkness fell, the hapless would-be refugees from Hitler's terror called at his surgery, were given an injection against whatever disease prevailed in the country they were supposed to be going to, and shown into a windowless concrete room. Here they died, while Petiot watched their death agonies through a little trap-door.

Like Landru, Petiot had a respectable upbringing, but turned early to crime. He, too, started with petty thieving—in the classroom, or from letter-boxes. In the army, in 1917, he stole drugs and sold them to addicts, yet managed to get invalided out with a pension and a certificate of psychoneurosis.

Petiot, as with his predecessor, combined criminal tendencies with high intelligence. Despite a background of petty crime, he became a doctor of medicine, practised at Villeneuve, and even became its Mayor, although no thought of civic dignity restrained him from pilfering from his own electric light meter, or being convicted of theft, even as Mayor, from a local store.

He was still collecting convictions for petty crime until the outbreak of World War Two, when he obtained the house in the rue Lesueur and got a builder to construct the cell-like annexe to his surgery in which his victims died.

It is sad to think of that long procession of terrified and oppressed people, longing to escape the concentration camps and Gestapo torture chambers, making their way in secrecy and silence to that house of death, carrying with them all their valuables, especially money and jewellery, which were to finance them in their new country.

As happened to Landru, neighbours once complained of the most nauseating, thick, acrid smoke belching from the chimney of his home. Petiot had, considerately, left a note on his door saying where he was to be found. An indignant policeman sent for him, but the stench was so unbearable that in the interval of waiting for Petiot the fire brigade was summoned, an entry effected, and an appalling charnel house with the dismembered remains of twenty seven people found inside.

Amazingly, Petiot, on his return to the house crowded with police, took the Inspector aside and managed to convince him that the dead were Nazis and collaborators, who had been executed by the French Resistance. The police accepted his story and left the matter there. Only after the fall of Paris in August 1944, was the truth discovered.

There have been many strange echoes, mostly macabre, of the Landru case in the ensuing years.

Landru was buried in a cemetery at Versailles, the place being marked by a small wooden cross inscribed merely 'Henri Désiré' and omitting his surname. After his execution his children claimed the body, as French law permits, intending to remove it from its ignominious corner to a setting reflecting the affection they still bore for him. The cost of exhumation and reburial proved, on the submission of the estimates, to be beyond the family purse, and Landru's remains were left where they were.

The cross has long since disappeared, and nothing now marks his resting-place.

Landru's two sons, and an unmarried daughter, changed their name more than once for from time to time somebody would appear to identify them and embarrass them in their vocational and personal lives. They are entitled to the anonymity that time has conferred upon them.

The objects that figured in the court proceedings, including the famous stove, were put up for sale after the trial. A gipsy bought the stove for 4,200 francs for exhibition in Luna Park, in Paris. In June 1923, some thieves made determined efforts to steal it, but were disturbed in their task, and escaped after exchanging shots with the night watchman.

Landru's villa at Gambais remained for a while unsold, but later became a restaurant and a place of morbid, commercialised attraction. It is now (as indicated in my Preface) an ordinary weekend home. The authorities forbade the sale of Landru's love letters to his various fiancées. Most of these letters disappeared, together with other records of the trial, when the Nazis stole the Versailles collection of Landru documents during the last war.

Various people described themselves, or were themselves described, as Landru's missing fiancées. Their claims were never proven. A Mme Heon who appeared in Montreal *after* her namesake had disappeared from Gambais could not be identified as the one who had known Landru. During a lecture on Landru in 1923, in Paris, a woman stepped on to the platform and claimed to be Mme Laborde-Line. It was quite a dramatic moment for the audience and lecturer—but there the matter ended.

At various times human remains have been discovered which seem to be linked with Landru. In March 1933, during the demolition of a house in the rue de Paris in the Paris suburb of St Denis, next to an apartment in which Mme Landru was then living and which had been Landru's home, the skeleton of a young woman was found beneath the kitchen floor. Her teeth were perfect, and beautiful. The house, according to the police, was rented from 1909 to 1925 by an old woman named Mme Henri, who kept a small grocer's shop and café there. She had a bad reputation, and her café harboured crooks of all kinds. Landru was one of her best customers.

Did Landru, with her knowledge and possibly her help, bury one of his victims in her home? Her name was not mentioned during the Landru trial, but shortly after his execution she became insane, and suffered terrible fits during which she would scream 'Blood! Murder! Assassin!' She died in 1925.

In 1958 another discovery connected with the Landru case was made. An Italian mason, M. Castelli, making excavations in the garden at 45, rue Paul Doumer, next to Landru's old villa at Vernouillet, found parts of two skeletons at a depth of about seventy centimetres.

These included the bones of two corpses, comprising vertebrae, humerus, cubitas and some broken ribs and bones of feet that appeared to have been dismembered. The two skulls were missing. They were considered to be the skeletal remains of a woman and a small-waisted child.

Were these the remains of Mme Cuchet and her son André? This house was adjacent to the villa from which they disappeared, and in Landru's day it was very easy to pass from one garden to another through a huge breach in the wall. I have asked the Préfecture if any definite link was established but, since the skulls are missing, and in the absence of any identifiable object found with the bones, all that can be said is that the woman seems to have been about thirty years of age and the boy about ten. Of course, it is not impossible that Landru had other victims.

There remains the curious case of the 'confession' by Landru discovered in 1963—nearly forty years after he took his secrets —his 'baggage', as he called them—to the guillotine. He had presented to M. Navières du Treuil a drawing he had done in the death cell. It was in a frame, and the fact that Landru had written on the back of the drawing was not discovered until it was removed from the frame for cleaning. Mme Denis, daughter of Navières du Treuil, who owns the picture, assures me that Landru did, indeed, write a message on the back of it.

The first discovery was made in my presence during the legal 'opening' after the drawing had been sequestered. The opening was carried out in the court of the Seine (department) in front of M. Bontonnier, President of the Barristers' Association, M. Lussan, a deputy, and others. A graphologist would have no difficulty in verifying the handwriting on the back of the drawing because on the front of it is a dedication to my father signed by Landru in his own hand. Besides, I possess several specimens of Landru's handwriting, including a long letter. After the unsealing, the drawing was handed back to me, as it is my personal property, and at no time did the court express any doubt about the authenticity of the drawing or of the explanation written on the back of it.

Mme Denis adds: 'I believe I have discovered the meaning of the somewhat ambiguous sentence that Landru wrote behind the picture in question.'

I have not seen the confession, or the writing which Mme Denis says is 'ambiguous'. *France Soir* reported the wording to be: 'These witnesses are all idiots. It took place in the house.' The London *Daily Express*: 'In pencil he had written "I did it. I burned their bodies in my kitchen oven." ' That doesn't sound ambiguous to me. *L'Aurore*: 'The witnesses are all idiots. It didn't take place outside the wall, but inside the house itself.' *What* 'didn't take place', I wonder? The *News-of-the-World*: 'The trial witnesses are fools. I killed the women inside the house.' And there I must leave the question of a 'confession'.

Mlle Segret, Landru's last fiancée and 'the one that got away', earned a living for a time in the concert halls until Landru's execution, then vanished until September 1965, when the film *Landru,* by Françoise Sagan and Claude Chabrol, was first shown. Mlle Segret objected to being represented in the film without permission, and claimed 200,000 francs damages. The judge awarded her 10,000 francs, the directors of the film claiming, with some justification, that they thought that she was dead.

In fact, she had left France, broken-hearted after her lover's execution, and had worked as a governess in the Lebanon for nearly forty years. It is scarcely surprising that she had been assumed dead. On her return, an old lady of seventy-two, she went to live in a little two-roomed flat in an old people's home in the rue Charenton, Flers-de-l'Orne. She seldom went out, and complained that on the rare occasions she did so people pointed to her as the woman in the Landru case.

The orthopaedic corset she was forced to wear because of a spinal complaint made her life such a misery that she penned a short note saying 'I still love him, but I'm suffering too much. I'm going to kill myself.' By her bedside were two framed photographs—of her mother, and of Landru. Every year since his execution she had had a Mass said for him.

Her note written, she made her way alone to the Normandy

castle of Flers-de-l'Orne and jumped to her death in the icy moat.

Her funeral was short and simple and private. Fernande Segret now lies buried in the Cimetière de Thais, near the Château. Her fate was summed up by a relative: 'This poor woman has been pursued by tragedy all her life. Now at last she has peace.'

APPENDIX A

Chronological order of disappearances and names of Landru's victims

	Name and domicile	Date of disappearance	Place from which victim disappeared
1	Mme CUCHET, née FAMAST, Jeanne, 65, rue du Faubourg St Denis	April or May 1915	VERNOUILLET
2	CUCHET, André George	April or May 1915	VERNOUILLET
3	LABORDE-LINE, née EURAN, Thérèse, 95, rue de Patay	25 June 1915	VERNOUILLET
4	Mme GUILLIN	3 or 4 August 1915	VERNOUILLET
5	Mme HEON	December 1916 – January 1917	GAMBAIS
6	Mme COLLOMB, née MOREAU, Anna, 15, rue Rodier	27 December 1917	GAMBAIS
7	BABELAY, Andrée Anne	12 April 1917	GAMBAIS
8	BUISSON, née LAIRE, Celestine	1 September 1917	GAMBAIS
9	JAUME, née BARTHELMEY, Louise 23, rue des Lyanes	26 November 1917	GAMBAIS
10	PASCAL, Anne Marie, divorcée GABRIEL, 2 Villa Stendhal	5 April 1918	GAMBAIS
11	MARCHADIER, Maria Thérèse	13 January 1919	GAMBAIS

Chronology of Landru's addresses and aliases, taken from the
records of the Préfecture de Police, Paris

Address	Period	Alias
60, rue Blomet	October 1912 – January 1913	—
Biezres	July, 1913	—
12, rue de Chantillon à Malakoff	October 1913 – September 1914	—
La Chaussée	April 1914 – September 1914	DIARD
Vernouillet	1 January 1915 – end of August 1915	CUCHET
152, rue du Faubourg St Martin	26 March 1915 – 27 July 1915	FREMYET
8, Place Budapest	9 August 1915 – 15 August 1915	FREMYET
15, rue Lamartine	27 August 1915 – 18 September 1915	PETIT
57, rue Tallier à Lavallois	October 1915 – January 1916	FREMYET
22, rue de Chateaudun	January 1916 – December 1916	FREMYET
69, Boulevard de Levrai Chateaudun	15 January 1916 – December 1916	FREMYET
32, rue Maubeuge	10 February 1917 – 30 April 1917	GUILLET
113, Boulevard Ney	April 1917 – October 1917	FREMYET
76, rue de Rochechouart	October 1917 – 12 April 1919 (the day of his arrest)	GUILLET
6, rue de Paris à Clichy	1916 until the day of his arrest	FREMYET
GAMBAIS	1 January 1916 to the day of his arrest, 12 April 1919	Raoul DUPONT

Index

Index

Time-Life Books Inc. offers a wide range of fine recordings,
including a *Rock 'n' Roll Era* series.
For subscription information, call 1-800-621-7026 or write
Time-Life Music, P.O. Box C-32068, Richmond, Virginia 23261-2068.